Theodor Adorno

Key Concepts

Key Concepts

Published

Theodor Adorno: Key Concepts
Edited by Deborah Cook

Gilles Deleuze: Key Concepts
Edited by Charles J. Stivale

Merleau-Ponty: Key Concepts
Edited by Rosalyn Diprose and
Jack Reynolds

Forthcoming

Pierre Bourdieu: Key Concepts
Edited by Michael Grenfell

Michel Foucault: Key Concepts
Edited by Dianna Taylor

Heidegger: Key Concepts
Edited by Bret Davis

Wittgenstein: Key Concepts
Edited by Kelly Dean Jolley

Theodor Adorno

Key Concepts

Edited by Deborah Cook

ACUMEN

First published in 2008 by Acumen

Acumen Publishing Limited
Stocksfield Hall
Stocksfield
NE43 7TN
www.acumenpublishing.co.uk

ISBN: 978-1-84465-119-1 (hardcover)
ISBN: 978-1-84465-120-7 (paperback)

British Library Cataloguing-in-Publication Data
A catalogue record for this book is available
from the British Library.

Typeset by Type Study, Scarborough, North Yorkshire.
Printed and bound by Cromwell Press, Trowbridge.

Contents

Contributors

Deborah Cook is Professor of Philosophy at the University of Windsor, Canada. Her books include *The Culture Industry Revisited: Theodor W. Adorno on Mass Culture* (1996) and *Adorno, Habermas, and the Search for a Rational Society* (2004).

Ståle Finke is Professor of Philosophy at NTNY, the University of Trondheim, Norway. His recent publications include *Approaches to Painting* (co-authored with art historian Holger Koefoed) on the Norwegian painter Håvard Vikhagen. His current research deals with Gadamer's hermeneutics, language and mimesis.

Fabian Freyenhagen is Professor of Philosophy at the University of Essex, having previously worked at the Universities of Sheffield and Cambridge. His research interests are in moral and political philosophy as well as in modern European philosophy (especially Kant and Adorno). He is currently writing a book-length defence of Adorno's ethics.

Espen Hammer is Professor of Philosophy at the University of Oslo, Norway. Recently a visiting professor at the New School for Social Research, he is currently teaching at the University of Pennsylvania. His publications include *Stanley Cavell: Skepticism, Subjectivity, and the Ordinary* (2002), *Adorno and the Political* (2006) and, as editor, *German Idealism: Contemporary Perspectives* (2007).

Pauline Johnson is Associate Professor and Head of the Department of Sociology at Macquarie University, Sydney. Her recent publications include *Habermas: Rescuing the Public Sphere* (2006). Her current research seeks to renegotiate the terms in which a contemporary sociology of intimacy conceives the intersections between the private and the public spheres.

Brian O'Connor is Senior Lecturer in Philosophy at University College Dublin. He is the author of *Adorno's Negative Dialectic: Philosophy and the Possibility of a Critical Rationality* (2004) and editor of *The Adorno Reader* (2000). Among his contributions to other aspects of German philosophy is *German Idealism: An Anthology and Guide* (2006), which he edited with Georg Mohr.

Alison Stone is Senior Lecturer in Philosophy at Lancaster University. She works in post-Kantian European philosophy, feminist philosophy and political philosophy. Her books include *Petrified Intelligence: Nature in Hegel's Philosophy* (2004), *Luce Irigaray and the Philosophy of Sexual Difference* (2006) and *An Introduction to Feminist Philosophy* (2007).

Marianne Tettlebaum is Visiting Assistant Professor of German at Hendrix College, USA. She is currently at work on a book-length study entitled *Adorno's Lightheartedness – 'Mozart's Sadness'*, which examines the role of the concepts of lightheartedness and childhood in Adorno's analysis of the German philosophical tradition.

Ross Wilson is a Leverhulme Trust Early Career Fellow in the Faculty of English, University of Cambridge, and a Fellow of Emmanuel College, Cambridge. He is the author of *Subjective Universality in Kant's Aesthetics* (2007) and of *Theodor Adorno* (2008).

Robert W. Witkin is Professor of Sociology at the University of Exeter, and a Fellow of the Centre for Cultural Sociology, Yale University. He is the author of *Adorno on Music* (1998) and *Adorno on Popular Culture* (2002).

Acknowledgements

First to be acknowledged is the sheer hubris involved in crafting essays that purport to introduce a thinker as complex and challenging as Theodor W. Adorno. If this book succeeds in serving as a guide through the intricate labyrinth of Adorno's work, its success is due to the attempts of its expert contributors to make Adorno accessible to a new generation of readers without, as they say in the current vernacular, "dumbing him down". A pleasure to work with, the Adorno scholars whose work appears here have managed to square the circle: to clarify Adorno's thought without simplifying it. They provide readers with the key concepts needed to decipher Adorno's often daunting books and essays.

Appreciation should be extended to others as well. Outstanding scholar Michael Walschots, who helped with editing, offered critical commentary from the refreshing perspective of someone encountering Adorno for the first time. Jeffrey Renaud, whose Masters thesis on Herbert Marcuse I am currently supervising, also offered insightful comments and criticisms. Librarian Johanna Foster was resourceful and diligent in tracking down many works cited in the references. Colleagues Catherine Hundleby and Marcello Guarini afforded me the luxury of several weeks in Toronto to work on editing when they agreed to serve in my place as acting head of the Philosophy Department. For his part, Tristan Palmer at Acumen was always helpful and encouraging in a quietly unobtrusive way.

Finally, the spirit of our own troubled age, the *Zeitgeist*, which deeply informs the essays in this volume, must be acknowledged.

Adorno remains relevant because the issues he explored are as pressing now as they were when he first began to subject them to his uncompromisingly critical gaze.

Deborah Cook

Abbreviations

The following abbreviations refer to frequently cited texts written by Theodor W. Adorno. Full bibliographical details are given in the References.

AE *Against Epistemology: A Metacritique. Studies in Husserl and the Phenomenological Antinomies* (1983)

AT *Aesthetic Theory* (1997)

CLA *Can One Live after Auschwitz? A Philosophical Reader* (2003)

CM *Critical Models: Interventions and Catchwords* (1998)

DE *Dialectic of Enlightenment* (1972), C: translated by John Cumming; *Dialectic of Enlightenment: Philosophical Fragments* (2002), J: translated by Edmund Jephcott

DLM "Democratic Leadership and Mass Manipulation" (1986)

EM *Essays on Music: Theodor W. Adorno* (2002)

HF *History and Freedom: Lectures 1964–65* (2006)

HPI "Husserl and the Problem of Idealism" (1998)

INH "The Idea of Natural History", *Things Beyond Resemblance: Collected Essays on Theodor W. Adorno* (2006)

IS *Introduction to Sociology* (2000)

KCPR *Kant's "Critique of Pure Reason"* (2001)

ME *Metaphysics: Concept and Problems* (2001)

MM *Minima Moralia: Reflections from Damaged Life* (1974)

ND *Negative Dialectics* (1973)

NLI *Notes to Literature*, Vol. I (1991)

NLII *Notes to Literature*, Vol. II (1992)

P   *Prisms* (1967)
PMP   *Problems of Moral Philosophy* (2000)
S   "Society" (1969–70)
TPC   "Theory of Pseudo-Culture" (1993)

PART I

Adorno's intellectual history and legacy

ONE

Theodor W. Adorno: an introduction

Deborah Cook

Adorno's professional life was bound indissolubly to the Institute for Social Research, which opened on 22 June 1924 in Frankfurt-am-Main, Germany. At its inception, Institute members engaged in inter-disciplinary studies devoted to the theory and history of socialism and the labour movement. However, after the first director, Carl Grünberg, resigned, Max Horkheimer took his place in 1930, giving the Institute a new orientation. In his inaugural address, Horkheimer stated that the work undertaken by the Institute would examine "the connection between the economic life of society, the psychical development of individuals, and the changes in the realm of culture in the narrower sense (to which belong not only the so-called intel-lectual elements, such as science, art, and religion, but also law, customs, fashion, public opinion, sports, leisure activities, lifestyle, etc.)".[1] Using both empirical research and philosophy, the Institute would develop a theory of contemporary society by analysing its prevailing tendencies, with the ultimate goal of transforming society along more rational lines.[2]

However, with the victory of Hitler's National Socialist Party in 1930, the Institute – nicknamed Café Marx[3] – would not remain in Frankfurt much longer. It was closed and its property confiscated by the Gestapo in 1933 on the grounds that it had communist leanings.[4] Having taken the precaution of placing the Institute's funds in Holland in 1931,[5] Horkheimer had the resources needed to estab-lish a branch of the Institute at Columbia University in New York in 1934, where he was soon joined by Friedrich Pollock, Herbert Marcuse and Leo Löwenthal. As they were settling in the United

States, Adorno was studying at Oxford with the philosopher Gilbert Ryle, who agreed to supervise a thesis he proposed to write on Husserl.[6] Although he was associated officially with the Institute in 1935, it was not until 1938 that Adorno left for New York with his new wife Gretel.

Adorno, who studied composition with Alban Berg in Vienna in the 1920s, had already published a number of essays on music.[7] Upon his arrival in New York, Horkheimer arranged for him to work with Paul Lazarsfeld in New Jersey as head of the music section of the Princeton Radio Research Project which was funded by the Rockefeller Foundation. Until 1940, Adorno was responsible for conducting empirical research into the psychological value of radio music for listeners.[8] But, by this time, it was glaringly apparent to the *émigrés*, some of whose family and friends were suffering horribly under Nazism, that anti-Semitism was rife in many other countries. In the early 1940s, then, Adorno began to study anti-Semitism, following the lead of Horkheimer in "The Jews and Europe".[9]

In a letter to the secretary of the Institute's Geneva office, Horkheimer declared in 1939 that all his earlier work was a prelude to a book he planned to write on dialectical logic.[10] He confided to Pollock as early as 1935 that Adorno was the ideal collaborator for this project.[11] By 1938 the project had become more concrete. Adorno reported to Walter Benjamin that Horkheimer was eager to "begin work on a book on the dialectic of the Enlightenment".[12] Yet this work really only began after the Institute moved most of its resources from New York to Los Angeles in 1941. Dedicated to Pollock, to mark his fiftieth birthday, the book was completed in the spring of 1944; it first appeared in 1947 in Holland under the title *Dialektik der Aufklärung*.

Dialectic of Enlightenment opens with a strident warning. If enlightenment was supposed to emancipate humanity, today the "fully enlightened earth radiates disaster triumphant" (*DE*, C: 3; J: 1). The first chapter tries to show that, for all its attempts to supersede the mythic worldview, enlightenment is just an outgrowth of myth and ends by reverting to it. Compulsively forcing natural objects into explanatory schema in order to dominate them, enlightenment confuses "the animate with the inanimate, just as myth compounds the inanimate with the animate" (*DE*, C: 16; J: 11). Allowing nothing to escape its conceptual grasp, enlightened thought not only exhibits an overwhelming fear of nature, but it continues to be driven by nature. The modern employment of reason makes nature "audible in its estrangement" because its very attempt to master nature shows only that reason remains enslaved to it (*DE*, C: 39; J: 31).

This theme of our embeddedness in nature, which is central to the later work of Adorno as well, is elaborated throughout *Dialectic of Enlightenment*. In an excursus on the *Odyssey*, the emergence of reason is itself traced back to the dawn of history. Bound to the instinct for self-preservation, reason developed as a means to the end of thwarting the powers of nature. Endorsing Freud's claim in *Civilization and its Discontents* that human history consists in the renunciation of instinct, Adorno and Horkheimer also observe that rational control over nature was achieved only by delaying the gratification of instincts, or by repressing them altogether. Mastery over nature

> practically always involves the annihilation of the subject in whose service that mastery is maintained because the substance which is mastered, suppressed, and disintegrated by self-preservation is nothing other than the living entity, of which the achievements of self-preservation can only be defined as functions – in other words, self-preservation destroys the very thing which is to be preserved. (*DE*, C: 55; J: 43)

Since survival instincts have propelled much of Western history, the official history of Europe conceals a subterranean history that "consists in the fate of the human instincts and passions repressed and distorted by civilization" (*DE*, C: 231; J: 192). Indeed, while greatly indebted to Marx, Adorno focused not just on economic conditions in the West, but on human psychology as well. As Martin Jay explains, "the unexpected rise of an irrationalist mass politics in fascism, which was unforeseen by orthodox Marxists", justified the incorporation of psychology into a critical account of society. Yet, even after the defeat of National Socialism, "psychological impediments to emancipation" remained in "the manipulated society of mass consumption that followed in its wake".[13] Concern about these impediments is forcefully expressed in a chapter of *Dialectic of Enlightenment* called "Enlightenment as Mass Deception", where the psychology underlying fascist propaganda is compared to the psychotechnology of the Hollywood-based culture industry. Extensive use is also made of psychoanalysis in the following chapter on anti-Semitism.

Nevertheless, it was not just the attempt to understand fascism and the culture industry that made Freud indispensable. What particularly recommended Freud to Adorno was his endorsement of the idea that nature and history are dialectically entwined. Originally advancing this idea in a 1932 lecture called "The Idea of Natural History" (INH: 260), Adorno later supported it by citing *The German Ideology*, where Marx declared that nature and human history would always qualify one another (*ND*: 358). But Adorno points out that Freud too described history as natural. On the one hand, Freud derived "even complex mental behaviours from the drive for self-preservation and pleasure". On the other hand, he never denied that "the concrete manifestation of instincts may undergo the most sweeping variations and modifications" throughout history.[14] Consequently, Freud's instinct theory not only helped Adorno to explain phenomena such as Nazi Germany and the culture industry, but also to elaborate in psychological terms on Marx's dialectical view of the relationship between nature and history.

Admittedly, Adorno was neither an orthodox Marxist nor an orthodox Freudian, and he never fully addressed the problem of reconciling Marx and Freud. Yet he examined the impact of capitalism on the psychological development of individuals in most of his work. According to Adorno, the rise of capitalism had fostered widespread social and psychological pathologies such as authoritarianism, narcissism and paranoia. And, as early as 1927, Adorno argued that these pathologies can be overcome, not by psychoanalysis, but only by completely transforming capitalist society.[15] Since psycho-pathologies have social roots, often connected to the predominance of exchange relations in human life, they can be dealt with effectively only by abolishing this predominance.

Yet Adorno distanced himself from both Marx and the orthodox Marxism of the former Soviet Union in his 1942 essay "Reflections on Class Theory". Since Marx's prediction about the concentration and centralization of capital was realized, capitalism had changed – particularly with respect to the composition of classes. Consisting of relatively independent entrepreneurs during the earlier phase of liberal capital, the bourgeoisie forfeited much of its economic power as monopoly conditions developed. The economically disenfranchised bourgeoisie and the proletariat now form a new mass class distinct from the class comprising the dwindling owners of the means of production (*CLA*: 99). In a Hegelian remark about the *Aufhebung* – the preservation and sublation – of classes under monopoly capital, Adorno states that Marx's concept of class must be preserved because "the division of society into exploiters and exploited, not only continues to exist but gains in force and strength". But the concept must be sublated "because the oppressed who today, as predicted by [Marxist] theory, constitute the overwhelming majority of humankind, are unable to experience themselves as a class" (*CLA*: 97, tr. mod.).

So, while class stratification persists, classes themselves have changed, and the subjective awareness of belonging to a class has evaporated. Marx's theory is no longer straightforwardly applicable to conditions today precisely because he was right about the emergence of monopoly conditions. Adorno also takes issue with Marx's theory of impoverishment, arguing that impoverishment can be understood only in a metaphorical sense because workers today have far more to lose than their chains. Compared to the situation of workers in nineteenth-century England, the standard of living of workers in the West has improved owing in part to the establishment of the welfare state. The work day is now shorter, and workers enjoy "better food, housing and clothing; protection for family members and for workers in their old age; and an increase in average life expectancy". Hunger no longer compels workers "to join forces and make a revolution" (*CLA*: 103, tr. mod.).

Borrowing a phrase from "The Communist Manifesto", Adorno argues that, with the welfare state, the ruling class effectively secures "for 'slaves their existence within slavery' " in order to ensure its own. Impoverishment now refers to the "political and social impotence" of individuals who have become pure objects of administration for monopolies and their political allies (*CLA*: 105). Survival depends on adaptation to a constantly changing and inherently unpredictable economic system. Adaptation is reinforced by the sophisticated psychotechnology of the culture industry and the prevailing positivist ideology which glorifies existing states of affairs. By these means, the needs of the new mass class are made to harmonize with commodified offers of satisfaction. Conformity to socially approved models of behaviour now appears more rational than solidarity (*CLA*: 97). This also helps to explain why prospects for revolutionary change have faded.

Some commentators claim that Adorno adopted Pollock's state capitalism thesis, which argues that there has been a transition in Western countries "from a predominantly economic to an essentially political era".[16] Yet, while acknowledging that political power had increased in the West, Adorno agreed with Marx's insistence on the primacy of the economy. At best, Pollock's thesis signalled ominous trends in other Western countries. What really changes with monopoly capitalism is that the ruling class becomes anonymous: it disappears "behind the concentration of capital". Capitalism now appears to be "an institution, the expression of society as a whole". Pervading almost every aspect of human life, the fetish character of commodities, which transforms relations between people into relations between things, ends in the socially totalitarian aspect of capital (CLA: 99). As Stefan Müller-Doohm remarks, the pervasiveness of reification today provides an answer to a question posed in the preface to *Dialectic of Enlightenment*, namely why humanity is sinking into a new kind of barbarism, rather than entering into a truly human state.[17]

The urgency of this question did not abate when Adorno returned to Frankfurt in 1949. Until his death, much of his work – including books and essays on music and literature – dealt with the problems of fascism and monopoly capitalism. What concerned Adorno above all is that conditions similar to those accompanying the rise of Nazism in Germany persist in the West. He believed that little had changed since the end of World War II: "The economic order, and to a great extent also the economic organization modeled upon it, now as then renders the majority of people dependent upon conditions beyond their control and thus maintains them in a state of political immaturity". In the interest of survival, individuals must "negate precisely that autonomous subjectivity to which the idea of democracy appeals; they can preserve themselves only if they renounce their self" (CM: 98).

Upon his return to Germany, Adorno's empirical study of personality traits in the United States – *The Authoritarian Personality* – was published, along with other volumes in a series entitled *Studies in Prejudice*. During the 1950s, Adorno also wrote articles dealing with research methodology in the social sciences.[18] Indeed, while criticizing empirical social research on the grounds that social science must be guided by the normative idea "of a true society",[19] Adorno engaged in empirical studies throughout the 1950s. In 1952, for example, he drafted a qualitative analysis of astrology columns in the *Los Angeles Times*, as well as two studies of television.[20] Back in Germany, he worked on a project examining the relationship between the manifest political opinions of Germans from different social strata and their latent attitudes.[21] Part of the study focused on how German citizens attempted to deny their recent past. Here again psychoanalysis was used to explore both the guilt experienced by Germans and the defence mechanisms that helped them to assuage that guilt.[22]

By the end of the 1950s, however, Adorno devoted himself almost exclusively to the elaboration of his critical social theory. Among the more important of his essays is "Progress", which he described as a "preliminary study" that "belongs within the complex" of his major work, *Negative Dialectics* (*CM*: 125). Here he develops an idea first advanced in *Dialectic of Enlightenment*, namely, that what counts as progress today is the domination of external and internal nature which, impelled by the instinct for self-preservation, threatens to destroy what it is meant to preserve. By contrast, genuine progress depends upon humanity becoming aware of its "own inbred nature" with the aim of halting "the domination that it exacts upon nature and through which domination by nature continues" (*ibid.*: 150). Catastrophe can be averted only if "a self-conscious global subject" develops and intervenes, using the "technical forces of production" to abolish all forms of material deprivation, and to establish "the whole society as humanity" (*ibid.*: 144).

But Adorno continued to develop his ideas. Among the more important of these are his notions of identity and non-identity thinking. As J. M. Bernstein remarks, identity thinking was discussed as early as *Dialectic of Enlightenment*, even if it was not given that name. What is called the principle of immanence in *Dialectic of Enlightenment* was later called identity thinking. This principle entails that an object is known "only when it is classified in some way", or "when it is shown, via subsumption, to share character-istics or features" with other objects. Similarly, "an event is explained if it can be shown to fall within the ambit of a known pattern of occurrence, if it falls within the ambit of a known rule or is deducible from (subsumable by) a known law". In turn, concepts, rules and laws have a cognitive value only when they are "subsumed under or shown to be deducible from higher-level concepts, rules, or laws".[23] Bernstein resumes: "[c]ognition is subsumption, subsump-tion is necessarily reiterable, and reiteration occurs through cogni-tive ascent from concrete to abstract, from particular to universal, from what is relatively universal, and thereby still in some respect particular, contingent, and conditioned, to what is more universal".[24]

By subsuming objects under concepts and laws, and concepts and laws under explanatory systems, we try to dominate nature in the interest of survival. In so doing, we wrongly substitute unity for diversity, simplicity for complexity, permanence for change, and identity for difference. Once particulars are effectively identified with universals, there is allegedly nothing more to be said about them. Identity thinking consists in the claim that diverse objects fall under concept "X"; it thereby obliterates the particularity of objects, their differences from one other, their individual development and histories, along with other unique traits. To counter identity thinking, Adorno proposed a new cognitive paradigm: non-identity thinking. He had already broached this idea in his lectures on Kant's *Critique of Pure Reason*. Kant implicitly endorses non-identity by insisting on "the obstacle, the *block*, encountered by the subject in its search for knowledge". Non-identity appears in the idea that our "affections" not only "arise from things-in-themselves", but that these things are irreducible to our concepts and categories of them (*KCPR*: 66–7).

Adorno devotes his *magnum opus*, *Negative Dialectics*, to exploring this alternative cognitive paradigm. Claiming that identity thinking merely "says what something falls under, what it exemplifies or represents, and what, accordingly, it is not itself", Adorno contrasts it to non-identity thinking, which "seeks to say what something is". By saying "it is", non-identity thinking does identify; it even "identifies to a greater extent" than identity thinking. But non-identity thinking identifies in "other ways" because it is not content merely to subsume objects under universal concepts with a view to manipulating and controlling them. Rather, non-identity thinking tries to make concepts consonant with non-conceptual particulars. In so doing, it reveals "elements of affinity" between the non-conceptual object and our concepts of it (*ND*: 149). This affinity exists because concepts are thoroughly entwined in non-conceptuality: they are "moments of the reality that requires their formation, primarily for the control of nature" (*ibid.*: 11).

In non-identity thinking, then, the "direction of conceptuality" is turned back towards non-conceptuality because concepts are generated in our embodied contact with material things, and they continue to refer to things by virtue of their meaning in which their relation to the non-conceptual survives (*ND*: 12). Yet concepts have a dual relation to objects. On the one hand, they depend on the non-conceptual matter that provides their content and is the source of their power to name. To convey "full, unreduced experience in the medium of conceptual reflection", then, non-identity thinking must immerse itself in things (*ibid.*: 13). On the other hand, concepts transcend objects by heeding "a potential that waits in the object", and intending in the object "even that of which the object was deprived by objectification" (*ibid.*: 19). In this case, non-identity thinking grasps objects by means of possibility to indicate what an object might become if the damaged conditions under which it developed were altered (*ibid.*: 52).

If concepts should be oriented towards the object's material axis, the object in turn should approximate concepts. Non-identity thinking involves the "[r]eciprocal criticism of the universal and of the particular". It must judge *both* "whether the concept does justice to what it covers" *and* "whether the particular fulfils its concept". These two critical operations jointly "constitute the medium of thinking about the nonidentity of particular and concept" (*ND*: 146). To rest content with the judgement that the concept does (or does not do) justice to objects would amount to leaving "behind the medium of virtuality, of anticipation that cannot be wholly fulfilled by any piece of actuality" (*MM*: 127). Objects will satisfy concepts only by making good on their own immanent potential – a potential that some emphatic concepts evoke or intimate. Non-identity can be said to contain identity in the prospective longing of the concept to become identical with the thing (*ND*: 149).

Non-identity thinking therefore "contains identity" in a peculiar fashion. Since particular objects do not currently realize their potential, no particular is "as its particularity requires" (*ND*: 152, tr. mod.). For Adorno, the "substance of the contradiction between universal and particular" is that the non-conceptual particular "is not yet – and that, therefore, it is bad wherever established". Holding fast to what concepts rob from particulars, non-identity thinking also retains "the 'more' of the concept" as compared to these particulars (*ibid.*: 151). To make good on "the pledge that there should be no contradiction, no antagonism" between the object and the thought of it (*ibid.*: 149), non-identity thinking prospectively identifies the object with the concept. In such thinking, emphatic concepts suggest changed conditions – like the condition of a free society where human beings might develop unfettered. Evoking conditions that do not yet exist, these concepts "overshoot" what exists in order better to grasp it (*MM*: 126).

Concepts can evoke something more than what exists owing to their determinate negation of existing conditions. The resistance of thought to "mere things in being" (*ND*: 19) is all the more powerful when concepts are forged in the negation of the negative conditions that damage human life. Adorno illustrates these ideas in his discussion of the concept of freedom: the shape of freedom "can only be grasped in determinate negation in accordance with the concrete form of a specific unfreedom" (*ibid.*: 231, tr. mod.). Ideas of freedom are derived from a negation of those aspects of reality that perpetuate unfreedom. Freedom is therefore "a polemical counter-image to the suffering brought on by social coercion; unfreedom as that coercion's image" (*ibid.*: 223). Here Adorno invites us to think of emancipatory movements such as abolitionism and women's liberation in which the unfree conditions that cause suffering point to their possible reversal by giving rise to the idea of a condition in which oppression would end. Ideas such as that of freedom arise within oppressive situations "as resistance to repression" (*ibid.*: 265); freedom arises historically in experiences of combating unfreedom.

Although he claims that determinate negation is "the only form in which metaphysical experience survives today" (*ME*: 144), Adorno rejects Hegel's view that it necessarily yields something positive. Since our conceptions of freedom are rooted in the very negativity they strive to overcome, they are also contaminated by that negativity. If critique indicates what is right and better, it does so only obliquely. The negation of negative conditions "remains negative" because positivity is only indirectly outlined by critique (*ND*: 158–9). A resolutely critical negation of existing states of affairs, determinate negation discloses something equally negative: what exists is not yet what it ought to be and what ought to be does not yet exist. In other words, a double negation yields only more negativity.

Emphatic concepts must be employed with other concepts in what Adorno describes as a constellation. As opposed to identity thinking, which abstracts from objects when it subsumes them under concepts, a constellation of concepts will illuminate "the specific side of the object, the side which to a classifying procedure is either a matter of indifference or a burden". In this context, Adorno praises Max Weber's employment of ideal types, or of concepts " 'gradually composed' from 'individual parts . . . taken from historic reality' " (*ND*: 164). To illustrate this procedure, Adorno turns to Weber's discussion of capitalism in *The Protestant Ethic and the Spirit of Capitalism*, where Weber gathers diverse concepts – such as acquisitiveness, the profit motive, calculation, organization – in order to express what capitalism "aims at, not to circumscribe it to operational ends" (*ibid.*: 166). Conceding that constellations are subjective constructs, Adorno nonetheless argues that this "subjectively created context" is "readable as a sign of objectivity", or of the "spiritual substance" of phenomena (*ibid.*: 165).

Adorno defines truth as "a constellation of subject and object in which both penetrate each other" (*ibid.*: 127). Even in this form, however, truth is not something static. Instead, thought must constantly renew itself "in the experience of the subject matter", and that matter, for its part, is first determined by subjective concepts. Enunciated in "a constantly evolving constellation" (*CM*: 131), truth manifests itself only in a progressive approximation of objects by concepts, and of concepts by objects. Thus objects are "infinitely given as a task" (*ibid.*: 253). Moreover, Adorno continues to stress the fallibility of emphatic ideas when he writes that "the truth of ideas is bound up with the possibility of their being wrong, the possibility of their failure". That the truth derived from determinate negation can always be revised, overthrown, even lost, further demonstrates that the negation of the negation fails to yield something positive (*ME*: 144).

Devoting much of his later work to devising an alternative cognitive paradigm to overcome identity thinking, Adorno was also drawn to aesthetics. Philosophy resembles art because, at their best, both aim to open up "a perspective on reconciliation" with nature (*AT*: 276). Yet, because it determines its object "as indeterminable", art "requires philosophy, which interprets [art] in order to say what it is unable to say" (*ibid.*: 72). If philosophy refuses to abandon "the yearning that animates the nonconceptual side of art", Adorno warns that a "philosophy that tried to imitate art, that would turn itself into a work of art, would be expunging itself" (*ND*: 15). He claims that "philosophy cannot survive without the linguistic effort" because the "organon of thought" is language. Consequently, one of philosophy's tasks is to reflect critically upon language in such a way that its use of language finally permits "a mutual approximation of thing and expression, to the point where the difference [between them] fades". In this, philosophy reveals the utopian bent that it shares with art because to want "substance in cognition is to want a utopia" (*ibid.*: 56).

While developing these ideas about non-identity thinking, and drafting his treatise in aesthetics, Adorno remained a staunch critic of oppressive socio-economic conditions. On his view, individuals now stand in relation to society in much the same way that material particulars stand to universal concepts. Indeed, he even refers to society as the "universal". While identity thinking falsely maintains the primacy of concepts over objects, society reifies individuals by subsuming them under abstract exchange relations. In this respect, identity thinking and exchange are isomorphic. Just as identity thinking expunges particulars by identifying them with universal concepts, exchange relations make "nonidentical individuals and performances become commensurable and identical". In both its conceptual and social forms, then, the principle of identification now "imposes on the whole world an obligation to become identical, to become total" (*ND*: 146 *passim*).

Adopting Marx's view that exchange relations have a life of their own to which human life is now forfeit, Adorno claims that bourgeois individualism, which celebrates the individual as the substance of society, masks an entirely different reality: the predominance of exchange relations and their homogenizing and levelling effects on needs, behaviour, thought and interpersonal relations. Although individuals have always been obliged to submit to economic conditions that determine whether they work, when, where, and how they work, today even their needs and instincts are manipulated to correspond to available offers of commodified satisfaction, and their behaviour is moulded to fit socially approved models. In fact, exchange relations now encroach upon areas of life that were formerly unaffected by them. Forced to adapt to a world "whose law is universal individual profit", we submit to forms of integration so complete and far-reaching that Adorno even compares them to genocide (ND: 362).

Individuals measure their own self-worth and the worth of others in terms of the value of the goods they possess and the places they occupy within the economic system; their possessions and occupations serve as social markers that position them within groups and distinguish them from other individuals and groups. In other words, individuals relate to one another as mere "agents and bearers of exchange value" (S: 148–9). At the same time, they are isolated and alienated from one another precisely because their interpersonal relations are often cemented by nothing more substantive than exchange. Indeed, Adorno is especially worried about prospects for social solidarity today. As the exchange principle degrades relations between people to relations between things, the solidarity needed to surmount these relations has evaporated. In other words, exchange relations undermine the very solidarity that is needed to overcome them.

Economic conditions also severely impair the autonomy of the family and the public sphere. Since individuals are completely dependent for their survival on the often fickle largesse of the state and the economy, it is far easier for public and private institutions to usurp the role the family once played as the primary agent of socialization. As the media and other institutions replace authority structures within the family, ego development suffers because individuals no longer measure their strength against their parents through rebellion and resistance. Now weakened, the ego's defences against the instinctual energy of the id and the superego are also weak. This ego weakness contributes to the marked increase in narcissistic pathologies, which Adorno was among the first to diagnose. Owing to the psychic economy of the reified and narcissistic personality, society "extends repressively into all psychology in the form of censorship and the superego".[25] Regressive forms of solidarity have emerged in movements (such as Nazism) where leaders attract followers by reanimating narcissistic superego introjects.

Of course, Adorno borrows from Freud in his analysis of phenomena such as Nazism. As Freud explained in "Group Psychology and the Analysis of the Ego", once individuals identify with a leader and become members of a group, they behave instinctually rather than according to their egocentric interests.[26] In his 1951 essay, "Freudian Theory and the Pattern of Fascist Propaganda", Adorno also adopted Freud's view that groups often act as a "negatively integrating force". Negative emotions towards out-groups (Jews, blacks, communists etc.) offer a narcissistic gain for followers because they believe that "simply through belonging to the in-group" they are "better, higher, and purer than those who are excluded".[27] Collective narcissism compensates for social powerlessness by allowing people to turn themselves "either in fact or imagination into members of something higher and more encompassing to which they attribute qualities which they themselves lack and from which they profit by vicarious participation" (TPC: 32–3).

While the family no longer serves as the primary agent for socialization, the public sphere fails to fulfil its role as "the most important medium of all politically effective criticism" because it has become so commodified that it currently "works against the critical principle in order to market itself" (*CM*: 283). Public opinion is imposed from above by "the overall structure of society and hence by relations of domination" (*ibid.*: 121). Opinions disseminated by the culture industry merely reflect those of the prevailing economic and political powers. Public opinion today is "indissolubly entangled" with private interests in profit and power that only masquerade as universal (*ibid.*: 117). Truth is replaced by statistically generated opinions, and the public has lost the capacity for the sustained reflection "required by a concept of truth" (*ibid.*: 114).

The loss of individuality, autonomy and freedom, which Adorno charts throughout his work, can be traced to the surrender of the task of self-preservation to the welfare state and the capitalist economy. Admitting that this surrender was necessary to enable individuals to survive "in more highly developed social conditions", Adorno nonetheless observes that, to survive under capitalism, individuals are compelled to become the involuntary executors of the law of exchange (*ND*: 312). For their part, however, Western societies neglect their living human substratum in their relentless pursuit of profit. As Simon Jarvis puts it:

> The more obvious it becomes that the economic basis of any individual's life is liable to annihilation, and the more real economic initiative is concentrated with the concentration of capital, the more the individual seeks to identify with and adapt to capital . . . For capital, however, the individual's self-preservation is not in itself a matter of any importance.[28]

Adorno complains that even reflective people, capable of taking a critical perspective on society, have little choice but "to make an alien cause their own" (*ND*: 311). But most individuals remain the unconscious and largely impotent pawns of an economic system that uses and abuses them with the sole aim of promoting its particular interests in profit and power. Once the "self-preserving function" of their egos was "split off from that of consciousness" and subordinated to economic and political agents and institutions, their attempts to preserve themselves effectively "surrendered to irrationality".[29] Since individuals are wholly dependent on society for their survival, capitalism can dispense with "the mediating agencies of ego and individuality" it had fostered under the earlier stage of liberal capitalism. It now arrests "all differentiation", while exploiting "the primitive core of the unconscious".[30] Substantially weakened, few individuals can resist the manipulation and exploitation of their instincts.

Openly admitting that he was exaggerating the "somber side" of our current predicament (*CM*: 99), Adorno tried to describe objective tendencies in the West where "the immense concentration of economical and administrative power leaves the individual no more room to maneuver", that is, where "society tends toward totalitarian forms of domination" (*ibid.*: 298). Still, individuals are not doomed to remain oblivious to the ways in which they perpetuate their own powerlessness. Although survival instincts have led us to do destructive things both to ourselves and to the nature on which our survival depends, things might have gone, and may yet go, differently. It may yet be possible to direct self-preservation consciously to the goal that it implicitly contains: the preservation of the species as a whole. In fact, Adorno argues that reason "should not be anything less than self-preservation, namely that of the species, upon which the survival of each individual literally depends" (*ibid.*: 273). Reason can never be "split off from self-preservation", not only because it owes its own development to this drive, but because the "preservation of humanity is inexorably inscribed within the meaning of rationality". Self-preservation "has its end in a reasonable organization of society" (*ibid.*: 272), or in a society that preserves its subjects "according to their unfettered potentialities" (*ibid.*: 272–3).

The goal of establishing a rational society that preserves and enhances the lives of each one of its members without exception was championed by all first-generation critical theorists. For his part, Adorno reiterates a point made by Herbert Marcuse in *One-Dimensional Man* when he declares that "the technical forces of production are at a stage that makes it possible to foresee the global dispensation from material labour, its reduction to a limiting value" (*CM*: 267). If it was once necessary to "struggle against the pleasure principle for the sake of one's own self-preservation", labour can now be reduced to a minimum and need no longer be tied to self-denial (*ibid.*: 262). A similar remark appears in *Negative Dialectics*: the state of productive forces is currently such that much of our labour is superfluous. Impelled by survival imperatives that continue to demand the sacrifice of instincts and the domination of external nature even after technology has made self-preservation "easy", the logic of history is logical no longer (*ND*: 262).

To be sure, capitalism appears to be second nature; it seems to have evolved naturally, and therefore to be unchangeable. But this appearance is illusory because "[t]he rigidified institutions, the relations of production are not Being as such, but even in their omnipotence they are man-made and revocable" (*CM*: 156). Although he has been criticized for failing to provide a blueprint for radical social change, Adorno recognized that radical change was needed to foster the reconciliation of the individual and society that would enable us to develop freely outside of constraints that are as unnecessary as they are irrational. He was also convinced that sustained critical reflection on our current predicament is the first step towards emancipation. According to Adorno, we "may not know what people are and what the correct arrangement of human affairs should be, but we do know what people should not be and what arrangement of human affairs is false". Only in this critical understanding of the negative aspects of the human predicament is "the other, positive, one open to us".[31] To acquire a sense of what a more rational society might look like, then, we first need to achieve a thorough understanding of the irrational conditions that continue to fetter us.

Notes

1. Max Horkheimer, "The Present Situation of Social Philosophy and the Tasks of an Institute for Social Research", *Between Philosophy and Social Science: Selected Early Writings* (1993), 11.
2. I am paraphrasing the Institute's description of its own history in an in-house publication. See *Forschungsarbeiten*, vol. 10 (September 1999), 7. Two excellent histories of the Institute are available in English: Martin Jay's *Dialectical Imagination: A History of the Frankfurt School and the Institute for Social Research, 1923–1950* (1973), and Rolf Wiggershaus's *The Frankfurt School: Its History, Theories, and Political Significance* (1994). A good biography of Adorno available in English is Stefan Müller-Doohm's *Adorno: A Biography* (2005).
3. Müller-Doohm, *Adorno*, 177.
4. Wiggerhaus, *The Frankfurt School*, 128.
5. *Ibid.*, 110.
6. Adorno revised this undefended thesis on Husserl and published it in 1956. The book was later translated into English as *Against Epistemology* (*AE*).
7. See, for example, Adorno's controversial essay "On Jazz", and "On the Fetish Character in Music and the Regression of Listening" in *EM*.
8. Wiggershaus, *The Frankfurt School*, 239.
9. Horkheimer, "Die Juden und Europa", *Zeitschrift für Sozialforschung* 8 (1–2) (1939), 115–37. In 1941, the Institute published a series of articles on National Socialism in the successor to the *Zeitschrift*, called *Studies in Philosophy and Social Science*.
10. Wiggershaus, *The Frankfurt School*, 177.
11. *Ibid.*, 160.
12. Jay, *Dialectical Imagination*, 254.
13. Jay, *Adorno*, 85.
14. Adorno, "Die Revidierte Psychoanalyse", tr. Rainer Koehne, *Gesammelte Schriften* 8 (1972), 22. This essay was originally given as a lecture to the Psychoanalytic Society in San Francisco in 1946; it was first published in *Psyche* VI(1), 1952.
15. Müller-Doohm, *Adorno*, 105.
16. Friedrich Pollock, "State Capitalism: Its Possibilities and Limitations", *The Essential Frankfurt School Reader* (1978), 78. See also Pauline Johnson's reading of Pollock's thesis in this volume (Chapter 7).
17. Müller-Doohm, *Adorno*, 267. See Horkheimer and Adorno, *DE*, C: xi; J: xiv.
18. See, for example, *The Positivist Dispute in German Sociology* (1976), which contains presentations that Adorno and Karl Popper gave at a workshop in Tübingen in 1961.
19. Adorno, *et al.*, *The Positivist Dispute in German Sociology*, 27.
20. See Adorno, "The Stars Down to Earth: The Los Angeles Times Astrology Column", *The Stars Down to Earth and Other Essays on the Irrational in Culture* (1994), 34–127. See also "Prologue to Television", and "Television as Ideology", *CM*: 49–57; 59–70.
21. Müller-Doohm, *Adorno*, 380. See Friedrich Pollock (ed.), *Gruppenexperiment: Ein Studienbericht* (1955).
22. Müller-Doohm, *Adorno*, 381–2.

23. J. M. Bernstein, *Adorno: Disenchantment and Ethics* (2001), 87.
24. *Ibid.*, 88.
25. Adorno, "Sociology and Psychology", *New Left Review* **47** (1968), 79.
26. Sigmund Freud, "Group Psychology and the Analysis of the Ego", *The Penguin Freud Library*, vol. 12: *Civilization, Society and Religion* (1985), 100.
27. Adorno, "Freudian Theory and the Pattern of Fascist Propaganda", *The Essential Frankfurt School Reader* (1978), 130.
28. Simon Jarvis, *Adorno: A Critical Introduction* (1998), 83.
29. Adorno, "Sociology and Psychology", 88, tr. mod.
30. *Ibid.*, 95.
31. Adorno, "Individuum und Organisation", *Gesammelte Schriften* **8** (1972), 456.

TWO

Influences and impact

Deborah Cook

Introduction

Two figures took centre stage on the philosophical scene in Germany in the 1920s: Edmund Husserl and Martin Heidegger. Focusing on Husserl in his 1924 doctoral thesis, Adorno continued to engage with his ideas in later work as well.[1] However, Adorno was neither a Husserlian nor a Heideggerian. He first criticized Heidegger's work in "The Idea of Natural History" (INH: 260–61), where he rejected Heidegger's notion of historicity, opting instead for a Marxist perspective on history. His critique of Heidegger became far more strident in subsequent work where, among other things, he charged that Heidegger's philosophy of Being devolves into "an irrationalist world view" (ND: 85, tr. mod.). Indeed, Martin Jay remarks that Adorno viewed phenomenology as a whole as "the last futile attempt of bourgeois thought to rescue itself from impotence". Content merely to reproduce existing conditions, phenomenology not only "turned against action in the world"; it had a "subterranean connection with fascism" because both "were expressions of the terminal crisis of bourgeois society".[2]

Adorno's formative influences were astute commentators on this crisis. They included the culture critic Siegfried Kracauer, whom Adorno met towards the end of World War I. Acquainting him with the work of Immanuel Kant, Kracauer taught Adorno to interpret all philosophical works as coded texts from which "the historical condition of the mind could be read" (NLII: 59). Kracauer also introduced Adorno to Walter Benjamin, who remained a close friend until

Benjamin's death in 1940. From Benjamin's *The Origin of German Tragic Drama*, Adorno borrowed the idea that truth is accessible through constellations of concepts. Following Benjamin, he adopted "the later Nietzsche's critical insight that truth is not identical with a timeless *universal*; . . . rather it is solely the historical which yields the figure of the absolute" (*P*: 231). As Simon Jarvis observes, Adorno also learned from Benjamin that philosophical interpretation should begin with "the material specificity of the minute particulars uncovered by historical and philological inquiry rather than the highest, most general, and hence emptiest concepts".[3]

In the early 1920s, Adorno was greatly impressed by Ernst Bloch's *Spirit of Utopia* as well as by Georg Lukács's *Theory of the Novel*, which, as Kracauer taught him, kept alive the longing for "vanished meaning" in a world bereft of gods.[4] Even more important for Adorno's critical social theory was *History and Class Consciousness*, where Lukács extends Karl Marx's critique of commodity fetishism to disparate aspects of human life. In this brief account of the major influences on Adorno, however, I shall narrow my focus to four thinkers whose ideas play a prominent role in his work: Kant, Hegel, Marx and Freud. Following this discussion, Adorno's impact on other thinkers will be examined. A first-generation critical theorist, Adorno influenced not just his contemporaries in the Institute for Social Research, but later generations of critical theorists as well, including the philosopher and sociologist Jürgen Habermas. After describing the impact of Adorno's radical critique of late capitalist society on Habermas and his successors, I shall comment briefly on his contributions to empirical social research, sociology, communications studies and literary theory.

Influences

Adorno endorses Kant's idea that there is an obstacle or "block" to our understanding of objects; this block points to "an irreducible residue", to something non-identical with thought. Unlike Kant, however, Adorno claims that the block that separates natural objects from our understanding of them is not completely unbridgeable. The major problem with Kant was that he radically separated things-in-themselves from concepts. As a result, "it turns out that what remains of everything independent of the subject, or that comes to the subject from outside, is at bottom completely null and void". Quoting Bertolt Brecht, Adorno complains that things-in-themselves are nothing more than a "noble feature" in Kant's work: they "survive as a reminder that subjective knowledge is not the whole story, but they are without further consequence themselves" (*KCPR*: 128). To be sure, a noumenal realm of things-in-themselves must be postulated on largely logical grounds. But Kant no sooner posits the noumenal realm than he bars all knowledge of it. He confines the cognitive subject to examining its inner perceptions because these are allegedly all it can know.

Interestingly, Adorno thinks that the greatness of the *Critique of Pure Reason* lies in the clash of two contradictory "motifs". On the one hand, Kant succumbed to identity thinking by reducing "synthetic *a priori* judgements and ultimately all organized experience, all objectively valid experience, to an analysis of the consciousness of the subject". Recognizing that our knowledge of objects is mediated, Kant wrongly concludes that we can apprehend only the concepts that we use to grasp objects. On the other hand, Kant was also a non-identity thinker. Rather than reducing objects to our understanding of them, he points to the obstacles that impede a complete understanding of objects. For Adorno, then, Kant's first *Critique* contains both "an identity philosophy – that is, a philosophy that attempts to ground being in the subject – and also a nonidentity philosophy – one that attempts to restrict that claim to identity by insisting on the obstacles, the *block*, encountered by the subject in its search for knowledge" (*KCPR*: 66, tr. mod.)

Adorno constantly stresses the non-identity of concept and object, mind and matter, the individual and society. Non-identity is the pivot on which his work turns. However, non-identity does not mean that mind and nature, concept and object, the individual and society, are radically distinct. Indeed, Kant's failure to recognize their affinity also mars his philosophy. After insisting that consciousness is "part impulse itself, and also part of that in which it intervenes", Adorno adds that, without the affinity between consciousness and its objects which Kant denies, there could be no "idea of freedom, for whose sake he denies the affinity" (*ND*: 265, tr. mod.). Freedom requires action, but we can act only because we are ourselves physical, non-conceptual objects, part of the natural and social worlds. Against Kant, who thought that reason alone motivates practical activity, Adorno counters that "practice also needs something else, something physical which consciousness does not exhaust", something both "conveyed to reason and qualitatively different from it" (*ibid.*: 229).

Still, Adorno greatly admired Kant's discussion of the antinomy of freedom and causality. On Adorno's view, the doctrine of determinism, which states that all human action is causally determined, implicitly endorses commodification and reification. Determinists act as though "dehumanization, the totally developed commodity character of labour power, were human nature pure and simple". But the champions of free will are equally wrong because they completely disregard the effects of commodification and reification on human behaviour. For Adorno, then, each extreme thesis is false because both "proclaim identity" (ND: 264, tr. mod.). His lectures on moral philosophy end with the claim that the "highest point" to which moral philosophy can rise today is "that of the antinomy of causality and freedom which figures in Kant's philosophy in an unresolved and for that reason exemplary fashion" (PMP: 176).

The antinomy of freedom and causality is instructive because it reveals the contradictions in which reason is entangled. Although Kant thought he could resolve this antinomy, Adorno claims that it actually reveals a contradiction in reality itself (ibid.: 30). In fact, he gives this antinomy a social interpretation while using it as model to clarify his dialectical practice. Since we can discover neither a positive freedom nor a positive unfreedom in ourselves, the truth content in Kant's antinomy consists in its disclosure of this ambivalent state of affairs (ND: 223). Adorno further argues that because "there can be no answer to the question of whether freedom or unfreedom of the will exists" (ibid.: 263), the antinomy indicates that the universal – in the form of existing socio-economic institutions and practices – and the particular individuals who make up its living human substratum have not yet been reconciled.

But Adorno also argues that the social conditions that currently obstruct freedom point dialectically to their own reversal. Moreover, he traces this idea back to Kant, who taught that "the entanglement of progress . . . in the realm of unfreedom, tends by means of its own law toward the realm of freedom" (CM: 149–50).[5] Progress is dialectical because "historical setbacks . . . also provide the condition needed for humanity to avert them in the future" (ibid.: 154). Calling this reversal of fortune the dialectic of progress, Adorno contends that experiences of oppression encourage some individuals to conceive of conditions under which oppression will end. In other words, oppression is actually "the prerequisite for settling the antagonism" (ibid.: 150, tr. mod.).

Adorno thinks that Hegel borrowed his own notion of progress – the cunning of reason in history – from Kant's idea that "the conditions of the possibility of reconciliation are its contradiction, and . . . the conditions for the possibility of freedom are unfreedom" (*ibid*.: 150). Applying Spinoza's famous dictum – all determination is negation – to the trajectory of spirit (*Geist*), Hegel shows that at each stage of its development, spirit determines itself and its objects more adequately and concretely when it acknowledges its own limitations, thereby enabling it to surpass them. On Adorno's own interpretation of Spinoza, a critical understanding of the negative aspects of the human predicament today makes it possible to conceive of an improved state of affairs. Although we shall never have a completely positive sense of "what the correct arrangement of human affairs should be",[6] Adorno frequently argues that "the false, once determinately known and precisely expressed, is already an index of what is right and better" (*CM*: 288).

Nevertheless, while Hegel thought that determinate negation allowed spirit progressively to acquire knowledge of the absolute, Adorno denies that it necessarily advances the human condition. Emerging in the negation of negative social conditions, our ideas about what is right and better are often flawed owing to their derivation from these very conditions. Although he employs these ideas himself in his trenchant and sustained critique of capitalist society, Adorno emphasizes their fallibility in his lectures on metaphysics when he states that critics have no choice but to work their way "through the darkness without a lamp, without possessing the higher [i.e. Hegelian] concept of the negation of the negation", by immersing themselves "in the darkness as completely as possible" (*ME*: 144).

Moreover, where Hegel thought world spirit was the motive force underlying history, Adorno views it as a cipher for "permanent catastrophe" because it implicitly discloses real antagonisms between the individual and society (*ND*: 320). Just as Kant's antinomies reveal real contradictions in society, so too Hegel's idea of a supra-individual spirit which determines the course of human history ultimately shows that individuals are "dictated by the principle of perverted universality" (*ibid*.: 344). Hegel's world spirit foreshadows our current predicament: a "world integrated through 'production,' through the exchange relationship" – a world that "depends in all its moments on the social conditions of its production, and in that sense actually realizes the primacy of the whole over its parts".[7] For Adorno, it is imperative to submit these oppressive conditions to a sustained and trenchant critique.[8]

Adorno also objects that Hegel ignores the "matters of true philosophical interest at this point in history", namely "nonconceptuality, individuality, and particularity" (*ND*: 8). Conceding that knowledge of non-conceptual particulars has never been attained, he criticizes Hegel for denying that such knowledge is attainable. More importantly, Hegel failed to understand that our conceptually mediated relationship to objects entails the existence of something that lies beyond concepts. Although our knowledge of objects is acquired in a mediated way, objects are immediate in the sense that they do not "require cognition – or mediation – in the same sense in which cognition requires immediacy". Here Adorno is not simply making a logical point: he also argues that experience itself posits the existence of something immediate because it discloses "that what it transmits is not thereby exhausted" (*ND*: 172, tr. mod.).

Despite this criticism, Adorno praises the dynamism of Hegel's system where critical reflection sets in motion Kant's antinomies of "form and content, nature and spirit, theory and praxis, freedom and necessity, the thing in itself and the phenomenon".[9] At the same time, he charges that Hegel ignored the preponderance or weightiness of the material world. For Adorno, mind is not ontologically distinct from matter, concepts from objects, or individuals from society. While they cannot be reduced to them, concepts are inextricably entwined in non-conceptuality, mind in matter, and the individual in society. If Kant's antinomies implicitly reveal both their affinity and their heterogeneity, Hegel failed to recognize that these antinomies "register the very moment of nonidentity that is an indispensable part of his own conception of the philosophy of identity".

Adorno's negative dialectics consists in a concerted attempt to surpass Hegel's dialectics by transforming it into a consistent sense of the non-identity of subject and object, individual and society, while simultaneously stressing that both are material in character.[10] Neither reductive nor dualistic,[11] his negative dialectics is material-ist because it reveals that both nature and history preponderate over human beings. At the start of a lengthy account of the history of materialism, Adorno states that there have always been two types of materialism: a social type, which focuses on society, and a scientific one, which focuses on nature. The two converge in their opposition to the "lie" perpetrated by the mind when it "repudiates its own natural growth".[12] Both types of materialism effectively locate "the origin of mind – even its most ostensible sublimations – in material scarcity".[13] Trying to accommodate the two types, Adorno claims that the material objectivity that weighs upon individuals is both natural and social, even though we largely ignore how these two dimensions of the material world preponderate over our thought and behaviour.

In fact, Adorno thought that society's influence on individuals had become so far-reaching that it could plausibly be described as total-itarian. Referring to society as the "universal", he invariably stresses its power over individuals. Today human beings must depend upon the performances of the state and the economy because these insti-tutions are responsible for their survival (*ND*: 311). If this increas-ingly totalitarian situation was prefigured by the transcendental subject in Kant and by world spirit in Hegel (*CM*: 248), Adorno agrees with Marx, who more aptly describes it as the "law of value that comes into force without individuals being conscious of it". This law, expressed in exchange relations, is the "real objectivity" to which individuals are subjected (*ND*: 300–301). Today, "the standard structure of society is the exchange form". The rationality of exchange now "constitutes people: what they are for themselves, what they think they are, is secondary" (*CM*: 248).

We have also been oblivious to the role that nature has played within our history. Adorno wants to correct our flawed understand-ing of ourselves as superior to the natural world by breaking through what he calls "the fallacy of constitutive subjectivity" (*ND*: xx). A critique of this idealist fallacy largely entails demonstrating that the mind is not primary. In setting himself this task, Adorno maintains that he is endorsing Marx, whose historical materialism became "the critique of idealism in its entirety, and of the reality for which idealism opts by distorting it" (*ibid.*: 197). On Adorno's view, Hegel himself derived self-conscious mind from its relationship to hetero-geneous matter in labour. Hypostasizing the mind, he was barely able to conceal the origin of the "I" in the "Not-I". Even for Hegel, then, mind implicitly originates "in the real life process, in the law of the survival of the species, of providing it with nutrients" (*ibid.*: 198, tr. mod.).

Again, this real-life process is both instinctually driven and shaped by the capitalist mode of production with its rapacious and exploita-tive relationship to nature. Citing a famous passage of *The German Ideology*, Adorno declares that in it, Marx stressed the "unending entwinement" of nature and history "with an extremist vigor bound to irritate dogmatic materialists". For Marx:

We know only a single science, the science of history. History can be conceived from two sides, divided into the history of nature and the history of humankind. Yet there is no separating the two sides; as long as human beings exist, natural and human history will qualify each other.

Adorno follows this quotation with the claim that the traditional antithesis between nature and history is true in one respect and false in another. It is "true insofar as it expresses what happened to the natural element" – namely, that nature has been concealed to such a degree that what now appears to be natural is actually social. However, the antithesis is false because "it apologetically repeats the concealment of history's natural growth by history itself" (*ND*: 358, tr. mod.).

Borrowing the idea of natural history from Marx, Adorno tries throughout his work to capture the important senses in which nature is always also historical and history always also natural. To avoid misunderstanding, however, he does not adopt the goal "of 'naturalizing' human beings and 'humanizing' nature". Instead, as Lambert Zuidervaart insightfully remarks, Adorno actually thought that "human beings already are natural, all too natural, and nature is unavoidably human, all too human". Human beings are "all too natural" because they "carry out domination as if they were beasts of prey", oblivious to the fact that survival instincts motivate their behaviour. For its part, nature has become thoroughly historical to the extent that it "has become a mere object of human control".[14]

To be sure, Adorno wants us to acknowledge both that we are inextricable parts of nature and that nature has always been (and always will be) entwined in human history. But, to adopt a controversial formulation, he simultaneously wants to "dehumanize" nature and "denaturalize" humanity. For even as he underscores both our natural creatureliness and our "humanization" of nature, he aims to foster the partial transcendence of nature by human beings, and of human beings by nature. If it is crucial for our self-understanding to acknowledge our affinity with nature, it is also the case that the non-identity of nature and human history must be given equal weight. In the final analysis, Adorno's goal is to develop a more fully dialectical conception of both human beings and nature.

To say that nature is always also historical does not authorize the reduction of nature to history. Conversely, the "naturalness" of human history does not mean that history can be reduced to nature. In fact, Adorno's former student Alfred Schmidt claims that Marx was the first to advance this non-reductive view of the relationship between nature and history. For Marx: "Natural and human history together constitute . . . a differentiated history". Precisely because they form an internally differentiated unity, "human history is not merged in pure natural history; natural history is not merged in human history".[15] As the material substratum of human life, nature remains something apart from its historical manifestations. Although it is always also historically and socially mediated, nature is not entirely identical with its mediated forms. For its part, human history has been impelled by natural forces both within and without, but it is something distinct from nature because our cognitive development has enabled us to distinguish ourselves from nature to a limited extent.

Charging that Marx often tended to focus on the preponderance of society over individuals, thereby failing fully to explore the preponderance of nature, Adorno nonetheless borrowed a great deal from his critique of capitalism. To return to an earlier point, he maintains that "freedom remains no less delusive than individuality itself" because the "law of value comes into play over the heads of formally free individuals" who have become "the involuntary executors of that law". Even in the earlier liberal phase of capitalism, the freedom and autonomy enjoyed by bourgeois entrepreneurs was essentially a function of economic conditions that fostered a certain measure of autonomy to improve its performance (*ND*: 262). Under monopoly capitalism, however, the ruling class itself is "ruled and dominated by the economic process". As Marx predicted, the ruling powers have become appendages of their own machinery of production (*CLA*: 116).

Against both Marx and Hegel, however, Adorno rejects the idea of necessity in history. After describing the continuity of history in terms of our growing capacity for destruction and self-destruction, Adorno insists that doubts about the inevitability of this trajectory cannot but arise for those who "want to change the world" (*ND*: 323). To be sure, he questions the extent to which the proletariat can act as an agent for radical social change today owing to its lack of class consciousness. But he also puts paid to those who view him as unremittingly pessimistic when he observes that relations of production remain "thoroughly antagonistic" in "their relationship to the subjects from which they originate and which they enclose". Owing to the antagonism between the individual and society, it is not possible for society "to extort that complete identity with human beings that is relished in negative utopias" (*CM*: 156).

While Marx tended to focus on the preponderance of society over individuals, Freud was obviously more concerned with the impact of instincts on human behaviour. Yet Adorno argues that Marx implicitly endorsed the idea that history has been instinctually driven: the truth content in his idea of natural history, its critical content, lies in

Marx's recognition that human history, which takes the form of the progressive mastery and domination of nature, merely "continues the unconscious history of nature, of devouring and being devoured" (*ND*: 355). Furthermore, if Marx thinks that the first premiss of human existence is that human beings must work to produce the means to satisfy their needs, Freud observes in *Civilization and its Discontents* that human life has as one of its foundations "the compulsion to work, which was created by external necessity".[16] For both Marx and Freud, then, history to date has consisted largely in the activities that provide human beings with the material necessities of life.

Adorno also agrees with Freud that "it is impossible to overlook the extent to which civilization is built up upon a renunciation of instinct, how much it presupposes precisely the non-satisfaction (by suppression, repression, or some other means?) of powerful instincts".[17] In Adorno's own words, the "idea of the renunciation of instinct . . . formulated in recent years by psychoanalysis goes hand in hand, or so I have been arguing, with the direction of civilization, and we could also say with the basic tendency of an urban civilization that is bourgeois in the broadest sense, that is to say, orientated towards work" (*PMP*: 136–7). Repressing their instincts in order to dominate external nature and other human beings, individuals rarely profit from their acts of renunciation. Consequently, "there is no real equivalence between renunciation of instincts in the present and compensation in the future". Society is organized "irrationally" because "the equivalent reward it always promises never arrives" (*ibid.*: 139).

Adorno also follows Freud's attempt to promote enlightenment by establishing a more accommodating relationship between ego and id. More generally, he maintains that rational insight into our affinity with nature "is the point of a dialectics of enlightenment" (*ND*: 270). Here he refers to the central thesis of *Dialectic of Enlightenment*, which states that a critique of our naturally driven subjugation of nature can "prepare the way for a positive notion of enlightenment which will release it from entanglement in blind domination" (*DE*, C: xvi; J: xviii). In Freudian terms, only when the ego acknowledges that it is not entirely master in its own house, that it is not omnipotent but subject to natural impulses, can it sublate its instincts by harnessing their energy to more emancipatory ends.[18] For Adorno, "we are no longer simply a piece of nature" only "from the moment that we recognize that we *are* a piece of nature" (*PMP*: 103). Paradoxically, perhaps, to rise above nature in any meaningful sense, we must first become fully conscious of ourselves as instinctually driven creatures.

Adorno was interested in Freud's account of narcissism as well, describing narcissism as the "new type of psychological affliction" characteristic of an era that has witnessed "the decline of the individual and his [sic] subsequent weakness".[19] Now that society assumes responsibility for our material survival, it can dispense with "the mediating agencies of ego and individuality" that it originally fostered in its more competitive liberal phase. It encourages the formation of weak and submissive egos by arresting "all differentiation" and exploiting "the primitive core of the unconscious".[20] In so doing, it fosters narcissistic pathologies where the "self-preserving function" of the ego is, "on the surface at least, retained but, at the same time, split off from that of consciousness and thus lost to rationality".[21] Since the narcissistic ego is too weak to accommodate its instincts, these can be exploited easily by politicians and the mass media. Given this ego weakness, effective resistance to society has all but disappeared.

Unlike Freud, however, Adorno thought that psychopathologies such as narcissism would be overcome, not by psychoanalysis, but only by completely transforming society. He also objected that Freud vacillates between criticizing "the renunciation of instinct as repression contrary to reality, and applauding it as sublimation beneficial to culture" (MM: 60). Still, Adorno developed a remarkably sophisticated psychoanalytic account of anti-Semitism and Nazism based on his discussions with Freudian social psychologists.[22] He gave pride of place to psychoanalysis in his criticisms of the culture industry and in much of his empirical work as well.[23] If he famously declared that "nothing in psychoanalysis is true but the exaggerations" (ibid.: 49), he also insists that what is essential to thought is just this "element of exaggeration" (ibid.: 126). Readily admitting that he too is exaggerating the sombre side of the human predicament, Adorno defends himself by stating that he is simply following the maxim that "only exaggeration per se today can be the medium of truth" (CM: 99). Exaggeration can play an important role in critical social theory by highlighting the destructive and self-destructive tendencies in contemporary society.

Impact

In keeping with the profoundly ethical thrust of first-generation critical theory, Habermas also orients his work towards the goal of a more rational society that would permit individuals to enjoy greater freedom and autonomy. Just as Adorno believed that a deep understanding of the present situation is needed to bring such a society to fruition, Habermas too endorses the view that only undiminished, critical insight into our current predicament can provide the basis for positive change. Like Adorno, he offers penetrating analyses of life in the West, examining problems such as the crises that periodically afflict capitalism, reification, civil privatism, democratic deficits in the West, and globalization. While far less critical of Western institutions, procedures and practices than Adorno was, Habermas continues to sound a distinctly Adornian note in *Between Facts and Norms* when he observes that, more than any other, the twentieth century has taught us "the horror of existing unreason". To banish that horror, reason must put itself on trial.[24]

Following Adorno, Habermas agrees with Marx's claim that "reason has always existed but not always in a rational form".[25] Moreover, in their respective critiques of Western reason, Adorno and Habermas declare themselves partisans of the enlightenment tradition described by Kant in "What is Enlightenment?"[26] Each sees himself as advancing this tradition with its emphasis on rational, autonomous and critical thought. For his part, Adorno claims that his work contributes to enlightenment by promoting the "self-critical spirit of reason" (*ND*: 29). Like Kant, he wants individuals to gain greater political maturity, to become capable of independent and critical judgement (*CM*: 281–2). Situating his own work within the enlightenment tradition, Habermas too wants individuals progressively to free themselves from superstition and authoritarian belief systems in order to submit to the unforced force of the better argument alone.

Although he denies that the proletariat can ever play the role of the universal subject of history, Habermas is indebted to Marx's critique of capitalism and the commodity form. In fact, he links his critical idea of the colonization of the lifeworld to the problem of reified social reality that Marx first targeted in his critique of commodity fetishism, and which Lukács subsequently adopted. As he told an interviewer: "When I was writing *The Theory of Communicative Action* my main concern was to develop a theoretical apparatus with which the phenomena of 'reification' (Lukács) could be addressed."[27] Furthermore, while criticizing the Marxist claim that the economy determines the political, social and cultural superstructure, Habermas accepts Marx's view that capitalism defines the development of Western society as a whole.[28]

Adorno constantly stresses the catastrophic tendencies in Western societies. For him, "the complete reification of the world . . . is indistinguishable from an additional catastrophic event caused by human beings, in which nature has been wiped out and after which nothing grows any more" (*NLI*: 245). By contrast, Habermas believes that the trajectory of Western society is double-edged. On the one hand, since the rationality that characterizes action within the economic and political systems now penetrates into the lifeworld, it unsettles communicative practices geared to reaching agreement about aspects of the objective, social and subjective worlds. On the other hand, these practices have become more rational in their growing reliance on good reasons – rather than on beliefs or dogmas that are immune from criticism – as the basis for validity claims. Indeed, given his positive view of the rationalization of the lifeworld, Habermas rejects Adorno's assessment of life under late capitalism – a view he describes as biased because it focuses on pathological tendencies in modernity to the virtual exclusion of countertendencies.[29]

Yet for Habermas as well, the reconciliation of society and the individual is key. He endorses the "idealizing supposition of a universalistic form of life, in which everyone can take up the perspective of everyone else and can count on reciprocal recognition by everybody" because this supposition "makes it possible for individuated beings to exist within a community – individualism as the flip-side of universalism".[30] Again, Habermas pursues the project that animates all the Institute's endeavours: to formulate a theory of society that examines the effects of economic and political institutions on social life and the development of individuals, with the ultimate goal of achieving "a reasonable organization of society that will meet the needs of the whole community".[31] Unlike his former professor, however, Habermas thinks that a radical transformation of society is unnecessary because conditions of life that will enable each individual to enjoy the same possibilities for self-realization and self-determination as all the rest are already latent in existing institutions. In other words, a more rational society is already within reach.

This more conciliatory view of Western society is echoed in the work of Habermas's successors, including the philosophers Albrecht Wellmer and Axel Honneth. Honneth, who is currently (2007) director of the Institute for Social Research, follows Habermas when he rejects Adorno's bleak view of prevailing tendencies in the West. Yet Honneth has recently defended Adorno, maintaining that he was not trying to explain capitalism, but to offer a "hermeneutic of natural-historical disaster"[32] that makes use of Max Weber's methodology of ideal types.[33] Moreover, Honneth continues to champion the goals of first-generation theorists, including Adorno. In a recent brochure, the Institute commits itself to examining contradictory tendencies in Western society, tendencies that have led both to greater freedom (in new familial arrangements, for example, or in the legal recognition of the equality of women, and ethnic and racial minorities) and to lesser freedom owing to the deregulation of labour markets and the arms race.

Never conceived as an exclusively theoretical enterprise, the Institute has also contributed enormously to the development of empirical social research. In fact, Adorno's own empirical work, as well as his many essays on empirical research methods, are exemplary in this regard. To be sure, projects such as *The Authoritarian Personality* came under critical fire, but this criticism by no means detracts from Adorno's pioneering role. As Jay rightly insists, to dwell on the problems with the methodology and conclusions of *The Authoritarian Personality* would "miss the tremendous achievement of the work as a whole". Jay also remarks that one astute reviewer described the eight volumes of *Studies in Prejudice* as "an epoch-making event in social science". These studies, which included *The Authoritarian Personality*, unleashed an enormous flood of research.[34] Moreover, the impact of this work on the social sciences was felt both in North America and Europe because Adorno brought back to Germany the research methodology that he helped to develop in the United States.

Adorno not only contributed to the development of the social sciences; his work on the culture industry had a significant impact on research in the field, initially influencing analysts such as Paul Lazarsfeld and Elihu Katz. Examining radio and the recording industry in the late 1930s, Adorno continued to study the mass media throughout his life, offering a highly critical account of the commodification of culture. In "Free Time", written in the 1960s,[35] he commented on the leisure activities of individuals in the West, offering a nuanced assessment of their reception of television. His assessment was based in part on an empirical study he conducted at the Institute in 1966 which showed that television viewers were more critical of what they watched than might otherwise have been expected. However, the importance of these studies of mass culture is largely overshadowed by the impact of Adorno's theoretical work on writers as diverse as Guy Debord and Stuart Ewen. Here too Adorno pioneered the exploration of many problems now treated in media studies and communications departments in Western countries.

If disciplines such as sociology and media studies have felt the impact of both Adorno's empirical and his theoretical work, it should also be noted that Adorno influenced the study of literature and music as well. Contemporary literary theorists, such as Terry Eagleton and Fredric Jameson, have certainly been drawn to his work. Indeed, Adorno's many essays on literary topics are taught with some frequency in departments of literature.[36] Still, Adorno was a far more prolific critic of modern music. His many essays and books on composers as diverse as Arnold Schönberg, Ludwig von Beethoven, Igor Stravinsky and Richard Wagner continue to interest critics and musicologists alike. Surprisingly, perhaps, given Adorno's denunciation of many aspects of mass culture, Max Paddison points out that some of his aesthetic ideas have been taken up by writers who study rock music, including Michael Coyle, Jon Dolan, Allan Moore and Simon Frith.[37]

Given the breadth of Adorno's impact, it is difficult to mention even briefly all the areas in which his influence has made itself felt. However, one thing remains to be said. Despite all the interpretive work that has been done on Adorno, Adorno scholarship is still very much in its infancy. No one can claim to have deciphered completely what Adorno described in *Dialectic of Enlightenment* as his message in a bottle. Indeed, Adorno remarks that, to ensure that it does not perish, his message about the hellishness of conditions here on earth is bequeathed, neither to the masses, nor to the impotent individual, but to an imaginary witness capable of turning his theoretical insights into emancipatory social practice (*DE*, C: 256; J: 213). Since this witness has not yet materialized, a definitive discussion of Adorno's impact is woefully premature. But his work is certainly rich enough to warrant the prediction that it will continue to influence philosophy and the social sciences for generations to come.

Notes

1. See, for example, *Against Epistemology* (*AE*). See Ståle Finke's essay in this volume (Chapter 5) for an extensive consideration of Adorno's engagement with Husserl.
2. Jay, *Dialectical Imagination*, 70.
3. Simon Jarvis, "Adorno, Marx, Materialism", *The Cambridge Companion to Adorno* (2004), 83–4.
4. Wiggershaus, *The Frankfurt School*, 67.

5. See Kant's fourth proposition in "Idea for a Universal History with a Cosmopolitan Purpose", *Kant's Political Writings* (1971), 44; emphasis in the text: *"The means which nature employs to bring about the development of innate capacities is that of antagonism within society, in so far as this antagonism becomes in the long run the cause of a law-governed social order."*

6. Adorno, "Individuum und Organisation", *Gesammelte Schriften* 8 (1972), 456.

7. Adorno, *Hegel: Three Studies* (1993), 27.

8. *Ibid.*, 87–8.

9. *Ibid.*, 8.

10. See Alison Stone's discussion of Adorno's logic in this volume (Chapter 3) for a more detailed discussion of the relationship between Adorno's and Hegel's dialectics.

11. Brian O'Connor was the first to point out that Adorno offers both a non-reductive and a non-dualistic account of the epistemological subject and its objects; see *Adorno's Negative Dialectic: Philosophy and the Possibility of Critical Rationality* (2004). But this characterization of the relationship between subject and object can be extended to Adorno's conception of the relationship between mind and matter, and the individual and society as well. More generally, it can also be applied to the relationship between nature and history.

12. Adorno, *Philosophische Terminologie zur Einleitung*, vol. 2 (1974), 172.

13. *Ibid.*, 173.

14. Lambert Zuidervaart, *Adorno's Aesthetic Theory: The Redemption of Illusion* (1991), 165.

15. Alfred Schmidt, *The Concept of Nature in Marx* (1971), 45.

16. Sigmund Freud, *Civilization and its Discontents* (1975), 38.

17. *Ibid.*, 34.

18. See Joel Whitebook's *Perversion and Utopia: A Study in Psychoanalysis and Critical Theory* (1996), especially ch. 2, for an illuminating attempt to reconcile two of Freud's most famous dictums: "where id was, there ego shall be" and "the ego is not master in its own house".

19. Adorno, "Freudian Theory and the Pattern of Fascist Propaganda", *The Essential Frankfurt School Reader* (1978), 120.

20. Adorno, "Sociology and Psychology", 87.

21. *Ibid.*, 88, tr. mod.

22. Müller-Doohm, *Adorno*, 292.

23. See, for example, Adorno, Else Frenkel-Brunswik, David J. Levison & R. Nevitt Sanford, *The Authoritarian Personality* (1950).

24. Habermas, *Between Facts and Norms: Contributions to a Discourse Theory of Law and Democracy* (1996), xli.

25. Seyla Benhabib quotes this comment, made by Marx in an 1843 letter to Arnold Ruge, in *Critique, Norm, and Utopia: A Study of the Foundations of Critical Theory* (1986), 34. Adorno cites this letter himself in "Critique": *CM*: 282.

26. See Kant, "What is Enlightenment?" *Foundations of the Metaphysics of Morals* (1959).

27. Habermas, "Morality, Society, and Ethics: An Interview with Torben Hviid Nielsen", *Justification and Application: Remarks on Discourse Ethics* (1993), 170.

28. Habermas, *The Theory of Communicative Action*, vol. II: *Lifeworld and System: A Critique of Functionalist Reason* (1987), 343: "Marx was right to assign an evolutionary primacy to the economy" in the West because "problems in this subsystem determine the path of development of the society as a whole". Yet Habermas also claims that the capitalist economy gained primacy only when the lifeworld had been sufficiently rationalized.

29. *Ibid.*, 391.

30. Habermas, "Individuation through Socialization: On George Herbert Mead's Theory of Subjectivity", *Postmetaphysical Thinking: Philosophical Essays* (1992), 186.

31. Max Horkheimer, "Traditional and Critical Theory", *Critical Theory: Selected Essays* (1972), 213.

32. Axel Honneth, "A Physiognomy of the Capitalist Form of Life: A Sketch of Adorno's Social Theory", *Constellations: An International Journal of Critical and Democratic Theory* 12 (1) (March 2005), 50.

33. *Ibid.*, 53–4.

34. Jay, *Dialectical Imagination*, 250.

35. See Adorno, "Free Time", *CM*: 167–75. For a far more detailed account of Adorno's views about Western culture, readers should turn to Robert W. Witkin's discussion of Adorno's philosophy of culture in this volume (Chapter 10).

36. See, for example, Robert Kaufman, "Adorno's Social Lyric, and Literary Criticism Today: Poetics, Aesthetics, Modernity", *The Cambridge Companion to Adorno*, 354–75.

37. Max Paddison, "Authenticity and Failure in Adorno's Aesthetics of Music", *The Cambridge Companion to Adorno*, 212–15.

Adorno's philosophy

Introduction

Deborah Cook

Following the general historical overview of Theodor W. Adorno's work offered in Part I, Part II focuses on its distinct philosophical dimensions. Contributors examine Adorno's philosophy under traditional rubrics: logic, metaphysics, ontology, epistemology and aesthetics; moral, social and political philosophy, as well as the philosophy of culture and the philosophy of history. Their examination reveals that Adorno completely rethinks these traditional areas of philosophical enquiry in his relentless critique of damaged life under capitalism.

Alison Stone's essay serves as an excellent introduction to Adorno's decidedly non-traditional mode of thought. After describing Hegel's transformation of Kant's transcendental logic into a dialectical logic, Stone explains how Adorno turns Hegel's dialectics into a negative dialectics. Adorno makes use of dialectics, not to trace the development of concepts, but to explore social phenomena such as myth and enlightenment, and more broadly still, to grasp the historical relationship between nature and culture. Although nature and culture have been entwined throughout human history, negative dialectics reveals that our historically conditioned ideas about nature do not exhaust it: nature remains stubbornly non-identical with respect to all our conceptions of it. Stone's account of Adorno's dialectically inflected non-identity thinking issues in an analysis of his employment of constellations of concepts to apprehend objects that are at one and the same time bound up with concepts and fundamentally heterogeneous with respect to them. Stone concludes that, while it does not accord with the traditional idea of logic, Adorno's negative dialectics has a logic of its own that attempts to do justice to nature – including human beings in so far as they are part of the natural world – while pointing to the prospect of a future reconciliation of concepts and objects, culture and nature.

Espen Hammer begins his thoughtful essay by contrasting traditional metaphysics with Adorno's conception of it. Adorno criticized the affirmative character of traditional metaphysics – its ideological legitimation of the existing world – when he argued that horrific events, such as the Holocaust, give the lie to the metaphysical claim that this world is, at bottom, morally good. For this very reason, however, Adorno wants to retain the idea of something that transcends this world. More surprisingly still, perhaps, Adorno contends that the metaphysical idea of transcendence can be retained only by adopting a materialist perspective, that is, by focusing on singular experiences of our fragmentary, transient world. Borrowing from Walter Benjamin as he develops his idea of metaphysical experience, Adorno thinks that such experience can offer a glimpse of transcendence only within immanence. Based on experiences of evil in this world, as well as on intimations of our own mortality, metaphysics as Adorno understands it may give rise to the idea of a condition in which human beings would eventually be reconciled with nature. Although he concedes that Adorno's conception of metaphysical experience is vulnerable to criticism, Hammer further argues that the alternative to it would be tantamount to accepting the view that life today is utterly meaningless and hopeless.

Ståle Finke addresses the thorny issue of the tension between ontology and epistemology in Adorno's thought. This issue is especially difficult because, for Adorno, "reality" is very much a function of the ways in which we think about it. Although he adopts a materialist position, Adorno certainly recognizes that nature (and the world of objects generally) is always also socially mediated. Focusing first on Adorno's extensive critique of Edmund Husserl, Finke shows that, among other things, Adorno targets his idea of subjectivity as pure intentionality and his idealist conception of objects. Like the objective world of which it is undeniably a part, the subject too is historically conditioned: it is both natural and social and, as such, invariably entangled in the things it tries to apprehend. But Adorno also criticizes the failure of Kant and Hegel to respect the weightiness, or preponderance, of objects in thought and experience. Although they both tried to come to grips with the "non-identical", Kant and Hegel ended by adopting idealist positions that wrongly subsume particular objects under universal concepts. At the end of his essay, Finke offers an interesting account of the role of mimesis in Adorno's work. According to Finke, by endorsing mimesis, Adorno attempts to make good on Husserl's famous dictum: to the things themselves.

Fabian Freyenhagen illuminates Adorno's non-traditional, negative moral philosophy. Since he views the existing world as radically evil, Adorno does not think it possible to live life rightly today. Freyenhagen considers Adorno's reasons for thinking that right living is currently impossible; he then reviews Adorno's criticisms of moral philosophies that claim to be able to underwrite right living by providing moral prescriptions, or by grounding morality on principles for generating moral duties, as in Kant's categorical imperative. Following a nuanced account of Adorno's critique of Kant, Freyenhagen proceeds to argue that Adorno does offer some ideas about how wrong life might be lived. At times, Adorno outlines ethical ideals based on his critique of our radically evil world, but he also offers negative prescriptions for living life today. In addition, Adorno advances what he calls a new categorical imperative: to live life in such a way that Auschwitz never happens again. Freyenhagen contrasts this new categorical imperative with Kant's, and ends with further discussion about the character of Adorno's negative and minimalist moral philosophy, paying particular attention to recent secondary literature with its conflicting accounts of the problem of normativity in Adorno's work.

As Pauline Johnson remarks, Adorno seems irredeemably pessimistic about our current social predicament. In what Adorno calls the totally administered world of monopoly (or "late") capitalism, society is fundamentally irrational because (among other things) it turns individuals into commensurable units of value that are traded as commodities on the "free" market, while exacerbating antagonisms between classes. Highlighting the concept of alienation in her discussion of Adorno's social philosophy, Johnson explores his concerns about society's intervention into virtually all aspects of human life, its manipulation and control of individuals, and its dehumanizing and levelling effects. If it was once a haven in this heartless world, the family no longer provides a sanctuary; the culture industry, which bolsters society's economic and administrative functions, now usurps the family's role as the primary agent of socialization. Searching amid the rubble of the administered world for signs of hope that wrong life might one day be lived rightly, Johnson thinks they may be found in the ambiguous needs that are expressed in the intimate sphere of human life. In an equally thought-provoking turn, she shows that a feminist politics which attempts to uncover the latent emancipatory potential in existing social institutions can both learn from Adorno's analysis and supplement it with its critical and utopian energies.

Marianne Tettlebaum opens her essay on Adorno's political philosophy by describing his personal experience of an early-morning house raid by the Gestapo. For Adorno, the relationship between the individual and the state continues to be extremely problematic. Individuals, who think of themselves as independent and autonomous, are now so abjectly dependent on the state and the economy for their survival that they tend to efface themselves as individuals. Moreover, prospects for reversing their subordination to state power have faded with the containment of revolutionary forces. And our nominal, or merely "formal", democracies only worsen an already bad situation with their authoritarian tendencies, propaganda and suppression of criticism. As a result, the conditions that led to Auschwitz may well recur. Although Adorno's call for critical reflection on our totally administered world – for theory rather than practice – has been condemned, Tettlebaum defends Adorno, explaining why he thought that reflection is the harbinger of a truly free and democratic society. Criticizing traditional ideas about freedom – Kant's in particular – for their complicity in perpetuating unfreedom, Adorno contends (as Freyenhagen also notes) that only the essentially negative freedom of resistance to existing conditions is possible today. Indeed, Tettlebaum ends by discussing the role that education may play in preparing individuals to think critically about the world around them, thereby fostering political maturity.

Adorno is also well known for championing the role of art in developing a critical consciousness of society. At the same time, however, as Ross Wilson insightfully observes, Adorno problematizes the traditional categories of art and aesthetics when he questions whether aesthetics can stand alone as an independent area of philosophical enquiry, and challenges the category of art itself. Beginning with a historical gloss on Adorno's aesthetic theory, Wilson describes his attempt to move beyond both Kant's subjective aesthetics and Hegel's objective aesthetics by showing that the subject is inextricably entwined with the object, or artwork. Given this entwinement, philosophers may play an important role in the interpretation of art as well. Wilson also addresses the contentious issue of socially critical tendencies in artworks. Rejecting Bertolt Brecht's and Jean-Paul Sartre's contention that art should serve explicitly political ends, Adorno believes that art is already indirectly critical of our contemporary predicament owing to its very existence as art, and to its refusal to succumb to the pressures of the capitalist marketplace. To be sure, art has an ideological dimension in so far as it legitimates existing conditions. But art also has a truth content when it points to conditions that transcend damaged life, to the prospect of a world that is no longer sullied by the antagonisms that rend society today.

Wilson's essay is complemented by Robert W. Witkin's evocative account of Adorno's philosophy of culture. Contrasting pseudo-culture to a more emancipatory culture that fosters the spiritual dimension of human life, Witkin reveals that Adorno based this distinction on Georg Simmel's views about objective culture and subjective culture. While all culture is entangled in material conditions, pseudo-culture differs from a culture that serves spiritual needs because it reinforces adaptation and conformity to these conditions by targeting regressive social and psychological tendencies in individuals. Moreover, because pseudo-culture does not develop dialectically from its elemental parts, it lacks a historical dimension that would nurture the human spirit. After remarking on Adorno's adoption of Max Weber's thesis that culture has succumbed to the disenchantment of the modern world, Witkin describes pseudo-culture as a fetishized, commodified culture that fails to participate in living relationships. He illustrates these ideas concretely by examining Adorno's critique of an astrology column in *The Los Angeles Times*, and by contrasting popular music, which is geared to producing effects that make it marketable, with serious music. Finally, Witkin situates Adorno's work in the context of other critiques of contemporary culture, while observing that his ideas about culture are themselves caught up in a historical dynamic which ceaselessly recasts and renews them.

Brian O'Connor examines Adorno's challenge to Hegel's idea of a progressive, universal history. Rather than simply rejecting this conception and asserting that history is discontinuous, Adorno tries to bring both ideas of history together, while holding them in dialectical tension, when he claims that history is characterized by constant disruptions. Following an engaging discussion of some of the problems with Adorno's view of history, O'Connor goes on to show that Adorno also fashions an idea of progress. As negative as his idea of freedom, progress would consist in preventing or avoiding catastrophe by disrupting the domination of nature that has characterized much of human history. Associated with this idea of progress is Adorno's idea of natural history, which sees human history as natural because it has been driven by survival instincts, and nature as historical to the extent that it is always also mediated by human beings. Although society continues to veer towards totalitarianism as it intervenes, with increasing efficiency, into every aspect of life in its ceaseless attempts to dominate nature, Adorno did not think that its historical trajectory was written in stone. As O'Connor argues, the direction of history can be changed by acting collectively to reconcile history and nature in such a way that the dualism of nature and history is finally overcome without summarily reducing one to the other.

Readers will discover that a single thread connects all the essays in this volume: Adorno engages with traditional philosophy – while challenging many of its central claims – to find ways to stem or reverse the damage done to life under late capitalism. In this respect, the contributors to this volume reveal that Adorno renews the philosophical tradition even as he radically contests and revises many of its premises. Indeed, few philosophers have been as uncompromisingly critical as Adorno was. Since thought itself (including philosophical thought) is shaped and conditioned by an increasingly irrational society, Adorno develops a new mode of thinking to counter historical tendencies that appear to be leading rapidly to a dead end, in more than just a metaphorical sense. Non-identity thinking; metaphysical experiences of transcendence which foreshadow new forms of intimacy, maturity and social solidarity; unwavering resistance to forces of integration and domination; the resolute critique of damaged life – not just in philosophy and social theory, but in art and culture as well; the disruption of prevailing societal tendencies – all these represent prospects for averting catastrophe.

THREE

Adorno and logic

Alison Stone

Introduction

Adorno and logic might seem to be a combination as unpromising as Nietzsche and democracy, or Sartre and Hinduism. Adorno has no logic in the sense of a theory of valid forms of argument and inference. He is also deeply hostile to any attempt to formalize thinking because, he believes, formal thinking disguises the complexities and ambiguities inherent in any subject-matter, making it impossible to reflect on them (*CM*: 245–6).[1] To encourage genuinely reflective thought, Adorno writes in a fragmentary and allusive style far removed from the logically formalized style of much twentieth-century analytic philosophy.

Yet Adorno does engage with an alternative tradition in logic which Kant and Hegel developed. Kant's transcendental logic studies the basic concepts – such as reality and causality – by which (Kant thinks) we structure our experience. Hegel transformed this transcendental logic into dialectical logic. Hegel's logic deeply influenced Adorno's approach to the study of socio-historical phenomena, especially his account of how enlightenment turns into its opposite, myth. But Adorno also criticizes Hegel, transforming his dialectical logic into a negative dialectic. In its most general form, negative dialectics applies to relations between concepts and objects, or between what Adorno calls "identity thinking" and the "non-identical".

To understand Adorno's thinking about logic in this Kantian–Hegelian sense, we need to examine a cluster of concepts – those of negative dialectics, of concept and object, of identity and the non-identical – as well as Adorno's concept of constellations which forms part of his account of negative dialectics. To make sense of these concepts, we must first reconstruct Kant's and Hegel's conceptions of logic.

Kant to Hegel: from transcendental to dialectical logic

In *Critique of Pure Reason*, Kant distinguishes between general and transcendental logic. General logic sets out the "rules of thought", without "regard to . . . the objects to which the understanding may be directed".[2] That is, general logic is purely formal and describes rules for how one must think – regardless of what one is thinking about – if one's thinking is to be valid. Thus general logic is what we ordinarily mean by logic.

By contrast, transcendental logic has meaning only within the framework of Kant's transcendental idealism, or his view that we cannot know objects as they are in themselves, but only as they appear to us when subjected to the forms of representation that we necessarily bring to experience. These forms are (1) forms of "pure intuition" (space and time) by which we structure our sensory impressions, and (2) concepts of understanding by which we organize the disparate materials of sensation into structured objects that interrelate in orderly ways.[3]

For Kant, forms of enquiry are transcendental if they investigate the conceptual and intuitive conditions that we necessarily bring to experience. Transcendental logic tries to identify which concepts structure *any* thinking at all about objects (or any thinking in which we order the materials of sensation).[4] These concepts are the "pure concepts of the understanding", or the "categories". They are "pure" because they are not derived from experience. Indeed, we need to employ these concepts to have any experience of objects at all.

So *which* concepts necessarily structure experience? For Kant, all concepts function to unify manifold impressions given in sensation; concepts are "functions of unity".[5] But judgements (such as "the rose is red") also unify: they unite a subject ("rose") with a predicate ("red"). Different kinds of judgement unite subjects and predicates in different ways: "the rose is red" unites them by affirming that the predicate belongs to the subject, while "the rose is not red" unites its terms by affirming that the predicate is "opposed to" the subject.[6] In Aristotle's logic – which was canonical in Kant's day – there are twelve kinds of judgement: twelve different ways of uniting subjects with predicates. Kant claims that this indicates what the categories are.

Since judgements can unite subjects and predicates in twelve ways, and concepts also unify sensory materials, there must be twelve pure concepts, each corresponding to one kind of judgement. For instance, the category "reality" corresponds to affirmative judgements such as "the rose is red", while the category "negation" corresponds to negative judgements such as "the rose is not red". Other categories include unity and plurality, causality, necessity and impossibility.

Kant takes himself to have worked out the categories systematically, from a sound principle.[7] But Hegel criticizes Kant for relying unquestioningly on Aristotelian logic. He holds that our basic categories must "be exhibited in their *necessity*, and . . . *deduced*".[8] Thus, Hegel accepts Kant's view that we must actively structure our experience in terms of certain basic categories. But philosophers must work out what these categories are by deducing them.

What does this deduction involve? First, we must show that a particular category is necessary for any thought. Then we show that this category has limitations such that an additional category is needed to provide the only possible – or, at least, the best available – corrective to those limitations. But this new category also proves limited, such that yet another category is required – and so on until we have deduced a complete chain of categories. Hegel sets out this chain of categories, or "thought-determinations", in his logic.

Unlike Kant, Hegel also thinks that logical categories are both forms of thought that organize our experience of objects, *and* basic structures or principles that organize things as they exist mind-independently. For example, causality is not just a category in terms of which we must think, but a basic principle that organizes all mind-independent things into causal relations.[9] Indeed, it is because these basic principles organize *all* things that they constrain the shape of human thought and experience. Thus categories are not merely subjective forms of thought but "the truth, objectivity, and actual being of . . . things themselves. [They] resemble the platonic ideas . . . which exist in individual things as substantial genera".[10]

Categories always follow one another according to higher-level logical structure, or a three-stage dialectical process.[11] The three stages are: abstraction or understanding – where we begin with a certain category; dialectic – where this category generates or turns into its opposite; and the speculative stage – which reconciles the first two categories.

For instance, Hegel's logic begins with the simplest category – being – then shows how being turns into nothingness because the category of being is so simple that being is entirely indeterminate and featureless.[12] Then the two categories are reconciled in this way: since both are equally featureless, nothingness does not really differ in content from being. In that sense, nothingness turns back into being.[13] But being and nothingness remain distinct because they prove to be the same from opposite starting-points: being goes from being to nothingness while nothingness goes from nothingness to being. It follows that being and nothingness are (1) distinct, but (2) interdependent, since each exists only inasmuch as the other constantly turns into it. Hegel concludes that this makes them aspects of a third category, becoming.[14]

This dialectical process regulates both the series of concepts with which we think and the metaphysical principles that govern reality. Thus Hegel transforms Kant's logic into a dialectical logic by (1) trying to derive the categories according to this three-stage dialectical structure and (2) interpreting the categories as not merely subjective but also metaphysical principles. We may now see how Adorno draws on and criticizes Hegel's logic.

Hegel to Adorno: from dialectical logic to negative dialectics

Adorno often applies Hegel's dialectical method to social phenomena. A notable example appears in *Dialectic of Enlightenment*, which claims that "enlightenment reverts to mythology" (*DE*, C: xvi; J: xviii). Here the enlightenment is subject to a dialectic whereby it turns into its opposite, myth.

By "enlightenment", Simon Jarvis notes, Adorno and Horkheimer do not mean the eighteenth-century intellectual movement, but rather a gradual process that characterizes the whole course of human history, a process of "demythologizing, secularizing or disenchanting . . . mythical, religious, or magical representation[s] of the world".[15] For Adorno, humanity repeatedly distances itself from previous systems of thought by criticizing them for being merely mythical. This progression is fuelled by humanity's desire to gain increased practical control over nature. Human beings have hoped that, by freeing themselves from mythical views of nature, and gaining greater insight into the real workings of nature, they could enhance their ability to intervene into these natural processes for their own benefit. The climax of this process has been the rise of modern science, which enables humanity to exercise unprecedented control over nature by representing nature as made up purely of extensive magnitudes that are understood using mathematics (*DE*, C: 24–5; J: 18–19).

Yet, the more human beings try to become enlightened by distancing their thought from myth, the more they fall back into mythic modes of thinking. This happens in many ways. For example, enlightenment thinkers try to avoid appealing to mythic beliefs – in gods, supernatural forces etc. – by sticking to the facts. These include the facts of how society is currently organized and the chain of historical events that led to society being organized in this way. But enlightenment thinkers cannot ask whether history could have been different, as this is not a simple factual matter. Their inability to ask whether things might have turned out differently conduces to an unthinking acceptance that current social arrangements are inevitable, a "fate" that no one can escape. And fatalism of this kind is a typically mythical form of belief.[16]

Underlying this dialectic whereby enlightenment reverts to myth is a dialectic whereby enlightenment reverts to nature. Enlightenment distances us from nature by positioning us as masters over – not parts of – nature and by enhancing our ability to use abstract concepts (*DE*, C: 13; J: 9). Nonetheless, we human beings remain partially natural since we each have an "inner nature" consisting of bodily impulses (*DE*, C: 39; J: 31). So part of the enlightenment goal is to make us masters of our own inner nature: to enable us to exercise self-control, to resist our own impulses, thereby freeing ourselves for dispassionate conceptual thought.

Human beings have sought to control nature in the hope that this control will enhance their ability to preserve themselves. The whole enlightenment effort to distance human beings from nature is fuelled by a *natural* desire for self-preservation. Thus, Adorno writes, "nature is reflected and persists" in thinking in so far as the latter serves as a "mechanism of compulsion", i.e. of domination (*DE*, C: 39; J: 31). The more earnestly people pursue the enlightenment project, and try to distance themselves from nature, the more they *submit* to their natural impulses. Hence "human history, the history of the progressive mastery of nature, continues the unconscious history of nature" (*ND*: 355).

We see, then, both the dialectic whereby enlightenment inverts into myth just when it tries to separate itself from myth, and the dialectic whereby enlightened humanity submits to nature just when it tries to stand above nature. Likewise, for Hegel, being turned into nothingness just when it assumed the form of a distinct category. Adorno thinks that many other social phenomena are subject to a similar dialectic. *Minima Moralia* gives many examples: intellectuals who withdraw from society because they are critical of its calculating and commercial nature end up becoming sanctimonious and just as hard-hearted as those who are calculating (*MM*: 26). What counts today as healthy and well adjusted rests on a pathological level of repression, in contrast to which sick or eccentric people are actually "healing cells". "Indiscriminate kindness to all [actually expresses] indifference and remoteness to each" (*MM*: 73; see also 62–3).

Adorno also seems to follow Hegel in hinting that the solution to the dialectic of enlightenment is a *reconciliation* between enlightenment and myth and, above all, between culture and nature. This latter reconciliation could take the form of a "remembrance of nature in the subject" (*DE*, C: 40; J: 32). If we could acknowledge, or "remember", that our pursuit of enlightenment is driven by instincts, then we could begin to free ourselves *from* subjection to them. Recognizing that these impulses have a hold over us, we could then ask whether we think it right to pursue them or whether other goals are more desirable. In other words, we could deliberate about what values to adopt, thereby gaining some independence from impulses.

Yet the paradox is that we can truly free ourselves from our instincts only by acknowledging that our thinking depends on them in the first place, and by admitting that the enlightenment project has expressed and grown out of them. But perhaps Adorno is simply following Hegel's idea that two opposed categories are reconciled by proving to be distinct but interdependent. By acknowledging that our thinking is not separate from but depends on – grows out of – nature, we truly distinguish ourselves from nature for the first time, whereas if we insist that our thinking is separate from nature, it remains driven by the impulses whose influence we are refusing to recognize.

However, Adorno's faithfulness to Hegel should not be overstated. A first obvious difference is that Adorno is studying dialectical processes within the historical and social world, not within basic categories. So when he suggests solutions to these dialectical processes, such as the reconciliation of nature and culture, he sees these solutions only as possibilities that humanity might – but may well never – realize in practice.

There are two further differences between these models of reconciliation. In Hegel, reconciliation occurs whenever a second category proves to be essentially the *same* as the first; its difference from the first is relatively superficial (e.g. being and nothingness). Culture and nature become reconciled when modern scientific and philosophical modes of enquiry establish nature as essentially rational.[17] Hegel therefore implies that when human beings use reason to control and transform natural things, they do no wrong but are actually helping nature to realize its inner rational essence.[18]

Adorno would object that Hegel disguises the fact that domination over nature *does* wrong nature. So his reconciliation of nature and culture takes a different form. We must acknowledge that our thinking depends on and grows out of impulses that are not wholly rational and cannot be understood exhaustively in rational terms. Even if nature and instincts can be partly understood through reason, they always have an additional non-rational aspect that resists understanding. Thus, by recognizing that our thinking depends on instinct, we see that thinking depends on a nature that differs irreducibly from rational thought (and which, therefore, is damaged when it is moulded in line with human reasoning).

A final difference between Hegel and Adorno is that Hegel thinks two items are reconciled when they prove to be interdependent. Just as being and nothingness depend on one another, reason depends on the nature out of which it grows while nature depends on the rational principles that structure it. For his part, however, Adorno stresses that culture, rationality and enlightenment depend on nature to a greater extent than nature depends on reason. He encapsulates this point by speaking of the "primacy [*Vorrang*] of the object" (i.e. nature) over thinking (*ND*: 192): any thinking, reasoning subject is always a particular object (a particular body, brain and set of impulses), but not all objects are reasoning subjects. Although objects have an intelligible structure, and in that respect depend on reason, they also have a non-rational element and so do not *wholly* depend on reason. By contrast, reasoning activity does wholly depend on objects.

These three points show how Adorno transforms Hegel's dialectics into a "negative" dialectics. Hegel's dialectics is positive because it reconciles two opposed items by showing that the second is essentially the same as the first (e.g. nature is rational, like culture) and that the first and second items depend on one another. Adorno's dialectics is negative because: (1) it suggests only possible – not actual – forms of reconciliation; and because reconciliation occurs when a first thing (e.g. culture) that tries to separate itself from and to dominate something else (e.g. nature) acknowledges both (2) that the other thing is irreducibly different from it,[19] and (3) that it depends on that other thing to a greater degree than the other depends on it.

Why does Adorno say that this dialectics is negative whereas Hegel's is positive? He does so because (from (2) above), two items are reconciled when they remain, and are acknowledged to remain, different from one another – to be *not* the same as, but the negation of, one another. "Dialectics" as Adorno practises it, "is the consistent sense of non-identity" (*ND*: 5). In its most general form, his negative dialectics obtains between concepts and objects. So, to better understand negative dialectics, we need to look at his ideas about relations between concepts and objects.

Concept and object; identity and non-identity

Concepts are such that they each apply to many different things: for example, the concept "dog" applies to all those things that are dogs. Thus, each concept grasps the things to which it applies as instances of a universal. If I conceive something as a dog, then I understand it as an instance of the universal kind "dog". Adorno therefore says that conceptual thinking is both (1) classificatory thinking (which says "what [kind] something falls under, what it exemplifies" (*ND*: 149)) and (2) identity thinking. Why "*identity*" thinking?

When I conceptualize something as an instance of a kind, I see it as identical to all other instances of the same kind. This means that conceptual thinking gives me no knowledge about what is unique in a thing, for example, about what is special about *this* dog as distinct from all other dogs. Having no access to what is unique, conceptual thinking sees it *only* as an instance of a kind. In that sense, one "identifies" things with the universal kinds under which one takes them to fall.

However, it is possible in principle to recognize that things are never simply identical to these kinds (or to the other instances of a given kind) but always have a unique side as well. Adorno does not assert that things are wholly unique. He believes that things can be brought under concepts. But falling under concepts is not *all* there is to things. Each thing is also unique; this aspect of things is the "non-identical" element in them – that element by virtue of which things are identical neither to the kinds they embody nor to other instances of those kinds.[20]

Adorno criticizes identity thinking for disguising the fact that things have a unique side, and – this is an ethical objection – for being linked to domination. This link itself has at least two aspects. First, when we conceptualize things, we dominate them in thought. Because conceptual thinking suggests that things are merely instances of universal kinds, and because we can understand universal kinds using concepts, conceptual thinking suggests that things are reducible to what we can understand of them. Conceptual thinking portrays things as lying wholly within the reach of our intellects.

Secondly, the whole purpose of conceptual thinking is to enable us practically to dominate the things that we have conceptually mastered. We began to conceptualize things – and have sought to do so ever more accurately and ever less mythically – so that we can grasp how things work and can intervene in their workings in ways that promote human self-preservation. So "*any* conceptual thought . . . is a kind of instrument and to that extent a form of mastery".[21] Even seemingly disinterested forms of enquiry such as mathematics belong within the project of science, which inherently aims to dominate nature.

Adorno holds, then, that things always have a non-identical element in addition to their universal side. But what *is* this non-identical element? Medieval philosophers held that what makes things unique is their *haeccitas*, or "thisness" – a property that makes each of them *this* individual thing that it is. The notion of *haeccitas*, though, seems not to solve, but only to mark the site of, the problem of what makes each thing *this* thing that it is. An alternative approach to uniqueness – adopted by Hegel in his *Encyclopedia Logic* – states that a thing's uniqueness consists in its distinctive way of instantiating a universal kind. A thing cannot instantiate a universal unless it does so in some particular way, and this way of instantiating a universal is what makes each thing a "singular individual". Here, how a thing instantiates a universal cannot be captured by mere reference to that universal.[22]

However, Adorno does not adopt Hegel's view: for he insists that he is not giving us a general concept, or definition, of non-identity or singular individuality (*ND*: 136). To give a concept of singularity would be to treat singularity itself as a universal kind that is instantiated by all things in so far as they have a singular side. To this Adorno objects that "as soon as we reflect upon the single . . . individual as an individual, in the form of a universal concept – as soon as we cease to mean only the present existence of this particular person [or thing] – we have already turned it into a universal" (*CM*: 251). But if the individual in its singularity is treated as an instance of the universal kind "singular individuality", then we forget that the singular side of things is, precisely, what makes them *more* than mere embodiments of universals (even of the universal kind "singular individuality").

Since Adorno's references to the non-identical in things do not provide, or rely on, any general definition of non-identity or singular individuality, what status do these references have? Perhaps he believes that we can gain immediate access to a thing in its uniqueness by approaching it solely through our senses. But Adorno is well aware that this view – that we can "grasp what constitutes the unique essence of the thing as an individual only if [we do] not use concepts in knowing that individual"[23] – was forcefully criticized by Hegel, who calls this view "sense-certainty" in his *Phenomenology of Spirit*.

Against sense-certainty, Hegel argues that to know something we must be able to pick it out.[24] At the very least, we must refer to a thing as "this", or as what is "here and now", or as "what I mean". Since even "this", "here", "now" and "I" are universal concepts that can refer to any number of things or people, one is still using concepts to try to know things. But these concepts cannot pick out the particular thing that I claim to know. Hegel concludes that knowledge of particular individual things cannot be obtained without concepts, but that we need finer-grained concepts than merely "this", "here", etc.

Adorno agrees with Hegel that objects cannot be known "immediately" (i.e. through the senses alone); we cannot apprehend objects without "mediating" them through concepts (*ND*: 186). This seems to leave Adorno in a dilemma. He wants us to recognize that things have a non-identical element without conceptualizing that element in universal terms, yet he denies that we can know anything without conceptualizing it. To solve this dilemma, Adorno sees the concept of the non-identical as a *limit-concept*. This concept does not give us any positive knowledge about things. It simply indicates the place where conceptual understanding encounters limits, or a side of things that concepts do not cover. But the concept of the non-identical also indicates that we cannot know anything about this side of things just *because* our concepts cannot cover it. Thus, it is possible, using concepts, to recognize that conceptual understanding is limited, and specifically that concepts are not adequate to the non-identical element in things.

By recognizing the limits of conceptual thought, we could bring about a reconciliation between concepts and objects. This would involve: (1) the recognition (using concepts) that concepts depend on objects to a greater extent than objects depend on concepts

(*CM*: 249–50). Objects depend on concepts because they always have a conceptually intelligible form. But objects also remain independent of concepts in respect of their non-identical side. In contrast, concepts depend entirely on objects: they arise only in so far as there are already objects that we seek to understand, and they also depend on objects of a particular kind – human brains and bodies. (2) Reconciliation would also involve the recognition (specifically using the limit-concept of the non-identical) that objects are never reducible to our concepts of them because objects always retain a non-identical element. (Indeed, it is because of this non-identical element that objects only ever depend on concepts partially and not to the same extent as concepts depend on objects.)

If concept and object were reconciled in this way, then their relation would have assumed a negatively dialectical form. The relation is dialectical in that the formerly antagonistic relation of concepts to objects would have been overcome (an antagonism manifested in our efforts to dominate and wholly understand things using concepts). It is negatively, rather than positively, dialectical because in the reconciled state objects would remain, and be acknowledged to remain, irreducibly different from – *not* the same as – concepts. So: "Reconciliation would release the nonidentical, . . . [and would] be the remembrance of the many [i.e. of items that are different from one another] as no longer inimical" (*ND*: 6).

However, there are obstacles to recognizing the limits of conceptual thought and bringing about a reconciliation. Whenever we recognize that a concept is limited, we shall inevitably try to produce a new, improved, concept to overcome this limit. This is where Adorno introduces the concept of constellations.

Constellations

For Adorno, once we recognize that our concepts are limited, we shall try to produce improved concepts to overcome those limits. This is inevitable because concepts enable us to control things practically by giving us accurate knowledge about them and about how they work. Thus, whenever a particular concept proves to give us incomplete knowledge about things – saying only "what something falls under . . . and what, accordingly, it is not itself" (*ND*: 53) – we shall try to produce a better concept that will give us fuller knowledge about things and enable us to dominate them better. Since this concept will prove limited in turn (as all concepts are inherently limited), we shall produce yet another concept, itself limited as well – and eventually we shall end up with a large range of concepts.

Adorno's claim that we inevitably strive to extend our concepts when they prove limited is indebted, again, to Hegel. In his *Phenomenology*, Hegel argues that when the concepts "this", "here" etc. prove to give us no knowledge of particular things, we must turn to richer concepts (e.g. "dog", "desk") that can do so. Moreover, Hegel argues that to grasp a thing as particular we must conceptualize it using a *range* of these relatively rich concepts. To pick out a particular dog, I must classify it not merely as a dog but also as light brown, friendly, excitable, middle-aged etc. Since no one thing has exactly the same range of characteristics as any other, we can grasp a thing in its uniqueness by using a range of concepts to specify the complete set of characteristics unique to that thing.

Adorno's idea of constellations may sound similar to Hegel's idea that we can grasp the uniqueness of a thing by using a range of concepts: Adorno suggests that the range of concepts that are gathered around a thing "illuminates" or gives insight into that thing. "Setting [concepts] in constellation . . . illuminates what is specific to the thing, to which the classificatory procedure is indifferent" (*ND*: 162). And since he expands on this point with the metaphor of unlocking something by using a combination of numbers rather than one single number (*ibid.*: 163), this suggests that he endorses Hegel's view.

But Adorno's constellations are unlike Hegel's ranges of concepts for two reasons. First, Hegel thinks that a range of concepts enables us to know an object *qua* singular because an object's singularity consists in its embodiment of a unique range of universals. But, again, because Adorno refuses to define singularity, he cannot accept Hegel's definition that the uniqueness of things consists in their embodying distinctive ranges of universals. Secondly, Hegel's definition implies that objects can be exhaustively understood if we use a rich enough palette of concepts. But Adorno insists that there are *inherent*, inescapable limits to conceptual understanding. He speaks of the "unavoidable insufficiency" of "thought" (*ND*: 5): for him all thought is unavoidably limited on account of being conceptual.

Yet the idea that constellations of concepts can illuminate a thing *qua* unique suggests that only single concepts are inherently limited, but that groups of concepts are not, or not necessarily. To be consistent, Adorno must admit that constellations too can only ever give us partial, non-exhaustive, insight into things *qua* unique. The problem then becomes how constellations can illuminate the non-identical element in things while illuminating it only partially. Introducing a second sense of "constellation", Adorno suggests that each object is *itself* a constellation of different past relations with other objects, all of which have shaped it.[25] On this account, an object is a constellation of historical processes, and a constellation of concepts is a range of concepts, each of which grasps one of the various historical relations that has left its mark on the object. Taken together, these concepts "gather around" the unique history of the object where this history makes the object the unique thing that it is.

In contrast to Hegel's ranges of concepts, Adorno's constellations capture the *particular* historical relations that have shaped an object, rather than whatever universal kinds the object may embody. And a constellation of concepts can only ever capture *some* of these relations. This is because the history of the relations and influences that affect an object continues for at least as long as that object exists. These ongoing relations and influences do not merely add to an object's history; they also make it possible to see further aspects of its past history, not previously appreciable. So no constellation of concepts can anticipate all the future influences and relations that will mark an object; and no constellation can grasp all the relations that have previously affected the object because many of these cannot be recognized in advance of the further unfolding of the object's history. Constellations, then, can never completely understand their objects.

When we construct constellations, we assume that objects are historically produced, and we use concepts to assemble narratives about aspects of these histories. This approach applies both to understanding human-made cultural and social artefacts, and to understanding natural things, in so far as these are all products of cosmic, geological, chemical, evolutionary and other kinds of processes. An example of this approach to an object (a cultural object in this case) is Hannah Arendt's "historical account of the 'elements' which 'crystallized' into totalitarianism".[26] Arendt sees totalitarianism as a constellation of elements which include Western imperialism and the "collapse of Western moral standards", modern anti-Semitism, and economic, industrial and social changes that left people in a rootless, alienated, condition.[27] Arendt's account of totalitarianism gathers together a plurality of concepts; each grasps one of these various elements (only some, not all, of the factors shaping totalitarianism).

There are at least two potential objections to Adorno's second account of constellations. First, it presupposes a definition of singularity – namely that an object's singularity consists in the total set of historical interactions that has marked it. Even so, this definition implies that no object can ever be exhaustively understood, because the history of each object is constantly ongoing. But this brings us to the second objection: it seems that constellations can never exhaustively grasp an object because of the nature of *objects*, specifically the fact that their histories – which make them the particular objects they are – are unfinished, ever ongoing. Concepts are incomplete because their objects are incomplete, embroiled in processes such that many aspects of their past histories are simply not available to be grasped.

Thus, Adorno's second idea of constellations is in some tension with both his reluctance to define singularity and his tendency to stress that concepts are limited in regard to objects (rather than stressing that concepts are limited *because* objects are incomplete). Despite these tensions, the second idea of constellations is promising. It opens up the prospect that constellations may reveal something about the singularity of objects without relying on the false assumption that concepts can exhaust objects.

Conclusion

This chapter has introduced two important aspects of Adorno's thinking about dialectical logic. On the one hand, Adorno describes the dialectical process whereby enlightenment and culture revert to their opposites, myth and nature, just when they try to separate themselves from myth and nature. On the other hand, he offers a model of how concepts and objects could be reconciled and enter into a negatively dialectical relationship which acknowledges that concepts depend on objects that differ irreducibly from concepts.

Moreover, enlightenment and culture become subject to this dialectic because their reversion to their opposites manifests the relationship in which they actually stand to myth and nature. They may deny their dependence upon myth and nature, but since that dependence actually exists it must manifest itself, and it will do so all the more in proportion as it is denied. Just as Freud thought repressed sexual desires must manifest themselves in the form of pathologies such as hysteria, Adorno thinks the asymmetrical relationship between concepts and objects, enlightenment and myth, culture and nature must manifest itself. It can do either benignly – when acknowledged – or destructively, when denied.

This reveals something else. Enlightenment and culture – and, more generally, concepts – stand to myth and nature – more generally, to objects – in a negatively dialectical relationship whereby the former depend asymmetrically upon the latter. Previously I suggested that concepts and objects would enter into a negatively dialectical relationship only if they were reconciled. But in fact, if concepts and objects were reconciled, we would be acknowledging the negatively dialectical relationship in which concepts and objects *already* stand to one another. This is a relationship whereby concepts depend on, but can never exhaustively understand, objects – a relationship that has been denied with the disastrous consequence that "the fully enlightened earth radiates disaster triumphant" (*DE*, C: 3; J: 1).

From this we see that Adorno's thinking about dialectics forms a coherent whole which revolves around his conception of the negative dialectics of concept and object. So, while he has no logic in the formal sense, near the centre of his thought are reflections on a range of topics: the concept/object relation, the limits of conceptual thinking, and the nature of dialectics. These topics do belong under the heading of logic in the expanded sense that Adorno inherits from Kant and Hegel. Adorno and logic may be an unlikely combination, but it is a surprisingly fruitful one.[28]

Notes

1. In places I have modified quotations from translations of Adorno's works.
2. Immanuel Kant, *Critique of Pure Reason* (1929), 93.
3. This position is idealist in the sense that it claims that we can know things only as we represent or form "ideas" about them, and not as they are in themselves.
4. Kant, *Critique of Pure Reason*, 95–6.
5. *Ibid.*, 105.
6. *Ibid.*, 108.
7. *Ibid.*, 114.
8. G. W. F. Hegel, *Encyclopedia Logic* (1991), 84. Ståle Finke also offers an account of Hegel's logic in this volume (Chapter 5).
9. *Ibid.*, 227–30.
10. Hegel, *Philosophy of Nature*, vol. 1 (1970), 200. One might object that Kant *does* see the categories as objective both in the sense that they are necessary for any thinking whatever and that they structure objects as we experience them. But Hegel argues that this makes objectivity depend on something merely subjective. See also *Encyclopedia Logic*, 81–6.
11. *Ibid.*, 125–33.
12. *Ibid.*, 136–9.
13. *Ibid.*, 139.
14. *Ibid.*, 141.
15. Simon Jarvis, *Adorno: A Critical Introduction* (1998), 24.

16. Here I am expanding on an argument made in Jarvis, *Adorno*, 25–6. See also *DE*, C: 27; J: 20–1.
17. See my *Petrified Intelligence: Nature in Hegel's Philosophy* (2004), chapter 3.
18. See John Passmore, "Attitudes to Nature", *Environmental Ethics* (1995), 135.
19. Adorno and Horkheimer do say that "myth is already enlightenment" (*DE*, C: xvi; J: xviii). Mythic thought already tries to understand nature with a view to controlling it, albeit in defective ways (e.g. by seeing nature as peopled by gods whose moods can be influenced through rituals and sacrifices). But if Adorno seems to follow Hegel when he claims that enlightenment need not – and cannot – separate itself from myth, he also believes that mythic thought is in part magical thought, and that magical thought draws on "mimesis" (*DE*, C: 9–11; J: 6–7). Mimesis is a non-rational, instinctual behaviour in which one imitates another organism or object (e.g. trying to harm someone by harming a doll that resembles him). This mimetic element is entirely non-rational, and because myth always has this non-rational aspect, it also remains irreducibly distinct from enlightenment rationality.
20. Indeed, Adorno objects to mass production on the grounds that it erases the singularity that is, or should be, proper to things.
21. J. Gordon Finlayson, "Adorno on the Ethical and the Ineffable", *Journal of European Philosophy* **10** (1) (2002), 4, emphasis added.
22. Hegel, *Encyclopedia Logic*, 240–41.
23. Robert Stern, *Hegel and the Phenomenology of Spirit* (2002), 45.
24. Robert Pippin, *Hegel's Idealism: The Satisfactions of Self-Consciousness* (1989), 119.
25. On the difference between these two conceptions of constellations, see Michael Rosen, *Hegel's Dialectic and its Criticism* (1982), 167–8. Adorno derives this second account of constellations from Walter Benjamin, *The Origin of German Tragic Drama* (1977).
26. Quoted by Seyla Benhabib, *The Reluctant Modernism of Hannah Arendt* (1994), 64. Like Adorno, Arendt derived this understanding of constellations from Benjamin.
27. *Ibid.*, 65.
28. I am grateful to Fabian Freyenhagen for his helpful comments on an earlier draft.

FOUR

Metaphysics

Espen Hammer

Introduction

Surprising as this may seem for a thinker steeped in Marxist theory and materialism, metaphysics was a key category in Adorno, and a concept around which his entire philosophical career revolved. By wresting this concept from its traditional associations with idealism, totality and affirmation, Adorno hoped to give it a new twist that would lead to its rehabilitation within the framework of a critical theory of society. Rather than understanding metaphysics as a purely theoretical and thus contemplative endeavour, Adorno urged his audience to think of metaphysics in social terms and ultimately as an element of unconstrained experience. He viewed metaphysics as a haven for truth: it is where experience leaps beyond the false totality of modern life and connects with the redemptive potentiality of real material being.

The history of Western metaphysics since Plato has been domi-nated by the attempt to distinguish between the temporal and the non-temporal, the world of finite objects in which we exist, and a suprasensible world of eternal or absolute objects. Behind the world of appearances and shadows there is a true, real and immutable world of essences about which philosophy has tried to speak. As the Greek word "metaphysics" (meta-physics, or that which exists before the science of the visible world, physics) intimates, the ultimate aim of this fundamental discipline has been to ground a science of the transcendent as opposed to the sphere of the imma-nent.

The classical expression of this project is, of course, to be found in Plato. In dialogues such as *Phaedrus*, *Phaedo* and *Politeia*, Plato claimed that the real, or what he called forms or ideas (*eidos*), is unchanging, transcendent and suprasensible – a world of pure essences in relation to which the sensible world is ontologically inferior and no more than a reflection or imitation.

Plato arrives at this view from many different directions. Among them, a particularly prominent one is epistemological. In order to tell that a thing is of a certain nature (that *this* is a car, or a scarf, or a horse), it is necessary to know something that cannot be derived from contemplating the particular thing itself. In order to know that *this* is a horse, one must have knowledge of what being a horse is, for otherwise one would not be able to identify *this* as a horse. One must know something about what all horses in the world have in common, or the conditions under which something may be said to be a horse. Once one arrives at the thought that these conditions cannot be arbitrary, changing and destructible (since if all horses disappeared, what it is to be horse would not be something tangible), then the conclusion is at hand that what a thing is must be determined by essences that exist beyond the empirical world, in a world of perfection that will never change.

For his part, Aristotle considers the forms to be inherent in objects as their animating rational principle. In his vastly influential *Metaphysics*, the universe is understood as an ordered teleological system in which every object strives to actualize its own nature. At the origin of this universe stands the "unmoved mover" – the *arché* on which everything else depends.

In the medieval world, metaphysics (in both its Platonic and Aristotelian variants) became the servant of theology, a means to articulate revealed truth in a rational language. With the early modern rationalists – including René Descartes, Gottfried Wilhelm Leibniz, and especially Christian Wolff – the medieval synthesis went through a process of further conceptual purification which led to the formulation of *metaphysica specialis* – the doctrine of suprasensible objects such as God, the soul and the origin of the world. *Metaphysica specialis* (literally: special metaphysics) was separated from *metaphysica generalis*, or the general doctrine of being. In Immanuel Kant and the British empiricists, however, this project was subjected to extensive and penetrating criticism and, ever since the downfall of German idealism, metaphysics has predominantly met with scepticism. Pragmatism, historicism, logical positivism, phenomenology, hermeneutics, ordinary-language philosophy, existentialism,

Marxism, naturalism – virtually all the major movements of modern philosophy – have not only reacted against metaphysics but considered it one of their main tasks to *overcome* it once and for all.

Adorno's critique of metaphysics

Adorno never dismisses the value and importance of the post-Kantian critique of metaphysics. He does not think that metaphysics can be rescued as a *rational science* of transcendent objects. Like Kant, he views the limits of what can be known as coinciding with the limits of possible experience; and since the objects of *metaphysica specialis* (God, the soul, the origin of the world) cannot be presented in experience, they cannot be known. Adorno will criticize Kant's conception of experience for being too narrow, but he never calls into question Kant's insistence that knowledge cannot transcend the experiential conditions of objecthood.

However, his critique of metaphysics does not centre mainly on its epistemological challenges. According to Adorno, the history of metaphysics can also be criticized on ideological grounds. In particular, Adorno raises three ideological charges against the history of metaphysics. First, it celebrates the immutable and non-temporal at the expense of the transient and temporal. On Adorno's account, this makes metaphysics complicit with a general historical trend towards increasing abstraction. This trend is problematic because abstraction is the main instrument in humanity's unchecked and destructive domination over nature.

Secondly, metaphysics is essentially affirmative because it holds that the existence of evil and chaos in the empirical world is compatible with the existence of a rational and moral order in the suprasensible realm. Metaphysics may therefore serve as a basis for the attempt to establish a theodicy: it tries to vindicate God's existence in the face of evil. Thirdly, metaphysics subordinates to its conceptions of totality the particularity of human experience and suffering, as well as the concrete material world. Adorno thinks that such conceptions should be criticized and exposed as expressing a disregard for everything that resists subsumption under categories and universals.

All this is brought together in Adorno's reflections on radical evil and death as represented by Auschwitz.[1] The historical event of industrialized mass murder means that traditional metaphysics is no longer possible. It is not just that metaphysical claims cannot be justified rationally; Adorno argues that metaphysics as it has been practised since Plato *has become incompatible with the course of human history*. To claim that there is some kind of deep meaning behind the phenomena, a divine principle or operation that, despite all the horror, shows the world to be good or in some sense morally acceptable, would be tantamount to mocking the fate of the victims of Auschwitz. In other words, what was always thought to be a purely *a priori* discipline – a study of final things and causes without any regard for the empirical world – turns out to be answerable to experience.

Extending this thought to theology, Adorno sides with influential post-Holocaust theologians such as Jürgen Moltmann when he holds that no conception of transcendence can survive such a horrendous demonstration of human evil unscathed. Auschwitz means that Western culture, including its highest achievements, has failed. Post-Auschwitz culture is "garbage' (*ND*: 367). The guilt it confers upon all the living generates a need for a radical rethinking of culture. It is no longer possible to entertain an affirmative conception of culture. Rather, from now on the only adequate cultural forms are those that testify to the despair and darkness of contemporary living.

Perversely, Auschwitz can be said to represent the historical realization of aspirations that were inherent in the metaphysical tradition itself. As a world unto itself beyond the exigencies of historical time, it aims to become a closed totality. In its destruction of every individuating feature of individuals, it subordinates particularity and transience to universality and immutability. More strikingly, Auschwitz is a world of radical immanence. There is no escape from the camps, no outside except death. The notion of such a context of immanence, Adorno argues, may even be viewed more generally as the organizing principle of modern, secularized society as a whole. While people are not murdered systematically under late capitalism, they are in thrall to systemic forces that mould their self-interpretations and action orientations so as to correspond to its irrational imperatives. Every feature of the modern individual – thoughts, senses, desires, body, actions – has become commodified. Immanence and identitarian reason reign uninterruptedly.

Rethinking metaphysics

We should now be in a position to see what the relevant considerations are for rethinking the notion of metaphysics. On the one hand,

the immanence of the camps, and of modern, rationalized life generally, calls for the construction of some account of transcendence.
More than anything else, what Adorno retains from the metaphysical tradition is its desire for transcendence – that is, the simple sense
that "this cannot be all". The only alternative to irredeemable
despair must consist in the possibility of witnessing some form of
alterity or otherness capable of resisting the closure effected by
formal–instrumental rationality. On the other hand, for transcendence to be possible, metaphysics must be stripped of its traditional
adherence to conceptions of the ideal, the immutable and the totalizing universal. For Adorno, this means that metaphysics must be
given a materialist twist. Metaphysics can only survive, he argues, in
so far as it accepts materialism as its ontological condition: "The
course of history forces materialism upon metaphysics, traditionally
the direct antithesis of materialism" (ND: 365).

Adorno hardly exaggerates when admitting that metaphysics has
traditionally been a direct antithesis to materialism. In the tradition
of materialism – from Democritus and Epicurus to Thomas Hobbes,
Julien de La Mettrie, Denis Diderot and Baron d'Holbach, as well as
in Marxism and later elaborations of naturalism – to believe in the
ontological primacy of matter has almost always implied a rejection
of the metaphysics of transcendence. Exceptions to this trend are few
and far between, but one such exception is Walter Benjamin, who
deeply influenced Adorno's thinking about metaphysics. For Benjamin and Adorno, transcendence must be sought, not in the order
of the immutable, but in the transient and fragmentary – in what
interrupts the patterns of repetition that mark historical time and
redeem phenomena in their sublime singularity. While both inherit-
ing and transforming the concepts he finds in Benjamin (especially
in his famous preface to *The Origin of German Tragic Drama*),
Adorno starts to construct a thinking very early in his career that
revolves around Benjamin's concepts such as mimesis, image, aura,
name and experience.[2] He uses these concepts, not in order to lapse
into irrationalism, or to find a vantage point entirely beyond reason,
but to expand the current notions of reason and experience to
include confrontations of alterity and otherness.

Adorno does not offer a *theory* of metaphysical experience. If
anything, what he has to say in this regard should be read as remarks
that, rather than seeking epistemological closure and completion, are
meant to encircle and anticipate the event of such an experience.
Many of them are negative, telling us what the antithesis to metaphysical experience might be. One particularly important concept is

that of "the name", or "naming". In his most manifestly theological writings, Benjamin had already defined the name as the identity of an object from the vantage point of an infinite being.[3] The name is the identity conferred on each object by Adam before the Fall. In the postlapsarian world, Benjamin imagines, the theological name, which exhausted the essence of the thing and was capable of redeeming it, is occluded by the invention of human language, which trades in concepts. Human language is structured around the capacity for predication; it subsumes the singular identity of an object under a universal concept, thereby determining it as a species of a given genus. As a result, human beings lose insight into the nature of reality.

Like Benjamin, Adorno believes that concepts have the ability to reify experience and turn us away from things as they are in their unique being. Naming, on the contrary, involves an experience of significance and expression that takes place in opposition to conceptual knowledge. Following Proust's notion of involuntary remembrance, Adorno sees such experience as taking place in connection with certain place-names – Illiers and Trouville in the French author; Monbrunn, Reuenthal and Hambrunn in the German. As names from his childhood, the holiday travels he made with his parents, they invoke a particular, yet indeterminate promise of happiness: "One thinks that going there would bring fulfillment, as if there were such thing" (ND: 373). Adorno is not so much interested in the object itself as in what we may think of as the *imagination* of it, especially as entertained in conjunction with the strong and passionate hopes of a child. Indeed, the village itself is likely to be both boring and grey in comparison with the dream-like anticipation of what it will have in store. Incorporated in the anticipation is the sense that only this particular village will be able to fulfil the child, and that no other village could replace it.

Adorno emphasizes that, rather than being real, the object of a metaphysical experience must be an illusion. If it were real, this would entail that reconciliation is possible within the false social totality of modern society. However, Adorno rejects this possibility. A reconciliation between subject and object, human beings and nature, would only be possible beyond the current history of domination (or what Adorno, following Benjamin, also calls "natural history"). It is a utopian concept. On the other hand, the illusion that is apprehended in metaphysical experience points beyond itself. In German, the word *Schein*, which is often translated as "illusion", means both something unreal *and* the appearance *of* the real.

Following Hegel, Adorno understands truth as the negation of *Schein*. Truth cannot be had directly; it must be mediated. This view sets him apart from Benjamin, for whom truth permits no mediation and hence no rationality or conceptuality. Metaphysical experience provides a promise of something which is not a mere projection; it is a transcendence *from within*.

It is important to realize that Adorno wants to position himself between two extremes. He is claiming neither that metaphysical experience involves an immediate, non-conceptual form of apprehension, nor that it calls for some kind of independent justification or determinate judging. Moreover, he is not claiming that for something to count as a metaphysical experience it must in some sense correspond to something that is real. Metaphysical experience is an intimation of transcendence, not its fulfilment.

In *Negative Dialectics*, Adorno compares his account of metaphysical experience to Kant's thinking about the conditions and limits of human experience. On the one hand, Adorno clearly seeks to criticize Kant for imposing narrow limits on human knowledge. For Kant, objective experience is only attainable in so far as the given is presented as synthesized in accordance with *a priori* rules provided by the human mind. Like many critics before him, Adorno sees the kind of experience for which Kant's transcendental mind legislates as coextensive with scientific experience. Kant uncovers the *a priori* conditions for objective judging in natural sciences such as geometry and physics, but fails to account properly for other forms of objective experience. Indeed, Adorno goes further than this and argues that Kant ideologically posits as universal what is only a particular historical form of human experience. Thus, rather than achieving a genuinely universal account of experience, what Kant expounds as experience is modelled on the abstract and reified relations to the world and others in it that spring out of social relations under capitalism. Ultimately, our imprisonment in the immanence of appearances follows from the mind's function as a means to secure self-preservation. Kant's vision of experience is one of domination and control.

On the other hand, however, Kant should be praised for his "rescue of the intelligible sphere" (*ND*: 385). Outside the world of appearances (to which human experience is objectively and necessarily indexed) there is an intelligible sphere, a world that can only be thought or, as Adorno puts it, imagined, but not known. Despite the ideological nature of his theory of experience, there is a deep speculative truth in Kant's understanding of metaphysics. He is aware that there must be something which transcends the (false) order of appearances. Yet Kant also resists the temptation, so prevalent in later idealists such as Fichte and Hegel, to postulate some kind of philosophical route to reconciliation.

While Adorno finds congenial this restrained show of awareness of something outside the world of appearances (or, for him, the social totality), he takes issue with Kant's ahistorical construal of it. For Kant, the distinction between the order of appearances and the order of things-in-themselves is impervious to social and historical change: it is an opposition that follows from the doctrine of *a priori* conditions of knowing – or conditions that generate a world of appearances against which one must countenance a world of things-in-themselves. For Adorno, however, the delusive context (*Verblendungszusammenhang*) of late modernity, which Kant's philosophy reflects, may seem to be eternal, but it must be understood as created by human beings. It is therefore contingent, rather than necessary. Kant is right in resisting an easy passage to the metaphysical object, yet wrong in hypostatizing the opposition between appearances and things-in-themselves.

We have seen that Adorno attempts to obtain markers for providing a materialist account of transcendence, and that one of the ways he does so is by introducing a notion of metaphysical experience understood in terms of naming. Another important concept, however, is mimesis. Like that of naming, the concept of mimesis can be traced back to Benjamin, who uses it to designate a form of imitative behaviour.[4] Before the acquisition of language, Benjamin argues, the infant responds mimetically to the environment. Rather than reducing, as Kant would have it, its experience such as to satisfy rational constraints, the infant assimilates itself to the object and takes part, as it were, in that object's own realization. For example, rather than stating that a bird sings, thereby turning the bird into an object, a baby will imitate the bird's song and communicate with the bird as a subject in its own right. It is this element of radical receptivity – a receptivity which is prior to our everyday practices of objectifying the other – that interests Adorno. He does not understand mimesis as the capacity to produce a copy of reality. Rather, mimesis is a form of apprehending the other which challenges the self-identical subject and exposes it to a sublime touch which effaces the distinction between touching and being touched.

Adorno strongly emphasizes that metaphysical experience promises a fulfilment, not just of the intellectual powers, but of the bodily subject. In Freudian terms, it involves at least the illusion

(*Schein*) of a reconciliation between the ego principle and the id or the unconscious. Indeed, Adorno takes very seriously the fact that human beings exist as radically embodied and therefore finite beings. The subject's normal relation to nature is dominated by the desire for self-preservation, which governs the ego's orientation in the world and translates into a relentless quest for dominion. Yet there are moments – threatening or exhilarating – when the repression is lifted and a "remembrance" may be conducted of the nature in the subject.

In *Negative Dialectics*, Adorno also associates the fact that we are natural beings with death. Like Ernst Bloch, he sees death as the absolute antithesis to happiness and fulfilment – the anti-utopian *par excellence*. According to Adorno, a very distinctive fact about death in modern society is its total absurdity, its complete incommensurability with life. Death simply cannot in any way be viewed "epically", i.e., as a meaningful end to an otherwise meaningful and full life. If society were such as to permit the existence of epic lives – of lives united around the pursuit of acknowledged forms of virtue – then death would appear to be meaningful. In particular, if the pursuit of virtue were combined with a strong metaphysical framework that provided a source of authority to the individual's quest for moral authentication as well as good reasons to believe in an afterlife capable of rewarding good conduct on earth, then death, though always frightening, would be an event with which members of society could reconcile themselves.

Contemporary society offers nothing of this. Instead, it leaves the individual with scant or no resources with which to integrate the fact of death in any comprehensive notion of a good and completed life. This is why Adorno thinks that any attempt to reconceptualize and reintroduce a conception of epic death would be ideological. He accuses Heidegger's metaphysics of death (*Todesmetaphysik*) of doing precisely such a thing. On Adorno's reading, Heidegger offers a "heroism of death": Being-towards-death is the heroic condition of complete authenticity whereby *Dasein* comes to terms with its own ungroundedness and finitude. It is thus capable of entering into a "resoluteness" which will make life as a whole meaningful. But Adorno objects that modern dying cannot be meaningful in this way, and when taking the death camps into account it becomes almost sacrilegious to hold that meaning can be obtained from death.

Adorno is much more sympathetic to Kant, who argued in his practical philosophy that, in contemplating death and the always existing possibility of evil triumphing over good, reason is inevitably led to postulate immortality and a benevolent God. Rather than suggesting that death can be a source of meaning, Kant held that the highest good, the unification of happiness and virtue, is made possible only if we suppose that the soul lives forever in a metaphysically just universe. But it would surpass possible experience to have knowledge in this area. So Kant argues that we can say only that it is in the interest of reason to suppose that we are immortal and that God exists because the highest good cannot be realized on earth with any certainty, yet must be able to motivate the moral will.

In the same way, Adorno insists that the experience of negativity – of death and radical evil, and indeed also of the utter loss of meaning which he thinks characterizes ordinary life in the rationalized social world – brings about a "metaphysical need". If we are honest and reflective, we simply cannot avoid desiring transcendence. Indeed, even to recognize how bad things are, we need a contrasting vision – a concept or experience with utopian implications – with which to oppose it. Adorno's thought here is that the dystopian and the utopian, immanence and transcendence, belong together: the one cannot be conceived without the other. Just as the idea of transcendence springs out of suffering, so "grayness could not fill us with despair if our minds did not harbor the concept of different colors, scattered traces of which are not absent from the negative whole" (ND: 377–8).

Conclusion

Adorno's vision of metaphysics in an evil world of radical immanence may appear to have much in common with gnosticism.[5] Indeed, he seems at least indirectly to acknowledge this when, referring to his literary hero Samuel Beckett, he writes that "to Beckett, as to the Gnostics, the created world is radically evil, and its negation is the chance of another world that is not yet" (ND: 381). For the gnostics, the material world, created by a dark spirit or devil, is uniformly evil; and the only possibility of salvation consists in negating one's implication with matter and finding the spark of divinity within, or *pneuma*. Obviously, if Adorno were a gnostic of some kind, then a pronounced tension would arise between his metaphysics, on the one hand, and his moral and political aspirations as a critical theorist in the Marxist tradition, on the other.

Much criticism of Adorno has focused on the apparent antinomy between claiming that the world is inherently evil – with change being possible only in so far as a wholly different world is created – *and* criticizing existing society with a view to reforming it. Critics have argued that Adorno's metaphysics is that of a melancholic conservative, locked inside his vision of the meaninglessness of life, who justifiably renounces any attempt at reform. How can this apparently desperate metaphysics support the effort to articulate a rational basis for social critique?[6]

Several points bear mentioning. First, Adorno places his metaphysics in close conjunction with morality. There is a metaphysical moment present in the simple acknowledgement of pain, in which the perception of pain in attentive individuals engenders a sense of commitment to offer support. Our moral life is founded not on universal principles but on the ability to empathize with others as unique and finite human beings with an endless capacity for both joy and suffering. This explains Adorno's anger at what he calls "bourgeois coldness", the prevalent form of moral attitude in late, post-Auschwitz modernity: it shuts itself off from the suffering of others, thereby promoting civilization's repression of nature. Rather than renouncing any attempt at reform, metaphysical experience generates a demand that suffering be resisted and a less violent social world created.

Secondly, Adorno is merciless in his critique of those, such as the theologian Karl Barth, who designs a notion of "the wholly other", completely untainted by culture (*ME*: 121–2). Such a notion, he argues, will necessarily fail: it will be abstract; it will draw on specific cultural resources; or it will dogmatically postulate what that "other" may be. There can be no unmediated absolute other. Finally, it is hardly the case that resignation or despair is the only option left to anyone who holds a view of contemporary society that is similar to that of Adorno. Adorno does not claim that change is impossible. His view is that it can only be possible in so far as the negativity and the irrationality of society are taken properly into account. Metaphysical experience is Janus-faced: while locating a moment of transcendence, it also makes us aware of the negativity of immanence. It offers a normative basis for social critique.

Finally, one may wonder how culture is supposed to sustain the possibility of such experience. Other forms of socially important experience – scientific, political, educational and so on – take place within institutions that possess technical, epistemic and organizational apparatuses geared towards making these experiences possible. Compared with scientific experience, for example, metaphysical experience seems hopelessly flimsy and non-committal.

Adorno's answer, however, is that cultural modernity does in fact possess such an institution. In advanced art practices, whether literary or musical, he finds that metaphysical experience is enacted at the level of the artwork's so-called "truth content" (*Wahrheitsgehalt*) (*AE*: 131ff).

When such an artwork, as in Arnold Schönberg's music or Beckett's dramas, succeeds in giving form to nature's own expression, it penetrates everyday experience and reveals a fragment of a shattered totality. Adorno argues that the artwork's truth content can be viewed as a mimesis of the beautiful in nature. Just as untrammelled nature provides an image of the non-identical, so artworks, when sublimating this experience into artistic form, are objects of metaphysical significance. Although they ought never to be administered, they provide sanctuaries for experiences that other modern institutions, science in particular, refuse.

In insisting on the need to "rescue metaphysics in the moment of its fall", Adorno stands out among his fellow associates of the Frankfurt School. Max Horkheimer, his close friend and co-writer of *Dialectic of Enlightenment*, was, with the exception of his Schopenhauerian reflections on suffering, more empirically inclined. So too was Adorno's assistant, Jürgen Habermas. The latter even introduces "postmetaphysical thinking" as a requirement placed upon all serious philosophical reflection in our time.[7] Philosophy, Habermas argues, should restrict itself to reconstructing a theory of rationality, all the while being in close *rapport* with the empirical social sciences. Although religious and metaphysical beliefs are often ineradicable sources of orientation in moral and ethical issues, they can only be taken seriously as claims in so far as they are filtered through a rational discourse.

Against such trenchant opposition to metaphysics, drawn mainly from Kantianism and pragmatism, Adorno's position may seem vulnerable and marginal. There are good reasons to believe that his rescue operation may not succeed. However, there are equally good reasons to think that it *ought* to succeed. According to Adorno, the most important reason why metaphysics ought to find some sort of haven in a world that seems to have rejected it is that the alternative would be a condition marked by a total nihilism. But, on Adorno's view, complete evacuation of meaning from the lifeworld would be unbearable. Meaninglessness is nothing to be cherished, as some of the most cynical postmodern thinkers would have it, but a predicament calling for resistance and hope. There is a strong element of hope in Adorno's fragile epiphanies of transcendent experience.

The apparent resurgence of religion, in both private and public life, would not have impressed Adorno. Although he was strongly oriented towards Catholicism in his early youth, he remained very sceptical of traditional religion. He argued that in a society such as ours, religion can offer nothing more than a false substitute, an artificial and hence unjustified injection of meaning into a meaningless universe. The danger, always, with the metaphysical impulse is its urge to affirm. Although post-Auschwitz culture cannot be affirmed, the desire to point beyond it will hardly be relinquished. If ours is a postmodern culture, a culture of the present, a culture without past or future, submerged in cycles of commodified consumption, then Adorno's work, which refuses to let go of the modernist values of truth, transcendence and meaning, is an anachronism. However, if these values are implicit in a larger project with which even contemporary humanity can identify, then Adorno's reflections on metaphysics will continue to be relevant for both ethical orientation and political struggle.

Notes

1. For further reflections on the importance of Auschwitz in Adorno's thought, see Fabian Freyenhagen's and Marianne Tettlebaum's essays in this volume (Chapters 6 and 8).
2. Walter Benjamin, *The Origin of German Tragic Drama* (1977).
3. Walter Benjamin, "On Language as Such and the Language of Man", *Selected Writings*, vol. 1 (1996), 62–74.
4. Walter Benjamin, "On the Mimetic Faculty", *Reflections: Essays, Aphorisms, Autobiographical Writings* (1978), 333–6.
5. For more on gnoticism, see, for example, Michael Pauen, *Dithyrambiker des Untergangs: Gnostisches Denken in Philosophie und Ästhetik der Moderne* (1994). See also Micha Brumlik, *Die Gnostiker: Der Traum von der Selbsterlösung des Menschen* (1992), 303.
6. See, for example, Wolf Lepenies, *Melancholy and Society* (1992), 196: "Both [Adorno and Arnold Gehlen] raise elitist claims and courageously suppress their longing for something better: melancholy appears as the atmosphere in which critique leaves things as they are. The comfortable 'Hotel Abyss', to which Georg Lukács referred so viciously, offers rooms to both thinkers."
7. See Jürgen Habermas, *Postmetaphysical Thinking* (1993).

FIVE

Between ontology and epistemology

Ståle Finke

Introduction

With our modernist commitments and problems, we cannot avoid epistemology. Epistemology represents the ways in which modern subjectivity and our rational, discursive self-conceptions are articulated and defended; it both preserves something authentic about subjectivity and conceals it. This concealment, Adorno thinks, results from a misconception that must be corrected since it neglects the dependence of both subjectivity and meaning on an embodied and finite experience of nature and things.

Adorno's critique of epistemology also involves rethinking the claims of ontology. Appreciating Kant's critique of ontology as something that transcends the bounds of possible sense or conceptual intelligibility, Adorno cannot revert to ontological assumptions in the Aristotelian tradition. Yet he does not endorse Kant's rejection of ontology, which makes intelligibility a mere question of the subject's conceptually articulated experience and normative self-authorization. Instead, Adorno presents us with a critical self-consciousness which reminds us that nature, our form of life, the lives of other beings, and the nature of things intrinsically evade our discursively articulated experiences and claims.[1] In the mature formulations of *Negative Dialectics*, the conception of ourselves as belonging to a natural life-world also involves acknowledging the problematic status of all ontological claims. We must acknowledge ourselves and our claims as indebted to an *affinity* with things and other beings which are recognized as finite individuals. An ontological claim to wholeness or completion cannot be defended; we can defend only individual expressions of particularity that invoke the whole without stating it.

A tension exists between epistemology and ontology in Adorno's thought. This tension cannot be resolved, or even presented co-herently, within philosophical systems since experience, and our discursive authorizations of it, are necessarily intertwined with nature. To balance the claims of thought and conceptuality with the unthought ontological assumption of nature's particularity, Adorno undertakes a critical reading of the premises of both epistemology and ontology in Immanuel Kant, G. W. F. Hegel and Edmund Husserl; these philosophers lodge a claim to systematic philosophy in the sense of *prima philosophia*, while simultaneously aiming to overcome the one-sidedness of the modern epistemological tradition. In their critique of epistemology and the philosophy of subjectivity, Kant, Hegel and Husserl implicitly exhibit a sense for what Adorno calls the *non-identical*. The non-identical, however, is merely a place-holder for several critical intuitions and claims that can be under-stood only by examining how different philosophies have tried to overcome the non-identity of concepts and things within experience.

In what follows, I shall address Adorno's arguments against epistemology, and his intention to both overcome and preserve it, by elaborating on the idea of the non-identical. We shall examine this idea in order to make sense of Adorno's attempt to recover a certain modified ontological claim, a claim for nature, or for individuals and their natural affinities. This reconstruction may rely upon arguments and conceptual resources that were somewhat alien to Adorno – not the least in order to make a case for his contemporary relevance. But, as I hope to make clear, we should not conceive Adorno's key concepts as fixed or analytically determined theoretical ideas. Instead, we should understand them by taking on the hermeneutic task of reinterpreting – or engaging in dialogue with – the central texts of the philosophical tradition so as to make these texts and Adorno's ideas our own, while at the same time disowning them, immersing ourselves in their ideas and ambivalent claims.

In the first sections of this chapter, I shall deal with Adorno's meta-critique of epistemology, with his attempt to recover, through a critical reading of Husserl's phenomenology, a conception of experi-ence and subjectivity that is embedded in a linguistic form of life and practice. Thereafter, I shall turn to Adorno's epistemic claims for the non-identical, and the way in which this notion turns on a phenom-enological sense of things and individual natures. Finally, I shall address his idea of a *mimetic* language of things – a language that expresses both subject and object, and the affinities between them prior to their conceptual form.

Metacritique, epistemology and language

Adorno's *metacritique* of epistemology is intrinsically related to his negative dialectics in a way that does not make the former a mere propaedeutic to the latter. Metacritique, as Adorno states, is "nothing other than the confrontation of judgement with the mediations inherent in it" (*AE*: 153). Epistemology, on the other hand, often takes the form of a philosophy of consciousness or subjectivity where the subject's "inner givens", or ideas, are considered fundamental for knowing external objects. But what is mediation in Adorno's conception of metacritique? And how does it apply to Husserl's phenomenology?

For Adorno, the foundational project of modern epistemology, which is based on the premisses of a philosophy of a subject that has privileged access to self-evident inner meanings, is untenable. Against this, he argues that the realm of mental representations is itself embedded in contexts of judging and conceptual inferences where subject and object are already interrelated and mediated through linguistic practices. Subjective meaning should be conceived as equiprimordial with *intersubjective* linguistic practices of expression and justification which provide for the intrinsic *correctibility* of all meaning and claims to knowledge. This criticism also applies to Husserl's phenomenology, which fails to acknowledge the importance of the grammatical or language-specific determination of thought when it treats all meaning as equivalent to inner givenness and immediacy. For Adorno, mediation through language entails the mediate character of even the supposedly immediate: "Husserl calls the mediate immediate because he believes in the datum: he wants to detach the mediate . . . from the mere possibility of being fallacious" (HPI: 132).

Now, this criticism might be thought to rest on a misunderstanding of Husserl's phenomenology and its explicit attempt to avoid the epistemic gap between mind and world, or the separation of experience into inner pictures and outer realities. According to Husserl: "Despite its transcendence, the spatial thing we see is perceived; we are consciously aware of it as given in its *embodied form*. We are not given an image or sign *in its place*."[2] Thus phenomenological reflection does not retreat into an inner realm, but simply treats the outer

realm as something in which consciousness always already participates – the objectivity of experience that is prior to subjective, inner
or private givenness.

However, Adorno does not overlook this important dimension of
Husserl's phenomenology. Instead, he objects to the epistemic or
foundational character of Husserl's methodology. To reveal phenomena in their originary givenness, Husserl prescribes an *epoché*, that
is, a withdrawal from all worldliness, or reality commitment in
judgement.[3] This withdrawal is not sceptical: it does not deny or
doubt the world, but attempts to recover its givenness *for* consciousness.

To clarify how everything can simultaneously be withdrawn and
yet recovered, Husserl appeals to an interesting analogy between
theoretical experience and aesthetic experience. When participating
in the play of aesthetic forms and lines, one brackets judgement –
with its commitment to articulate things or objects as being *thus* and
so – and turns towards subjectivity.[4] As aesthetic consciousness tears
itself away from an intramundane reality orientation, and becomes
theoretical in the sense of being reflexively occupied only with itself,
an internal play of forms is disclosed. Similarly, the phenomenolo-
gist brackets the object in its *thus* and *so* existence, and attempts to
reveal the forms of intentional consciousness that constitute the
experience of it.[5]

For Husserl, then, there seems to be a privileged realm of analysis
related to the givenness of the inner – and a corresponding reflection
or phenomenological "seeing" – which finds its "ultimate source of
justification" in the mere idealities or possibilities of intentional
directedness.[6] Against this, Adorno agrees with many of the conclusions reached in the post-Wittgensteinian philosophy of language,
such as the impossibility of disclosing a cognitively relevant sense of
inner meanings from which knowing can proceed to conclusions
about objective "states of affairs".[7] Cognition is already part of an
expressible linguistic practice; it manifests procedures of justification,
judgement and the reflexive authorization of inferential entitlements,
and intrinsically refers to the *externalities* of things beyond the scope
of mere subjective meaning.

What Adorno calls "peephole metaphysics" abstracts from contexts in which expressions such as "this looks to me such and such",
or "appears as so and so", reflexively modify claims in accordance
with an understanding of the limitations of a specific viewpoint or
epistemic situation. As is clear from practices such as these – which
involve judging and modifying a claim – the determination of the

inner depends upon conceptual practices that determine the outer world of things. Hence Adorno declares: "There is no peeping out. What would lie in the beyond makes its appearance only in the materials and categories within" (*ND*: 140, tr. mod.).[8]

Although Husserl explicitly wants to close the epistemological gap between mind and world, Adorno argues that his phenomenology becomes a victim of its own methodology. By turning consciousness into a self-sufficient realm of meaning, Husserl withdraws it from the lived experience he wants to recover, thereby neglecting the ways in which ordinary language is embedded in forms of life and practice. In ordinary conceptual practices, meaning is always revisable and subject to unique authorizations through singular judgements and inferences that cannot be conceived as given, or evidentially enclosed, within the realm of pure subjectivity.

For Adorno, there can be no ultimate fulfilment in a natural language of what is thought, or taken to be, such and such, since the very act of judging entails commitments to further acts of judging to reveal the meaning of what is expressed. To vary one of Adorno's own examples (HPI: 129): arguments for or against a liberal government (for example: "a liberal government is the only human form of government") rely upon agreement about what "liberal", "government" and "human" mean – together with the common understanding presupposed in claiming a liberal government as the only human one. Now, such agreements and understandings are not self-evident or immediately revealed to me in reflection on what I meant by my claim. They cannot be understood in abstraction from contexts in which agreements are claimed and achieved. For Adorno, rather, "the notion of intentionality implies only that we can mean the objective essences in the stream of consciousness; it implies nothing about their being" (HPI: 129).

Meaning something thus implies a claim to attunement with others in judgement, meaning something *rightly*; it implies common commitments to further applications and uses of concepts, and to the meanings that words may acquire. Again, the point is that I cannot articulate an "original" meaning – and its essential fulfilment (*Evidenz*) – in abstraction from the practices of expression, judging and sense-giving that make up the *grammar* of an ordinary language. Meaning is something to be *achieved* rather than already fixed or intuitively determined.[9] In agreement with Adorno, Ludwig Wittgenstein notes the following: "We want to say: 'When we mean something, it's like going up to someone, it's not having a dead picture (of any kind)'. We go up to the thing we mean."[10] In other words, meaning something does not proceed from self-authorizing inner givens, but is something attained, fulfilled or confirmed through living practice as it develops. The meaning of concepts cannot be determined independently of such practice.

Subjectivity in judgement

Adorno's problem is not with the central place that Husserl gives to subjectivity in experience, but with his adoption of an epistemological or foundational construction of subjectivity. In a certain sense, Husserl retains too little of subjectivity because he views it as transparent to itself and its meanings in phenomenological reflection: "Too much subjectivity in Husserl implies at the same time too little of the same. By assuming it is itself a pregiven and constitutional condition of all objectivity, this subject renounces intervention in both knowing and practice; it merely registers, in contemplative and uncritical passivity, the world of things."[11]

Moreover, Husserl draws a sharp distinction between pure meaning (*Bedeutung*) and its grammatical variability, or the dependence of meaning on concrete contexts of expression.[12] His descriptive analysis concerns objectivity as a formal possibility; it brings into pure eidetic intuition only the formal structures of possible meaning and intentionality. His turn "to the things themselves" (*zur Sachen selbst*) explicitly turns against the factical judgements and conditions of subjectivity, or the "unsteadiness of meanings", and tries to recover meanings as "ideal unities".[13]

Against this, Adorno argues that Husserl ignores the subject's place within conceptual practices and thus neglects its unique responsibilities. The propositional and conceptual articulation of a thing, which gives it a logical form or structure, is inseparable from the conditions under which that thing is articulated and conceived to be *thus* and *so*. This articulation is the result of certain commitments to *factical* inferences, as well as to judgemental and conceptual orientations; it also exhibits attunement in judgement, achieved agreement. Knowing the meaning of words implies forming judgements – or material inferences[14] – in which intersubjective linguistic practice as a whole determines what is meant. Linguistic intentions are subject to criteria that belong to this practice – not to inner convictions or fulfilment. Again, the fulfilment of meaning is accomplished only in linguistic practice itself. Through participation in such practice, I become aware of the sense of my intentions, of what is entailed in meaning something with a determinate sense.

Hence Adorno objects that formal articulation by conceptual consciousness requires *subjective* judgement and *factical* inference in which meaning is continually articulated, determined and revised in light of authorizations made in each singular or *unique* judgement, or the claims to rightfulness or appropriateness in each execution. The conditions of execution are themselves of a practical nature, and are thus not available in a reflective and descriptive analysis that concerns itself with pure meanings. In this way, the subject attains to both *more* and *less* than Husserl's pure eidetic subject since it does not merely register objective meanings, but must be conceived as spontaneity all the way through to the discriminations and judgements which make consciousness responsive to experience:[15] "The thought of truth . . . demands the relation of the subject to states-of-affairs. And this relation – and thus the objectivity of truth – likewise comprises thinking subjects . . . The objectivity of truth really demands the subject. Once cut off from the subject, it becomes the victim of sheer subjectivity" (*AE*: 72).

Importantly, then, even if all inner modifications of subjectivity – that is, all its inner apprehensions – are mediated through the external constraints of an expressive form of linguistic practice, one cannot avoid subjectivity because the subject's orientation towards meanings and things expresses its unique responsiveness to things. This responsiveness also involves recognition of a thing's independent existence outside thought. The inner and the outer evade one another. Genuine experience is attained by acknowledging thought's dependence on its other – the world of natural objects and things. And this acknowledgement is a subjective accomplishment, so that a sense of the inner must be retained because it refers to a unique relation. A reconstruction of Adorno's conception of experience will thus have to balance a twofold claim: that subjectivity is embedded in linguistic practices of expression, interpretation and a normatively authorized space of inferences, and that it has an epistemic responsibility for its relation to the world.

Historicality and genetic phenomenology

The factical dimension of subjectivity entails a history of conceptual practices and their constitutive role in language and meaning. And it was precisely this perspective on experience to which Husserl wanted to draw attention in his later work.[16] To be fair to Husserl, then, one ought to show how his phenomenological method itself motivates a turn towards a genetic phenomenology, and rejects an epistemological stance altogether. Indeed, Husserl seems to have been the first to undertake a metacritique of the epistemological premisses of his own thinking.

For instance, in his 1927 *Natur und Geist*, the conceptual articulation of an object or object-domain is conceived as a rationalization of an originary and unitary stream of "mute experience" from which conceptual consciousness emerges.[17] Hence, according to Husserl, the constitution of objectivity first finds its fulfilment in being referred back to this unity of worldly experience – which makes the idealities of intentional consciousness less a matter of givenness than of genetic or historical becoming. In the late work, this explicitly involves a critique of what Husserl calls "the sedimented conceptual system" from which phenomenological reflection begins in order to "animate concealed historical meaning" in its unattained becoming.[18] All this could be matched to aspects of Adorno's own thinking: he calls for a critical hermeneutics which discloses sedimented historical life and meaning within conceptual forms that present themselves as givens, as forms of nature. He wants to grasp *"historical being in its most extreme historical determinacy, where it is most historical, as natural being"* (INH: 260, emphasis added).

Even if Adorno was not taking on board later developments in Husserl's thought and its affinities to his own thinking, his argument remains relevant to the extent that there is a conflict in Husserl's phenomenological methodology and its search for a foundation – a search retained even in *The Crisis of European Science and Transcendental Phenomenology*. For Adorno, the turn to the "things themselves" cannot consist in the analysis of the fulfilment of phenomena: meaning and aboutness are constituted in conceptual practices and their historicality. And the medium of such mediation is language.

Accordingly, what is crucial in Adorno's reading of Husserl's philosophy – with respect to both its critique of epistemology and its importance for the development of Adorno's work as a whole – is how Husserl also challenges the premisses of a philosophy of consciousness. For Adorno, Husserl's philosophy both remains "within the range of subjective immanence", and prepares for a hermeneutics or mode of reading which aims "to use concepts to unseal the non-conceptual, without making it their equal" (*ND*:

10–11). When performing the *epoché*, Husserl tries to disclose the field of pure meaning, things in their possibility and abstract ideality – which is analogous, as we have seen, to the contemplative stance or attitude underlying experiences of the beautiful in art. Yet the analogy between the experience of beauty and the phenomenological attitude can also be turned against Husserl.

The idealities of meaning disclosed in an artwork certainly withhold judgement about the factical being of the things they represent (as Kant makes clear, a judgement about beauty is based exclusively upon disinterested and free pleasure). Thus, attention is drawn to the *play* of these meanings within the compositional whole which makes up the canvas. In this sense, it is correct to speak of figurations and motifs as mere possibilities, abstract *idealities* whose sense is determined as aesthetic play unfolds. Yet, even if they disclose important aspects of things – as well as their sense and importance to us, our encounters with them, and their proximity to our form of life – aesthetic forms and appearances cannot be said to grasp or disclose things themselves since the latter are *outside* art.

One might say that the artwork pays attention to things, even lets them show themselves, but not that they are somehow fully grasped in virtue of the art-immanent forms of aesthetic subjectivity. What art discloses depends on the meanings derived from conceptual and interpretive practices; these practices determine the conditions under which concepts acquire meaning. But, if art discloses an "essence", this essence is not fulfilled in art; its truth lies beyond the scope of immanent appearances. Similarly, the truth of phenomena is not revealed in pure phenomenological description; truth manifests itself only when the phenomenological attitude is broken, that is, in the return to a linguistic form of life, to factical existence in language.

In this sense, Husserl's epistemic ambition amounts to what Adorno calls an *identity philosophy* in which the objects of philosophical explication are identified with an epistemically defined subject. Adorno writes: "The identity of spirit with itself and the subsequent synthetic unity of apperception, is projected on things by the method alone . . . This is the original sin of *prima philosophia*" (*AE*: 10). To heed Husserl's ambition to "break through the walls of idealism" (HPI: 133), to continue his announced "breakthrough to the things themselves", requires a different turn in thinking, an acknowledgement of things as determining thought from without.

The preponderance of things: beyond Kant and Hegel

By now it should be clear that Adorno never subscribed to the premisses of a philosophy of consciousness.[19] Indeed, the aim of *Against Epistemology* is precisely to show the limits of this sort of philosophy in the case of Husserl. Importantly, though, Adorno's reading of Husserl is not intended merely to unmask the false premisses of his philosophy of consciousness by pointing to the inter-subjective nature of conceptual consciousness or, say, to the grammar involved in the inferential entitlements that are authorized and justi-fied in linguistic practice. Adorno thus cannot be said to agree with recent pragmatism in the philosophy of language which exhausts the meaning of experience in a discursively articulated idea of objec-tivity.[20] For Adorno, "[t]he criterion of truth is not its immediate communicability to everyone . . . Truth is objective, not plausible" (*ND*: 41).

As already noted, Adorno was sympathetic to Husserl's ambition of recovering a sense of things themselves in experience. However, he was critical of Husserl's ideal sense of things, their reduction to inner givenness. Adorno's turn towards things themselves is con-ceived as the need to acknowledge the "preponderance of the object": "Carried through, the critique of identity is a groping for the preponderance (*Vorrang*) of the object" (*ND*: 183).

Doubtless, the project of negative dialectics requires an under-standing of this preponderance. As we shall see, the development of Adorno's negative dialectics, and the very idea of non-identity as a placeholder for a retained epistemic claim, rest on the turn towards things themselves. What Adorno retains in this phenomenological turn is just the idea of a thing as an "in-itselfness", as non-identical to thought. But how is non-identity to be recovered? And, how does thingliness constitute itself for conceptual consciousness? Since *Negative Dialectics* centres more around Kant's and Hegel's concep-tion of experience than Husserl's, we should remind ourselves of their idealist commitments, and of why Adorno finds them *both* superior to Husserl's conception *and* insufficient in view of the promise to rescue things.

Adorno tries to show that the things to be rescued are prey to idealist premisses – either to the epistemic construction of experience, as in Kant, or to an ontological sublation of things to their logical form, as Adorno holds against Hegel (arguably, somewhat insensi-tively). With Kant, the whole problematic of experience is detached from substantive or ontological concerns, so that what is at stake is

how concepts and intuitions are brought into an epistemically justi-
fiable relation. The object is the result of a "synthetic unity" of
possible judgement.[21] It is a *projected* unity, that is, a unity presented
in sensibility by the productive imagination of a disparate manifold
(itself merely epistemic in character). As such, no ontological claims
about the nature of individual things can be made.[22]

The problem with this, for Adorno, is that it neglects the substan-
tiveness of things in their *bodily presence*. This presence is not to be
conceived as an ultimate given (and, in this, Kant was right): "What
we may call the thing itself is not positively and immediately at hand.
Whoever wants to know it must think beyond . . . the 'synthesis of
the manifold' which is no thinking at all. Yet, the thing itself is no
product of thought: it is nonidentity through identity" (*ND*: 189).
The conception of intuitions as a disparate manifold dissolves things
into a manifold of subjective impressions and intuitions, thereby
separating *form*, as accomplished by consciousness and the imagination, from *content*, or sensible givens without substantive coherence
(*ibid.*: 187).

To retain substance, Kant had to introduce the "thing-in-itself" as
a mere *limiting* concept, the idea of a *ground* beyond appearances.[23]
Yet, for Adorno, who follows Hegel here, this idea is incoherent to
the extent that (1) any possible sense of a thing's in-itselfness must
be demonstrable within the bounds of sensibility if it is not to be
empty. The idea of the *noumenon* thus entails only a formal recognition of something heterogeneous to thought, a "recognition of
non-identities in form" (*ND*: 26). Moreover (2), the conditions of
possible experience are turned into *subjective* conditions, so that
experience cannot be said to be objective, but concerns only *appearances* (and there is no meaningful or epistemic sense in which appearances can be related to their ground).[24] Kant is therefore incapable
of overcoming the premises of the epistemological tradition; he
reintroduces into his analysis of consciousness a view of cognition as
picture-thinking when he claims that the productive imagination,
after apprehending impressions, brings "the manifold of intuition
into the form of an *image*".[25]

Hegel offers an alternative conception of experience in *Phenomenology of Spirit*. His idea of testing knowledge claims – their standards,
as measured by the ideal of exhausting the conceptual and normative
conditions under which possible experience and objectivity make
sense – discloses objects as conceptual determinations which unfold
through critical presentation. Thus self-consciousness becomes the
ground of objectivity. This "self-recognition in otherness" achieves

what Kant's transcendental critique could not: the conformity of the object of experience to the conditions of experience. These conditions are no longer subjective, but *objective* determinations of thought and spirit. As Hegel proclaims in his *Science of Logic*: "As science, truth is pure self-consciousness in its self-development and has the shape of the self, so that the absolute truth of being is the known Notion and the Notion as such is the absolute truth of being."[26]

With Hegel, a thing's particularity is recognized as *Dasein* (there-being, sometimes rendered as "being there") in its own right, and not merely as a manifold to be unified by conceptual consciousness.[27] However, as Hegel's idealist conception of discursivity and logic unfolds, particularity is not conceived in abstraction from conceptual determination, but is itself a moment or aspect of the concept.[28] By turning particularity into a logical moment, Adorno thinks that Hegel again repeats the idealist mistake (implicitly an epistemological one) of subordinating a thing under a conceptual form; a thing merely expresses a conceptual articulation of self-consciousness – the latter thus has priority. Adorno states: "The Hegelian system in itself was not a true becoming; implicitly, each single definition in it was already preconceived." Moreover, Hegel failed to acknowledge the integrity or non-identity of things, since "the thought he discusses always extracts from its objects only that which is a thought already" (*ND*: 27). Although Hegel may be read more generously, he does not turn conceptual consciousness against itself so as to release a thing's particularity.[29]

Yet Adorno's turn towards things as non-identical to thought must take its departure from Hegel's idea of experience: since "the concept is experienced as nonidentical, as inwardly in motion, it is no longer purely itself; in Hegel's terminology, it leads to otherness without absorbing that otherness" (*ND*: 157). Again, things are supposed to have priority, not conceptual consciousness. The meaningfulness of experience is therefore not exhausted in the discriminating relations of inferentially and propositionally determined thought which make it possible for conceptual consciousness to be *about* something in the epistemic sense. Instead, such aboutness entails its own fulfilment in what is other than thought, in a unique nature and in-itselfness that limits consciousness from without. The determinations and transitions of conceptual consciousness, its logic, are indebted to a thing's nature, to its power of showing itself, so that a thing's givenness or in-itselfness is not a unity of conceptual discriminations, but rather their limiting condition. The thing enacts its own capacities for change and sameness.

But would the priority of a thing over and against its conceptual determinations not simply regress behind Hegel's insight into the determination of all particularity by conceptual consciousness? And if it is prior to conceptual thought, what is a thing? For an adequate understanding of Adorno's epistemic and ontological claim for the non-identical and the preponderance of the object, we shall return to his concerns with Husserl's phenomenology.

Non-identity and things themselves

Husserl attempts to preserve things in their givenness for conscious-ness. Hence a thing is not the result of a conceptual synthesis of the manifold, but an individual, an "embodied presence": "The spatial thing to which we attend is, in its transcendence, a perceived, cor-poreal given for consciousness."[30] Thus a thing is conceived both as an individual and in its "mode of givenness". This corresponds to Aristotle's sense of a thing, its *tode ti*, which involves its individual being-thereness (its "thisness") and its "whatness", that is, its being thus and so. The crucial question is whether the *ti*, or "whatness", in *ti einai*, is revealed adequately through its mode of givenness, or whether one must at the outset presuppose that the *being* of the thing is an individual nature prior to form, that is, a *hypokeimenion* (that which grounds).[31] In Husserl, this problem is conceived as involving a duality between the form of intentionality and the embodied presence of a thing.[32]

Husserl's appeal to the difference between the mode of givenness of a thing and its transcendence is ambivalent. In *Ideen* II, his account of things makes them the result of a passive form of consti-tution; this involves the embodied interaction between a subject and things and the causal influences of things upon an experiencing subject: "Reality, or what is the same, substantiality and causality belong together inseparably ... Real properties are thus *eo ipso* causal ones. To know a thing therefore means to know through experience how it behaves ... in the nexis of its causalities."[33] A thing's mode of being is not exhausted in its ideality for conscious-ness: since it is constituted through the passive apprehension of causal capacities, a thing seems to be a self-presence in virtue of its causal coherence, or of a mode of being that is not brought about by intentional consciousness in the active sense.[34]

An embodied "thing-experience" also underlies Adorno's idea of "non-identity": "[T]he non-identical moments show up as matter, or as inseparably fused with material things. Sensation [is] the crux of all epistemology ... There is no sensation without a somatic moment" (ND: 193). In keeping with this, one might say that Adorno wants to take Husserl at his word by preserving the transcendence of things that is inherent in their embodied self-givenness. Yet Adorno objects that Husserl's retreat to the premisses of a philosophy of consciousness undermines the recovery of things in their "originariness" (Urgegebenheit). For the unity of a thing as a transcendent object is understood as an accomplishment of consciousness that confers unity on an infinite manifold of adumbrations (Abschattungen). A thing's transcendence is thus effected by consciousness, and is part of the sphere of what presents itself in evidential givenness.

For Adorno, the phenomenological recovery of things must go all the way to express things in their integrity, or their mode of being; it must not rest content with abstract conceptions of things as intentional correlates of consciousness, as mere forms, or the result of a fulfilment of form, because such conceptions strip things of their "dignity" as "absolutely existing" entities (AE: 140). Here Adorno is rehearsing an objection, already much debated by Husserl's own students (by Hedwig Conrad-Martius, among others), which points to an immanent problem in Husserl's constitutional analysis: that of the duality of the mode of being and the givenness of a thing. Importantly, though, Adorno's argument is not primarily ontological – it does not concern the duality of being – but rather deals with experience and the non-identity of things qua individuals.

The attribution of an invariant eidos – essence or form – to the tode ti has a long history. Agreeing with Aristotle, Husserl conceived the essence of an individual thing to be what it has yet to become (to ti en einai). A thing is always in the process of becoming, of actualizing itself. In this sense, the embodied and conceptual histories of things are intertwined. For Adorno, however, it is crucial that the becoming of a thing not be conceived as a conceptually articulated unity, but preserved in all its individuality. Conceiving of a thing in dynamic terms, as having been and being in becoming, entails a perspective in which conceptual determinations are turned inside out by showing their dependence on things.

According to Adorno,

> when things in being are read as a text of their becoming . . . idealistic and materialistic dialectics touch. But while idealism sees in the inner history of immediacy its vindication as a stage

of the concept, materialism makes that inner history the measure, not just of the untruth of concepts, but even more of the immediacy in being. The means employed in negative dialectics for the penetration of its hardened object is *possibility* – the possibility of which their reality has cheated the objects and which is nonetheless visible in each one.

(*ND*: 52, emphasis added)

Without pretending to unravel this passage in detail, one should note its concern for possibility, for the individual nature of things as being always *not yet*. In their capacity for change, things reveal their non-identity. Their non-identity is the condition of the possibility of any discursively articulated experience.

Hence there is a phenomenological sense of the mode of being of things that transcends the limited standpoint of epistemology. As conceived by conceptual consciousness – and this corresponds to an epistemic determination – a thing is a transcendent idea (and its unity is ideal), but, as bodily presence, a thing is transcendent in virtue of its possibilities and self-presence. This non-identity of a thing is not epistemological since a thing makes a claim to having a being or nature of its own – a being or nature that differs from that of concepts. Adorno's epistemic ambition, however, is to reverse the idealizations of epistemology, and preserve the otherness of things. The question is whether this makes any difference to experience, or whether things should be sacrificed for the sake of the autonomy of concepts.[35]

Mimesis and "The Language of Things"

By preserving Husserl's idea of turning to the things themselves beyond the scope of conceptual consciousness, Adorno hopes to show that embodied experience promises to recognize things in their own right, expressing them mimetically rather than representationally.[36] By invoking the classical notion of *mimesis*, he wants to rehabilitate a mode of presenting things by likening – that is, by expressing things through forms of sensuous presentation in which they appear, or are made present in their absence – as a form of knowing. Such knowing is based neither on the epistemic model of picture-thinking nor on Kant's idea of a discursively articulated objectivity. Rather, in mimesis, the subject immerses itself in the things it attempts to present; it strives to disappear in things (*ND*:

189). Only through the subject's involvement in its presentation of things, which also involves the things presented, can the modern epistemological stance be overcome (*AE*: 144).

Mimesis is an attitude towards things; it is effected by an *epoché* which allows things themselves to come into view. This mimetic and expressive turn to things is in fact a *return*, since conceptually articulated experience already presupposes that language and things are sedimented in our form of life. Indeed, things are not merely *seen* (or "seen-as"), but require a language of their own if they are to be known at all. And this language would feed on a sensitivity to words, to how things dwell within them – a sensitivity that is not argumentative, inferential or strictly analytical, but attentive to the ways in which things show themselves *in language*. As Adorno states: "to comprehend a thing, not just to fit and register it in its system of reference, is nothing but to preserve and confirm (*gewahren*) the individual moment in its immanent relations to other things". Negative dialectics, then, ought to reverse conceptual idealizations and recall "the coherence of the nonidentical" (*ND*: 25–6, tr. mod.).

To discriminate between things and to conceptually articulate such discriminations, a subjective responsiveness is needed to provide "a haven for the mimetic element of knowledge, for the element of elective affinity between the knower and the known" (*ibid.*: 45). This allusion to Goethe is, of course, not superfluous, as diverse elective affinities are based upon mutual attractions and resistances. In mimetic acknowledgement, things are experienced as limiting conditions, and as individual natures interwoven both with other individual natures and with the experiencing subject.

To defend a mimetic language of things, Adorno must counter Plato's one-sided solution to the ancient quarrel between philosophy and poetry, his downgrading of mimesis to either arbitrary wilfulness or mythical dependence. Surely a mimetic presentation of things has its originary form in mythical invocations of natural powers through rite and play. Released from its mythical context, however, and transposed into forms of artistic beauty, mimesis recovers an experience of things that has been displaced by *logos*. Natural beauty reveals things in their physiognomic aspects, values and forms that recall or reinstate our dependence on them.[37] Hence Adorno pays special attention both to the "expressive moments" of art and to the subject's receptivity (which underlies the physiognomic nature in which things reveal themselves). Subjective expression makes things present and, as such, retains its significance for knowledge of objects (*CM*: 250).

In artworks, things show themselves through a second nature, which consists in the logic of the materials inherent to the medium that reveals their physiognomic aspects. The artwork is thus a doubling of nature to the extent that it relies upon its own disclosive power to make the hidden visible. Mimesis is thus conceived as a form of participation in which the subject transcends itself towards things so as to release them in their otherness to subjectivity. Through mimesis, a thing both withdraws and reconstitutes itself. Only as absent, as determining the mimetic presentation by simultaneously withdrawing from it, are things present at all. As Aristotle also made clear, in poetry, things and figures are articulated as mere possibilities.

Mimetic presentation thus has an *ideality* of its own. Kant, Husserl and the neo-Kantians showed that consciousness continually strives towards objects, objects that are to be conceptually and mathematically grasped and articulated as ideas. However, Adorno argues that these formal idealizations of consciousness – while constitutive for an epistemically determined objectivity – neither exhaust objects, nor are they ontologically preponderant.[38] Instead, the object preponderates: it exists prior to form as a limiting condition, or there-being, constituting the ground of all conceptual determination, and of the elective affinities between things. In natural beauty, itself a residual moment within artistic form, Adorno finds an original articulation of things, not as "givens", but as possibilities (*AT*: 66).[39]

The sensuous forms of physiognomic traits – which shift with the expressive attentiveness of the experiencing subject – reveal things in their otherness to conceptual consciousness. That is, they reveal things as conditioning appearances. In this sense, mimesis is a reminder of the mutuality of things and language; it also reminds us that language can never be entirely sublimated into pure forms. For Adorno – and this brings him close to thinkers such as Wittgenstein, Martin Heidegger and Hans-Georg Gadamer – this limitation is not an obstacle to knowing but a salutary corrective to an epistemic (metaphysical, according to Wittgenstein) misconception.

Whether Adorno transcends epistemology towards ontology is a difficult question. It cannot be answered fully without considering his criticisms of Heidegger's phenomenological ontology in some detail. Without pursuing this topic here, however, we may conclude by noting that Adorno, at least in his later writings, gradually seems to become more sympathetic to Heidegger's thought, in particular to his famous turn towards things in his essay on art.[40] Unlike Heidegger, however, Adorno does not infer ontological commitments

93

from the nature or being of things. If being is historical, sedimented historicality in concepts, the being of beings can neither be expressed as a whole, nor dissolved into a primordial stream of life. Rather, the elective affinity of things is based on their individuality, and non-identity demonstrated only in its individual manifestations. As such, nature is dappled diversity, not unity.[41]

Consequently, Adorno's metacritique of epistemology cannot be conceived in ontological terms, either in the classical or the Heideggerian sense, since its aim is to avoid unity and dwell only with particularity. Still, as we have seen, Adorno cannot rest content with epistemology, as epistemology fails to do justice to things themselves. The turn towards things themselves obtains its evidential authority only through *experience*; and experience for Adorno is something to be achieved rather than something given, an achievement of "togetherness in diversity" (*ND*: 150). Experience entails a promise to things of remembrance and acknowledgement.

Notes

1. Still, Adorno denies neither the idealist claim to normative self-authorization, nor the attempts to articulate a normative self-conception within epistemic, moral, political and aesthetic contexts of experience which Robert Pippin defends in *Modernism as a Philosophical Problem* (1990).
2. Edmund Husserl, *Ideas: General Introduction to Pure Phenomenology* (1969), 136 (*Ideas* I). Translations of this, and other texts, are altered where appropriate.
3. *Ibid.*, 98.
4. Edmund Husserl, *Ideas Pertaining to a Pure Phenomenology and to a Phenomenological Philosophy. Second Book: Studies in the Phenomenology of Constitution* (1989), 10–11 (*Ideas* II).
5. Husserl, *Ideas* I, 107.
6. *Ibid.*, 75.
7. Most prominently formulated, perhaps, by Wilfrid Sellars: "in characterizing an episode or a state as that of knowing, we are not giving an empirical description of that episode or state; we are placing it in the logical space of reasons". *Empiricism and the Philosophy of Mind* (1997), 76. See also Charles Taylor, "Overcoming Epistemology", *Philosophical Arguments* (1995).
8. Sellars formulates this as follows: "The point I wish to stress . . . is that the concept of *looking green*, the ability to recognize that something *looks green*, presupposes the concept of *being green*, and that the latter concept involves the ability to tell what colours objects have by looking at them." *Empiricism and the Philosophy of Mind*, 43. Hence there is no privileged description of what "looks to me such and such" that does not already imply the conceptual practice in which things are determined as "being such and such

or *thus* and *so*": "looks-talk" is derived from linguistic practice; it is not a non-inferential premiss for knowing.

9. For a similar analysis, see Herbert Schnädelbach, "Phänomenologie und Sprachanalyse", *Philosophie in der modernen Kultur* (2000), 240ff.

10. Ludwig Wittgenstein, *Philosophical Investigations* (1953), §455. Fruitful comparisons can be made between Adorno's metacritique and Wittgenstein's grammatical investigations. See, for example, Christoph Demmerling, *Sprache und Verdinglichung* (1994).

11. Adorno, "Zur Philosophie Husserls", *Gesammelte Schriften* 20.1 (1998), 63.

12. Edmund Husserl, *Logical Investigations*, vol. 1 (1970), 258. (The English vol. 1 includes vol. 2 of the German edition.)

13. *Ibid.*, 322–3.

14. Sellars introduced this notion of material inference to capture the non-formal use of "subjunctive conditionals" in ordinary language. Their use permits inferences on the basis of our interaction with natural objects (in an interest-related perspective), such as "If I drop a stone on this piece of chalk, it will break". Sellars claims that material rules of inference are "essential to the language we speak, for we make constant use of subjunctive conditionals". See *Pure Pragmatics and Possible Worlds: The Early Essays of Wilfrid Sellars* (1980), 273. The conception of material inference is here extended to include the inferential nature of all judging as embedded in human life, capturing the grammatical sensitivity for revisability and judgement-bound authorization that governs the use of concepts in ordinary linguistic practice.

15. This point echoes an argument by John McDowell: "Experience enables the lay-out of reality to exert rational influence on what a subject thinks", *Mind and World* (1994), 26.

16. Yet some commentators argue that Husserl's early methodological aim – his Cartesian claim to have a self-evident and self-sufficient foundation – conflicts with his later genetic phenomenology which undermines the insistence upon a Cartesian foundation. See Iso Kern, *Kant und Husserl* (1964), 196ff.

17. Edmund Husserl, *Natur und Geist* (2001), 15.

18. Edmund Husserl, *The Crisis of European Science and Transcendental Phenomenology: An Introduction to Phenomenological Philosophy* (1970), 71.

19. Here I am arguing against Peter Dews in *Logics of Disintegration: Post-structuralist Thought and the Claims of Critical Theory* (1987), 227ff.

20. Cf. Robert B. Brandom: "[T]alk about the representational dimension of the conceptual content of intentional states should be understood in terms of the *social* dimension of their inferential articulation." See *Making it Explicit: Reasoning, Representing, and Discursive Commitment* (1994), 586.

21. Kant, *Critique of Pure Reason* (1929), B161.

22. *Ibid.*, B148–9.

23. *Ibid.*, B311.

24. Cf. G. W. F. Hegel, *Science of Logic* (1969), 46ff. For an excellent account of Hegel's case against Kant's "subjectivism", see William F. Bristow, *Hegel and the Transformation of Philosophical Critique* (2007), 38ff.

25. Kant, *Critique of Pure Reason*, A120.

26. Hegel, *Science of Logic*, 49.

27. *Ibid.*, 115. Adorno remarks: "to Kant, multiplicity and unity were already categories side by side; Hegel, following the model of the late Platonic

dialogues, recognized them as two moments of which neither is without the other" (*ND*: 158).

28. *Ibid.*, 39.

29. Some readings of Hegel's conception of experience and his logic avoid the strong idealist claim of a philosophy of consciousness by viewing the category of reality as a form of fullfilment in practices that retain their particularity and contingency. See, for example, Paul Franco, *Hegel's Philosophy of Freedom* (1999).

30. Husserl, *Ideas* II, 90.

31. For an excellent discussion of this problem in the context of Husserl's *Ideas*, see Roman Ingarden, *Einführung in die Phänomenologie Edmund Husserls – Osloer Vorlesungen 1967* (1992), Lectures 6–8.

32. Husserl, *Ideas* I, 113–14.

33. Husserl, *Ideas* II, 48.

34. *Ibid.*, 61: "*in all perception and experience, the body is involved . . . as* [a] *freely moved totality of sense organs*, and . . . on this original foundation, all that is thingly-real in the surrounding world of the Ego has its relation to the Body".

35. This question, I take it, underlies much of Robert Pippin's criticism of Adorno. Pippin rejects the idea that experience entails commitment to an otherness or non-identity prior to concepts since the preponderance of things undermines the idealist commitment to autonomy and normative self-authorization. See, for example, *The Persistence of Subjectivity* (2005), 98–120. While I share Pippin's worries about Adorno's rather abrupt claims regarding the "falseness" of idealist philosophy in general (and its complicity with a culture distorted by the commodity-form), the following section tries to make sense of the claim that respect for the non-identity of things offers an experience of finitude and self-limitation; such respect acknowledges, rather than knows, things and their proximity to our form of life (in language).

36. Martin Seel speaks of an "acknowledging cognition" (*anerkennenden Erkenntnis*) which employs concepts by "taking up a relation of recognition in which the knower and the known are there for one another without dominating the other". *Adornos Philosophie der Kontemplation* (2006), 59. Espen Hammer also discusses Adorno's ideas about mimesis in this volume (Chapter 4).

37. Ernst Cassirer, who figures in Adorno's polemic against neo-Kantianism, provided an analysis of "expressive-perception" which demonstrates its importance for the objective constitution of natural things. For Cassirer and Adorno, this level of expressivity, entwined with the physiognomic appearances of things, underlies aesthetic experience. See, in particular, Cassirer's "Mythischer, ästhetischer und theoretischer Raum", *Gesammelte Werke* 17 (2004), 411–32.

38. Adorno would therefore be sceptical of Günter Figal's attempt to conceive the non-identical as entailed by the "open identity" of language (Plato's *dialogos* as infinite articulation) because the thought of unity – even if endlessly postponed – implies a sense of "wholeness" that would displace the sedimentation of particulars within concepts (in a natural language). From a Platonic perspective, non-identity would retain its significance only as an idea (of the Good). However, the ideality of the non-identical through

mimesis needs to be understood, not as an unattained idea in Plato's sense, but as an unattained promise to things, the promise of recognizing finitude, or *Einmaligkeit*. See Wolfram Ette *et al.* (eds), *Adorno im Widerstreit* (2004), 13–23.

39. Adorno's notion of natural beauty is thus more indebted to Friedrich Schiller than to Kant or Hegel (who dismiss natural beauty and mimesis, or the *Nachahmung der Natur*, in favour of the pure expressive significance of artistic beauty). According to Schiller, "natural beauty is not nature itself but its imitation in a *medium* which is completely different from the imitated material. *Imitation* is the formal affinity of materially different things". See J. M. Bernstein (ed.), *Classic and Romantic German Aesthetics* (2003), 178.

40. Cf. Martin Heidegger, "The Origin of the Work of Art", *Poetry, Language, Thought* (1971). For Adorno's comments on Heidegger, see "Art and the Arts", *Can One Live after Auschwitz?* (2003). For a detailed account of the importance of this turn in Heidegger, see Günter Figal, *Gegenständlichkeit* (2006), 126–41.

41. Interestingly, Adorno's implicit pluralistic endorsement of "individual natures" agrees with at least some aspects of recent neo-Aristotelian work in the philosophy of science, such as Nancy Cartwright, *The Dappled World* (1999).

SIX

Moral philosophy

Fabian Freyenhagen

Introduction

Moral philosophy used to be full of promises. In ancient times, it aimed at providing a guide to the good life that integrated moral matters with other concerns (such as our intellectual, aesthetic and prudential interests). In modern times, it set out to present a supreme principle of morality (such as Kant's categorical imperative, or the greatest-happiness principle of utilitarianism) from which a full-blown system of obligations and permissions was meant to be derived, guiding or constraining our conduct.

However, if Adorno is to be believed, the promises of moral philosophy have not been fulfilled: neither the good life, nor even the moral life, is currently available. In this sense, his position can be characterized as a negative moral philosophy. What makes this position interesting is *why* Adorno thinks that both the good life and the moral life are blocked and *what implications* he draws from this in terms of criticizing the dominant strands of modern moral philosophy and suggesting how we should live our distorted and deformed lives.

In this chapter we shall look at each of these aspects and ask the following questions:

1. Why can no one live the right life in our current social world?
2. Why does the task of moral philosophy today consist essentially in the critique of moral philosophy?

3. Does Adorno say anything about how we should live, or is his negative moral philosophy devoid of any practical guidance?

The impossibility of right living today

Adorno is not alone in thinking that something is problematic about ethical practice and theory in the modern social world. For example, contemporary Aristotelians often lament the breakdown of traditional social practices which (supposedly) underwrote the exercise of the virtues.[1] Yet Adorno's thesis that "[w]rong life cannot be lived rightly" (*MM*: 39) is distinctive in a number of ways.

First, Adorno's thesis is distinctive because of his particular conception of the modern social world. One way to describe this conception is to say that the modern social world (especially in the post-1930s stage of "late capitalism") is *radically evil*. This is not to invoke theology, where talk of "radical evil" traditionally had its place, but to express this twofold claim: (1) late capitalism is evil to the root (evil is not accidental to it, or only a surface phenomenon); and (2) this evil is particularly grave (it does not get more evil than this).

The clearest example of why Adorno thinks that late capitalism is radically evil is the genocide of the European Jews. For Adorno, this genocide was not an accidental relapse into barbaric times, or due to the fact that modern civilization had not fully taken root in Germany. Rather, these events mean that enlightenment culture *as a whole* has failed in important respects (*ND*: 366f). This culture, and the modern social world that gave rise to it, are deeply implicated in the moral catastrophe of Auschwitz. They constitute the "objective conditions" for its occurrence and, unless they are overcome, a moral catastrophe of the same kind is possible again (*CLA*: 20f). More generally, what happened to the victims in the concentration camps is what late capitalism is moving towards: the liquidation of anything individual, the degradation of people to things, and the triumph of bureaucratic rationality at the expense of deeper reflection about ends and means. Here is a clear example in which late capitalism is radically evil in the two senses mentioned: Auschwitz was a moral catastrophe of the gravest kind and its occurrence (and the threat of its recurrence) is systematically connected to our current social world.

Adorno says that right living is not possible because, in a radically evil social setting, whatever we do short of changing this setting will probably implicate us in its evil – either indirectly in so far as we contribute to maintaining this social setting where it should be changed, or directly by actually participating in and furthering particular evils within it. In other words, in most cases we can only hope that we do not participate actively and directly in evils. However, even if we do not participate actively and directly, to think that this would constitute right living would mistake a lucky and merely partial escape for more than it is. Even then, we would still be part of a guilt context; that is, we would still contribute to the continuity of an evil world.[2]

Secondly, Adorno's thesis that we cannot live rightly in this social world is phrased in a distinctive way. Adorno always speaks of "right life" ("*richtiges Leben*"), rather than the more traditional "good life" ("*gutes Leben*").[3] He does so deliberately. With the phrase "right life", he can exploit an ambiguity between the normative sense of "right" which contrasts with "wrong" (as in "this is not the right thing to do"), on the one hand, and the factual sense of "right" which contrasts with "false" or "counterfeit" (as in "this is a false beard"), on the other. Exploiting this ambiguity allows Adorno to say both (a) that *moral* living is not possible today, and (b) that no real *living* is taking place. While these two aspects are dialectically entwined, I shall begin by analysing them separately before considering the underlying explanation for both.

The possibility of morally right living is blocked, partly because we are caught in the guilt context of our evil society, but partly for further reasons. First, within this guilt context we almost always get caught in ideologies, that is, we hold a set of beliefs, attitudes and preferences which are distorted in ways that benefit the established social order (and the dominant social group within it) at the expense of the satisfaction of people's real interests. To defend our behaviour (e.g. holding on to our possessions while others face severe deprivation), we often end up implicitly defending what should be criticized, namely, late capitalism or elements thereof (e.g. its property regime).[4] And even where we do not attempt to justify our way of life, we tend to fall prey to ideological distortions, so that we accept social arrangements as they are, instead of changing them as we should (this is true even of those who are most disadvantaged by these arrangements). Thus, either by endorsing or by unreflectively accepting distorted truths or half-truths, we entrench the social *status quo* and fail to do what we should.

Morally right living is also impossible because we face practical "antinomies". Adorno uses this Kantian term, which traditionally denotes "irresolvable conflicts", in this sense: we are faced with conflicts that are not fully resolvable within the current social system, so that whatever we do, we cannot do the right thing. One example of such conflict involves compassion (*PMP*: 173f). On the one hand, while compassion is the right reaction to the suffering of others, it often only mitigates injustices and suffering within the current social system. It might thereby contribute to their persistence. On the other hand, working towards overcoming (not merely mitigating) injustices and suffering might mean that we do not always show people in need the compassion required by their situation. This is not just owing to a lack of imagination, but because of the social structures in which we find ourselves.

In effect, Adorno thinks that we constantly face practical antinomies of this kind, and that, while tragic conflicts exist in all societies, at least some of these antinomies are irresolvable only within (or only occur because of) the social world we live in. Their pervasive existence is another reason why life in this social world is wrong and why right living is blocked.

The second aspect of Adorno's thesis involves the thought that what we normally refer to as the life we live actually falls short of life (what might be called "surviving" or "getting by"). "Life does not live" (*MM*: 19)[5] for two reasons. First, under a capitalist economy and culture, life becomes more and more uniform and impoverished (and this is true even of that small part of humanity who can make full use of the goods and opportunities afforded by late capitalism). Secondly, and related to this point, life does not live because we do not actually and actively live it. We lack autonomy because we cannot exercise our capacity for self-determination. At most, we merely *react* to external or internal pressures, and this is connected to the social world that surrounds and forms us. Even where we seem to act against society by following our self-interest, we are, in fact, serving and maintaining a social system that often relies on people acting in this way.[6] In other words, Adorno turns Adam Smith on his head: instead of capitalism's invisible-hand mechanisms making possible a prosperous and moral society, they enable a radically evil society that depletes natural and human resources to sustain itself.

Finally, this points to Adorno's distinctive explanation for why right living (in both senses of the term) is impossible. It is not merely that traditional social practices are lacking, or that the boundless reflection characteristic of modern reason destroys ethical knowledge. Rather, right living is also blocked because society undermines our autonomy. This marks an interesting shift from traditional philosophical conceptions of obstacles to freedom: instead of first nature (natural events or our psychological make-up) endangering our freedom and autonomy, "second nature", or society, is the main obstacle. In other words, Adorno agrees with Kant and the tradition that "human beings are unfree because they are beholden to externality". But this "externality" is not independent of human beings (as nature is said to be) but made and sustained by them as part of society (*ND*: 219, tr. mod.). As Adorno puts it: "the intertwining of man and nature is also the intertwining of man and society" (*PMP*: 176).

The "intertwining of man and nature" has two social dimensions. First, the prevailing way of thinking about first nature – as a closed, determined system – does not adequately reflect it. Rather, it reflects a particular social reality and its impact on our relationship with nature. For Adorno, our conception of nature is shaped for the purposes of domination and exploitation, and this is why we think of nature as a closed system (*ND*: 269). Thinking about nature in this way serves our purposes by facilitating predictions (and control) of natural events. However, if we abstract from the way we conceive of nature for the purpose of dominating it, we have no good evidence for thinking that nature – whether external nature or internal nature (our physical impulses and psychological make-up) – determines us in a way that endangers our freedom or autonomy.[7] So we need not appeal to Kant's metaphysical thesis of a different world underlying nature to make room for freedom. Rather, we should concentrate on the real factors that block our autonomy: autonomy is blocked by society, not first nature.

Secondly, the intertwining of human beings and nature has a social dimension because we mistake determination by society, which we do in fact experience, for determination by nature. We do so partly because capitalist society is not the product of a consciously made history, but of something approximating natural growth – it is part of our natural history as vulnerable creatures who aim to master our surroundings to gain security. We also make this mistake because capitalism presents itself as if it were first nature, as if its "laws" were as fixed as the law of gravity. For example, capitalism operates mainly in an impersonal way – it is not a warrior elite that forces people to work and lead a certain life, but market pressures and other structural forces. It is therefore natural to overlook the real obstacles to our autonomy and to right living. To uncover these obstacles requires the kind of complex analysis of the underlying structure of capitalism that Karl Marx presented in *Capital*.

In this section, we have seen what Adorno means by "wrong life cannot be lived rightly" and his reasons for making this claim. Now, we should turn towards its implications for moral theorizing and for whatever practical guidance Adorno can offer us.

Moral philosophy as critique

So far I have presented Adorno as saying that modern society creates the obstacles to moral living. Yet, even so, his moral philosophy might not differ greatly from traditional ones that theorize about examples, or conceptually analyse, say, the faculty of volition, to generate practical guidance in the form of principles for action, duties and permissions, or ideals and aspirational virtues. However, Adorno is sceptical of such projects. Although we shall see that he does not completely exclude the possibility of moral theory containing some limited practical recommendations and prescriptions, he questions whether philosophers can offer us more than a minimalist ethics. In other words, he rejects the idea that moral theory could currently provide or underwrite a full-blown morality or a canonical plan for the good and right life.

Adorno's scepticism is broadly Hegelian in nature: the good and right life would actually have to be realized and institutionalized in the current social world to a significant degree for moral theory to provide a fully worked-out conception of the good life or morality.[8] Otherwise, we are faced either with highly abstract, indeterminate and ultimately empty ideals, without any detailed practical guidance; or we are stuck with a substantive ethics built on the wrong kind of social practices and institutions, so that we end up entrenching or legitimizing unjust or bad states of affairs. Instead of adopting either of these extremes, Adorno thinks that the dialectical relations between them should be played out.

If one combines these Hegelian concerns with Adorno's premiss that right living is currently impossible, then scepticism about moral theorizing is the natural conclusion. From this perspective, problems of moral practice (right living) affect moral theorizing, and the latter cannot directly solve these problems – only a change in social practices would help. Indeed, this is why Adorno says that moral philosophy today should consist mainly in the critique of moral philosophy: however much modern moral philosophers might differ, mainstream philosophers tend to suggest that complete practical guidance is possible. Adorno's scepticism is directed against this confidence.[9]

With respect to moral theories, Adorno both criticizes and values Kant's. This ambiguous stance is explained by the fact that he thinks Kant's ethics reflects better the problematic state of affairs of moral theory and practice in the modern social world. Kant's ethics is the most fruitful moral philosophy because, even where it gets things wrong, it captures best the antinomies and problems of moral living and theorizing in the modern world.

To see this more clearly, let us consider two of Adorno's criticisms of Kant. For Adorno, Kant's ethics is characterized by its focus on principles (morality is anchored in a supreme principle, the categorical imperative[10]); by its formalism (its supreme principle is not a substantive, but a formal principle); by its emphasis on intentions rather than consequences; and by the idea that we can (and often should) act independently of our desires and physical impulses. Adorno objects to all these characteristics, but let us concentrate on Kant's formalism and on his idea that we acquire moral worth in virtue of our good intentions (our "good will").[11]

With respect to formalism, Adorno rejects Kant's claim that the categorical imperative generates a set of specific duties. Equipped with this imperative alone, that is, with the demand that our subjective principles for action ("maxims") be suitable as universal laws, we shall either be left completely in the dark about what to do in specific circumstances; or, if we do hit upon specific obligations and guidelines, we shall have to import them from somewhere else, for example from the social norms we internalized as children.[12]

Secondly, Adorno criticizes Kant's idea of an ethics of conviction or intention as follows. If moral worth lies in intentions, then there is the grave danger that people may behave self-righteously and irresponsibly by simply aiming at morality without any sense for the havoc they might cause in doing so. Adorno illustrates this by discussing Henrik Ibsen's play The Wild Duck,[13] where the main character, Gregers Werle, seems in many respects a perfect example of a Kantian moral agent in that he consistently strives for the good – even at the expense at his own self-interest. However, as Werle exposes what he perceives as moral wrong-doing, his actions (and thereby the Kantian idea of moral agency) are called into question when they drive an innocent person to suicide.

Far from suggesting here that we should not aim to eliminate moral wrongs, Adorno argues that we need to be sensitive to consequences as well – moral worth cannot be uncoupled from consequences.[14] Moreover, in developing this objection to Kant's ethics,

Adorno also questions the very idea of having a pure intention to act morally. Making use of Freudian insights, he argues that, more often than not, what looks like a purely moral intention is actually the result of repressed drives or feelings of guilt (*PMP*: 162f).

These examples also illustrate that Kantian ethics might be interesting and reflect some truth, even where it is (allegedly) wrong. For Adorno, Kant's formalism is in part the natural extension of criticisms of traditional, premodern moral systems and in part a response to the breakdown of these systems which once provided people with exemplary roles and practical guidance. Many of these systems were too narrow in their conception of moral agents or rights-holders. The breakdown of these systems meant that a broader conception of moral agents or right-holders as well as new ways of generating moral duties were needed. Many critics (including Kant) thought that abstract equality (expressed, for example, in the universality requirement of Kant's categorical imperative), and the principles based on it, would be suitable for these tasks. Their mistake did not come into full view until the breakdown was complete. In this sense, Kant, who lived during the transition, might not have fully realized that his ethics both eroded and relied upon the substantive moral systems that preceded him.[15]

Similarly, it is natural to adopt an ethics of intention, given that we can be even less assured of how the consequences might work out in the modern world than in a traditional society where roles and responsibilities were clearly assigned (*PMP*: 98f). Adorno thinks that whatever we do in late capitalism, we get caught in the guilt context of our radically evil society. If, in these circumstances, it is natural, and even to some extent admirable, to try to save morality by consigning it to the "sphere of interiority", or intentions, this can also have the unacceptable consequence that what actually happens to people is not assigned sufficient importance by ethical theory and its adherents (as in the example from *The Wild Duck*).

However, an ethics more sensitive to consequences and less based on formal principles is not a better solution. As an alternative, Adorno considers Hegel's idea of "ethical life", which has consequentialist elements while tying morality to social norms and practices. According to Adorno, adopting Hegel's substantive ethics of responsibility today would make morality too dependent on the way of the world; it would surrender morality, which tells us what we ought to do, to what is the case. Moral norms would then lose much of their critical edge and individuals would be subordinated to the way the world actually is (*PMP*: 163–6). Hence a substantive ethics of responsibility, rooted in the current social world, cannot underwrite right living either – for it is complicit in what makes right living impossible: the radically evil society that overwhelms us.

Apart from these two options – a formal ethics of conviction and a substantive ethics of responsibility – Adorno does not discuss moral systems in detail. This is presumably partly because he thinks that these two options exhaust most of the space of (credible) moral theories, so that if they cannot offer us a guide to right living in our current social world, then this is also true of moral theory generally.[16]

However, Adorno makes some dispersed and brief remarks on other options. For example, he objects that Nietzsche's proposal to proclaim new values does not take seriously his own critique of morality (*ND*: 275; *PMP*: 172–4). He has nothing good to say about existentialism, whose notion of choice and talk of authenticity he rejects as ideological.[17] And he thinks that "the concept of virtue has taken on an archaic sound" because of the breakdown of the social practices and institutions that made the exercise of virtues possible (*PMP*: 98).[18] With its emphasis on character and dispositions, virtue ethics tends to detract from real problems and their real cause, namely, the radically evil and overwhelming capitalist society (*ibid.*: 10–16). Finally, Adorno would probably not have accepted a full ethics based on compassion, since, as we have seen, compassion gives rise to an antinomy in this society.

In sum, Adorno contends that the problematic nature of living in late capitalism affects moral theorizing deeply and cannot be fully addressed by such theorizing. His moral philosophy mainly takes the form of fighting the illusions and pretensions to which moral philosophy itself gives rise, namely, its claims to guide, or underwrite, right living. However, Adorno's own moral philosophy is not restricted to this critical function, as we shall now see.

How to live wrong life

Adorno's moral philosophy may seem to consist solely in critique, lacking any positive views or practical recommendations. And this is, indeed, a widely held view, among both his critics (who think that it is problematic for a theory with emancipatory intent not to have practical import),[19] and some of his defenders (who think that his theory is merely explanatory, not normative).[20] However, there are both textual and other grounds that speak against this view. And, in the last decade, some authors have argued that Adorno's philosophy contains an ethics, or even that it is ethical through and through.[21] What speaks for the claim that Adorno's philosophy contains an ethics is that he puts forward an amalgam of ethical ideals, prescriptions and even a categorical imperative of his own.

For example, Adorno suggests that, in the absence of the possibility of living morally, one should aim to live one's life in such a way that "one may believe oneself to have been a good animal" (*ND*: 299, tr. mod.). Among other things, a good animal would identify with others and their plight, as well as show "solidarity with the tormentable body" (*ibid.*: 285). Such solidarity arises out of the abhorrence of physical suffering, which has direct motivational force for human animals (*ibid.*: 365), and for other animals as well in so far as Adorno situates this abhorrence within the context of natural evolution.

What is at issue here is not a rationalized form of pity, motivated by thoughts of reciprocity or reward, since such thoughts would undermine identification-based solidarity.[22] At issue, rather, is natural compassion – a "physical impulse" (*ND*: 285) of which other animals are allegedly capable (though perhaps only in exceptional circumstances, as in the rare instances of an animal raising young of a different species). Adorno thinks that one of the problems of modern society, and the pre-eminence of instrumental reasoning within it, is that such solidarity is disappearing. Our social context engenders the opposite of identification-based solidarity, namely, bourgeois coldness. It is this coldness – the ability to stand back and look on unaffected in the face of misery – that made Auschwitz possible (*ibid.*: 363). Identification-based solidarity is, therefore, important for counteracting bourgeois coldness and finds its expression in the moral impulse against suffering (*ibid.*: 286, 365). At the same time, solidarity is something to which we can only aspire; it is not fully achievable.[23]

Without a socially institutionalized and fully functioning ethical life, the conditions for the cultivation of solidarity are not given. In this sense, Adorno is not so much advancing a prescription as describing an ethical ideal. And one can find other ethical ideals in Adorno's writings, such as his suggestion that modesty might be the only suitable virtue in our current predicament. By suggesting this, he means to say that we should "have a conscience, but not insist on our own" (*PMP*: 169f; *ND*: 352); that is, we should make ethical demands on ourselves and others, but without behaving self-righteously. Adorno is not confident that we shall succeed in this delicate balancing act – it is again something towards which we can only strive.

Adorno also advances "negative prescriptions" of how to live wrong life. In particular, he puts forward the prescription that we should resist what society makes of us (*PMP*: 167; *ND*: 265). Although resistance will be futile most of the time, trying not to join in (or, where joining in cannot be avoided, at least not to do so full-heartedly) is something we are obligated to do, given the radical evil of our current social world.[24]

In one instance, Adorno further suggests that we face a "new categorical imperative", namely, "to arrange our thoughts and actions so that Auschwitz will not repeat itself, so that nothing similar will happen". This new imperative is unlike Kant's in many ways: it mentions Auschwitz (and a set of events), rather than being merely formal and ahistorical; it refers explicitly to actions and consequences, rather than focusing on principles or intentions; it is only negative, minimalist and strict in its prescription, rather than enjoining wide, positive duties and underwriting a full-blown morality; and it is "imposed by Hitler upon human beings in their state of unfreedom", rather than being the self-legislated principle of autonomous, individual agents. Nonetheless, Adorno's categorical imperative, arguably, shares one property with its Kantian predecessor: it is categorical in the sense that the normative force of its prescription to stop another Auschwitz from happening is not dependent on whether we have the requisite inclinations, ends or attitudes. For even if "morality survives" only "in the unvarnished materialist motive" that (bodily) suffering should cease (*ND*: 365, tr. mod.), the new categorical imperative applies also to those who ignore, repress or lack this motive.[25]

In sum, Adorno advances both ideals and negative prescriptions, including one of a categorical nature. Hence he does subscribe to an ethics of sorts, giving whatever guidance is possible about how we should live and how we should *not* live our wrong lives. This ethics offers only negative and minimalist guidance in so far as it tells us mainly what we should avoid and provides us with only a general sketch, not a fully worked-out picture. Yet Adorno would say that nothing more than this limited guidance can be offered today. In the absence of the possibility of right living, and the inability of moral philosophy to underwrite it, the most we can do is *to live less wrongly*.

However, one might object that no practical recommendations or prescriptions, even if they were merely of a negative and minimalist nature, could flow from Adorno's philosophy. If individuals are determined by society, how can they resist it? And how can moral theory prescribe resistance to society? Does this not violate the principle "ought implies can", that is, the principle that people are obligated to do something only if they are able to do it?

In reply, we must extend our understanding of Adorno's conception of freedom. As we saw earlier, autonomy involves the capacity for self-determination, but such autonomy (or, as Adorno also calls it, positive freedom) is currently denied to us.[26] However, along with this idea of autonomy, Adorno takes from Kant a more limited conception of freedom, namely, negative freedom as independence from external determination.[27] As we have also seen, Adorno denies that external determination comes from first nature. Rather, we have to make ourselves independent from determination by society in order to be negatively free. And while autonomy is completely blocked in late capitalism, Adorno does not reject the possibility of negative freedom within it. As he writes, "There has been as much free will as people who willed to free themselves" (ND: 265, tr. mod.).

Now, to admit that negative freedom is possible (at least sometimes, and to some extent) is not sufficient for a full-blown morality, as Adorno is well aware. Instead, it is possible only to make negative and minimal prescriptions. Such prescriptions are compatible with Adorno's conception of freedom because they simply ask us to use our negative freedom to resist society and the forms of wrong life within it. Still, negative freedom will never be sufficient for living autonomously: even on the few occasions where we resist determination by society, we are not directing our lives, but merely reacting to "changing forms of repression" (ND: 265).[28] Moreover, while negative freedom might make resisting wrong life possible in some instances, there will be too few of them to add up to right living. Hence this defence of Adorno is compatible with his negative moral philosophy presented in the first two sections of this chapter.

However, problems remain. For example, even if the possibility of negative freedom sufficed to underwrite a minimalist ethics, Adorno would owe us an account of how individuals are capable of such freedom. Sometimes he makes it sound as if the social world determines us to such an extent that even resistance to it is impossible.[29] Either this is an exaggeration meant to bring to our attention the precarious nature of our predicament, or Adorno has to tell us how it is possible for some individuals, when they are lucky, to see through the workings of late capitalist society and resist it (ND: 41).

Moreover, Adorno faces perhaps an even graver problem. He has long been criticized for not being able to underwrite the normativity contained in his philosophy, for being unable to account for the standards with which he operates in criticizing late capitalism and prescribing resistance to it.[30] In particular, his philosophy is thought to be too negative. Critics argue that any account of normative standards requires knowledge of, and an appeal to, the good – for example, we can only say a sculpture is bad if we invoke the idea of a good sculpture. However, within Adorno's philosophy, knowledge of the good (or the right) is impossible for the following reasons: late capitalism is deeply evil and we therefore cannot learn about the good from this world. Since our conceptual capacities are deeply implicated in this evil, they are of no use either in gaining such knowledge. Even our imaginative capacities are too damaged to acquire any determinate idea of what a free society and the good life would be like (*ND*: 352).

This might be called the problem of normativity. It is especially pressing when it comes to Adorno's moral philosophy: to deny that right living is possible and to prescribe certain forms of living seem to require knowledge of the good. In the literature, a number of responses have been suggested, ranging from (1) a denial of the problem, to (2) the suggestion that the good (or a good) can be known within Adorno's philosophy and used to underpin his ethics, to (3) the claim that Adorno can account for the normativity inherent in his philosophy without appeal to the good or the right.[31] Still, this is a very live issue in contemporary debate and more needs to be done to solve it, if, indeed, it can be solved.

Conclusion

We have seen why Adorno thinks that (right) living has become problematic in the modern world. We have also seen that moral theory cannot point to a way out of these problems, but is deeply affected by them. However, Adorno does offer us limited guidance on how to live and what to do in our current predicament. In this sense, the objection that his moral philosophy is devoid of practical recommendations can be rejected, as emphasized by a wave of publications over the last decade. While other objections may not have been fully answered in the literature, it is fair to say that Adorno presents us with an important challenge to the way we normally think about our lives and moral theory. It may not be a systematic theory and it may not give us all we expect from a moral philosophy, but we have seen that there are reasons why this is the case and why moral philosophy cannot provide or promise anything more in our current predicament.

Notes

1. See A. MacIntyre, *After Virtue*, 2nd edn (1985).
2. This raises the complex issue of individual responsibility. Since society determines individuals, it would seem that they are not responsible for their wrong-doing (see, for example, *ND*: 219). In fact, Adorno was sceptical of conceptions of freedom (such as Kant's) in which people can be held responsible and punished (see, for example, *ibid.*: 215, 232, 255). Yet he also rejects the suggestion that those who do evil should be let off, specifically the perpetrators of Nazism (see *ibid.*: 264f, 286f). Hence his thinking appears to be inconsistent. Yet Adorno responds that this inconsistency expresses an "objective antagonism" (*ibid.*: 286) or "antinomy" (*ibid.*: 264) between the legitimate desire (and social need) not to let crimes go unpunished, and the impossibility of pinning evil acts on individuals as agents responsible for them.
3. Unfortunately, some translators (such as Rodney Livingstone) use "good life" and "bad life" for "*richtiges Leben*" and "*falsches Leben*", obliterating the ambiguity with which Adorno plays.
4. See, for example, *MM*: 39.
5. This is a quotation from the nineteenth-century Austrian writer Ferdinand Kürnberger; it is employed by Adorno as a motto for the first part of *Minima Moralia*.
6. See, for example, *ND*: 261f.
7. Admittedly, this does not fully settle the matter, for even a non-deterministic nature may be inhospitable to human freedom. (For further discussion of this problem, see my "Adorno's Negative Dialectics of Freedom", *Philosophy and Social Criticism* 32(2) (2006), 429–40.)
8. Hegel expresses this view in the preface of *Elements of a Philosophy of Right* (1991).
9. For an excellent discussion of how Adorno's views differ from the central claims of the dominant strand of modern moral philosophy, see Raymond Geuss, *Outside Ethics* (2005), ch. 1.
10. In its universal law formulation, the categorical imperative states: "act in accordance with a maxim that can at the same time make itself a universal law". See Kant, *Practical Philosophy* (1996), 86.
11. *Ibid.*, Part I.
12. See, for example, *PMP*: 81–3; *ND*: 270f; on formalism, see also *ND*: 235–7.
13. See *PMP*: Lecture 16.
14. For an interesting Kantian reply, not to Adorno's objection specifically, but to objections of this type, see B. Herman, *The Practice of Moral Judgment* (1993), especially Chapter 5.
15. See *PMP*: 116f; see also *ND*: 243. We encounter here what Adorno calls "metacritique", that is, his attempts to supplement the philosophical

critique of other theorists with sociological considerations that show why they got things wrong, or could develop only a limited point of view. It is important to note that for Adorno "metacritique" is a supplement to philosophical critique; it cannot replace it (*PMP*: 152; *ND*: 197). On Adorno's conception of metacritique, see also Simon Jarvis, *Adorno: A Critical Introduction* (1998), 12, 153–7, and Ståle Finke's chapter in this volume (Chapter 5).

16. Thus, a more formal consequentialism (of the sort familiar from contemporary ethics and as intended by Max Weber in his "ethics of responsibility") is not a live option for Adorno either, though it is less clear why this is so. Perhaps he accepts the Kantian criticisms of such a moral theory (e.g. that it is too demanding) as true in respect to the current society; he might also be worried that such an ethics is open to the formalism objection (either it is empty, or it implicitly relies on current social norms, for example in using a particular conception of welfare as its criterion for measuring the goodness of consequences).

17. See Adorno, *The Jargon of Authenticity* (1973); see also *ND*: 49–51, 276–8; *PMP*: 13f, 176.

18. See also C. Menke, "Virtue and Reflection: The 'Antinomies of Moral Philosophy' ", *Constellations: An International Journal of Critical and Democratic Theory* 12(1) (March 2005), 36–49. There are, hence, some parallels after all between Adorno's and the Aristotelian accounts of the problematic nature of moral life in the modern social world.

19. The charge that Adorno's theory has no practical import was made by his New Left critics in the 1960s and 1970s, but is not restricted to them. It also played an important role in the reorientation of the Frankfurt School by second- and third-generation theorists; see, for example, Axel Honneth, *Critique of Power: Reflective Stages in a Critical Social Theory* (1991), Chapter 3, especially 95f.

20. For a recent example of the latter view see G. Tassone, "Amoral Adorno: Negative Dialectics Outside Ethics", *European Journal of Social Theory* 8(3) (2005), 251–67.

21. For the first of these views, see J. Gordon Finlayson, "Adorno on the Ethical and the Ineffable", *European Journal of Philosophy* 10(1) (2002), Section 3; for the stronger view, see J. M. Bernstein, *Adorno: Disenchantment and Ethics* (2001).

22. See, for example, *MM*: 33.

23. Espen Hammer and Alison Stone also comment on bourgeois coldness in this volume (Chapters 4 and 3).

24. Adorno never explicitly and directly prescribed the overthrow of society (as one would expect him to do). This might have to do with a number of factors: the cold war context in which he mainly wrote; his fear that this prescription could backfire (e.g. by provoking a repressive backlash); and his belief that currently only resistance is possible because the moment for a revolution is missing.

25. However, this interpretation of Adorno's categorical imperative does not answer further puzzles about it, such as whether a particular historical event can give rise to a prescription of a categorical nature and whether this prescription is meant to hold indefinitely.

26. See, for example, *MM*: 37f; *ND*: 231f, 241.

27. See Kant, *Practical Philosophy* (1996), 94. Note that negative freedom for Kant and Adorno includes both freedom of action from external constraints and freedom of thought from such constraints (that is, it includes the idea of *Mündigkeit*: the courage to think for oneself without direction from others). Marianne Tettlebaum also discusses negative freedom in this volume (Chapter 8).

28. See also *ND*: 231. Perhaps the idea of negative freedom allows us to rescue a limited notion of individual responsibility: if we are negatively free, we are responsible for our acts to the degree that we can be obligated to act in certain ways (such as resist the pressures to join in) and be blamed (albeit not necessarily legitimately punished) for failing to do so. Full responsibility would require that people (a) live in a social arrangement where their acts would have real, attributable effects (*ND*: 264); (b) are able to avoid living wrongly; and (c) are autonomous, not just negatively free.

29. See, for example, "Unfreedom is consummated in its invisible totality, which no longer tolerates an outside from which it might be seen and broken" (*ND*: 274, tr. mod.). See also *ibid.*: 243.

30. Jürgen Habermas was perhaps the first to state this criticism explicitly in "Theodor Adorno: The Primal History of Subjectivity: Self-Affirmation Gone Wild", *Philosophical-Political Profiles* (1983), 99–110, especially 106.

31. The first strategy is implicit in the non-normative reading of Adorno's philosophy; see Tassone, "Amoral Adorno". For the second, see Finlayson, "Adorno on the Ethical and the Ineffable" (2002). I have been working on the third strategy in an unpublished manuscript, "The Good, the Bad and the Normative".

SEVEN

Social philosophy

Pauline Johnson

Introduction

The failure of socialist revolution in Western Europe is often viewed as the key to understanding Adorno's diagnosis of modern society.[1] The very first sentence in his main work, *Negative Dialectics*, reads: "Philosophy, which once seemed obsolete, lives on because the moment to realize it was missed" (*ND*: 3). Socialist revolution, which might have overcome the irrationality of the existing bourgeois order and established a rational world, failed to materialize. This is why philosophy remains necessary as a vehicle of radical critique.

Horkheimer and Adorno witnessed the complete victory of fascism in Europe. The Institute for Social Reasearch's empirical studies under Erich Fromm in the 1930s had already discovered the pervasive influence of the authoritarian personality among the German working class. This problem was compounded by the apparently successful reorganization and stabilization of monopoly capitalism under the New Deal in the United States.[2] Its success ensured that a burgeoning consumerist culture was never problematized as a way of life but hailed as a truly democratic expression of the popular will. The multiple crises of the interwar period in Europe and the worldwide Depression appeared to have been overcome, but only at the cost of increased state intervention into the economy and the adoption of a greater planning and regulative role.[3] The Bolshevik revolution in Russia had stagnated into a totalitarian form of state oppression. Rosa Luxemburg's fears about the bureaucratization of the Communist Party seemed to be realized. The possibility of a socialist future seemed closed for the foreseeable future.

Horkheimer and Adorno summed up the historical configuration of the postwar world with the idea of the totally administered society. In their view, all contemporary economic systems – liberal democratic, fascist and socialist – manifested a frightening convergence in their basic logic and structure; they were characterized by the planning and manipulation of all spheres of life. Faced with a completely administered world, in which political regimes could be distinguished only by the means they used to produce totally compliant populations, Horkheimer and Adorno felt compelled to abandon their early allegiance to a Marxian vision of history as an emancipatory process towards humanity's increasing self-conscious mastery of nature and its own fate. They looked upon the totally administered present as both an essentially irrational configuration and as a product of the triumph of the enlightenment reason that was assimilated by Marxism. In *Dialectic of Enlightenment*, they insisted that the historical Enlightenment's vision of a humanity able to steer its future by converting capricious nature and blind history into its own controlling purposes had turned hope for human freedom into the nightmare of an unleashed will that was bent only on domination.

Adorno's mature social philosophy has routinely been described as adopting a melancholy, sometimes blackly pessimistic, posture on the present and future. We might wonder, though, what Adorno thinks we still have to lose. What emancipatory interests can survive his fulsome repudiation of an Enlightenment vision that equates freedom with the dominating aspirations of a self-asserting will? If all we have left is the lament of "reason's other", then how can Adorno's own social philosophy offer itself as a critique of the irrational social order? To answer these questions, we need first to reconstruct what Adorno means by calling society irrational, and then explore his assessment of the human costs of this irrational social formation. Finally, we shall take up what Adorno says about our chances for a rational way of life.

Society

Adorno never abandoned the critical purposes that charged the early days of the Institute for Social Research. He says to German students in the late 1960s that sociology "is insight into what is, but it is

critical insight, in that it measures that which 'is in case' in society
... by what society purports to be, in order to detect in this contradiction the potential, the possibilities for changing society's whole
constitution". What can Adorno mean when he proposes that
insights into the "essential" nature of society can be weighed as the
frustrated potentials of a bad present even as he remains sceptical of
the interest in "all general, comprehensive definitions" (*IS*: 15)? Not
at all concerned to answer this riddle in terms that his audience can
"write down and take home", the single clue that Adorno offers is
that only by "doing" the theory can the answer be understood. The
theme of "learning by doing" was always dear to Adorno.

The essential nature of society has to be discovered by reconstructing the "social mediations" that emerge when we try to make sense
of "elementary needs and problems" that seem to "have nothing
directly to do with society" (*IS*: 16). The theory of society begins,
then, with the attempt to understand the suffering of the concrete
individual. Society, one might say, "becomes directly perceptible
where it hurts". For example:

> one might find oneself in certain social situations, like that of
> someone who is looking for a job and "runs into a brick wall"
> has the feeling that all doors are shutting automatically in his
> face; or someone who has to borrow money in a situation in
> which he cannot produce guarantees that he can return it
> within a certain period, who meets with a "No" ten or twenty
> times in a definite, automated manner, and is told he is just an
> example of a widespread general law, and so on – all these, I
> would say, are direct indices of the phenomenon of society.
>
> (*Ibid.*: 36)

Adorno is interested in those "hurts" that seem to betray antici-
pations that our social interactions might be different, or that might
facilitate individual wishes and purposes instead of crudely refusing,
remodelling and homogenizing them. This suffering awareness that
one is dependent on others, and that this dependence is not felt as
simply an alien power, is not based on a plan for a better way of
living together, just resentment at what is. The authors of *Dialectic
of Enlightenment* make the point: "Hope for better circumstances –
if it is not a mere illusion – is not so much based on the assurance
that these circumstances would be guaranteed, durable, and final, but
on the lack of respect for all that is so firmly rooted in the general
suffering" (*DE*, C: 225; J: 186).

Adorno thinks that the word "alienation" captures the general character of a mode of integration that provokes suffering as a way of life. For him, the term evokes the contradiction of living "within a totality which binds people together", not on the basis of solidarity, but "only through the antagonistic interests of human beings" (*IS*: 43). The "profit comes first" logic of the market system ends in the "domination of the general over the particular, society over its captive membership" (S: 148). The pathology of capitalist society is not just that the principle of commodity exchange sweeps the individual into an alienated system of relations, but that its driving imperatives reproduce savage class inequalities.

Even towards the end of his life, Adorno was telling us: "Society remains class struggle today, just as in the period when that concept originated" (S: 148). He is persuaded that capitalism is an irrational mode of integration because its arrangement of society runs counter to society's purpose: "the preservation and the unfettering of the people of which it is composed" (*ibid.*: 133). This account of the purpose of society is not rooted in a background anthropology. It is, rather, a generalization that emerges from the sociologist's efforts to reconstruct how people live and suffer in the modern world. "Alienation" expresses the general condition of a life damaged by social interactions that do not sustain and unbind the people who compose it but that stands over them with all the blind power of the world of nature.[4]

From this derivation of the "seemingly anachronistic irrationality of society", Adorno supposes that a "proper sociology" needs to explore the irrational ends that are served by instrumentally rational institutions and practices in society because "the irrational conditions of society can only be maintained through the survival of these irrational functions" (*IS*: 133). His account of the institutions that serve the "stubborn irrationality of a society which is rational in its means but not in its ends" guides the investigation into the truly administered character of contemporary society (S: 149). The totally administered society appears as an instrumentally rational response to, and a manifestation of, the irrational and self-contradictory character of capitalism.

Even as it models the whole of modern life after the interests and norms of the market, capitalism fosters the ideal of the independence of each individual. However, the attempt to construct a principle of social interaction out of the expectations of competitive, isolated individuals ends up with a dislocated, impotent individuality confronting a hostile, anonymous power. "Within repressive society",

Adorno tells us, "the individual's emancipation not only benefits but damages him. Freedom from society robs him of the strength for freedom" (*MM*: 150). This endemic irrationality is articulated and "managed" in different ways in the distinct epochs of capitalist development.

Nineteenth-century capitalism had "maintained a certain equilibrium between its social ideology and the actual conditions under which its consumers lived".[5] At least for the entrepreneurial capitalist, the liberal epoch of free enterprise had underpinned the construction of a "free" self-responsible individuality with some kind of, limited, practical conditions. The liberal expectation that the private will might be enough to direct the life and fortunes of the particular individual was experienced as suffering, but also as an ideology that made sense of a new general standard of rational action. Horkheimer puts it this way: "Liberalism at its dawn was characterized by the existence of a multitude of independent entrepreneurs, who took care of their own property and defended it against antagonistic social forces." Though isolated "by moats of self-interest", individuals "nevertheless tended to become more and more alike through the pursuit of this very self-interest".[6] The construction of society as a network of interactions between private, self-interested individuals produces a culture of conformist motivations, and with this, an effective management of the tensions between the individual and society.

However, in the epoch of monopoly capitalism, individuality loses its economic basis and this transforms the mode in which the relationship between the individual and society is regulated. In the age of big business, "[t]he future of the individual depends less and less upon his own prudence and more and more upon the national and international struggles among the colossi of power".[7] The great economic crises of the 1920s and 1930s fuelled the rise of corporate power and created the objective conditions for dependence which robbed individuals of their self-sufficiency and exposed them to unprecedented manipulation.

Friedrich Pollock provided the economic dimension of the Frankfurt School's diagnosis of the totally administered character of late twentieth-century capitalist societies.[8] The crux of his argument was that capitalism had entered a new phase in which competition had given way to government intervention and corporate planning. According to the totally administered society thesis, the liberal age of bourgeois society – with its competitive economic relations, democratic political institutions and contractually legal arrangements – masked the domination implicit in the capitalist system. But these liberal forms of freedom are now historical memories. They are increasingly replaced by an overtly authoritarian system. With the advent of modern totalitarian regimes, the typical liberal dualisms of individual and society, private and public spheres, the economy and politics are blurred – even liquidated – in the service of direct control and command.

Traditional capitalist entrepreneurs, who controlled their enterprises and lived off the profits, were reduced to mere rentiers and removed from a direct management function. Government intervened to control prices and wages, to encourage technological innovation, to enforce full employment and avoid over-accumulation through the expansion of military and defence requirements.[9] This control, exercised by the state in league with the large monopolists, forestalled the worst excesses of periodic downturns in the economic cycle. Coupled with the direction of the new mass media, it opened up the possibility of a new system of ubiquitous control and manipulation (*DE*, C: 38; J: 30). Political cliques that controlled the state apparatus in the interests of the economically most powerful groups could now exercise naked power, backed by all the forces of modern administration and bureaucracy, and aided by the subtle yet insidious pressures of the mass media.

The authoritarian state becomes a vehicle of new modes of capitalist organization. No longer relying on competition and the market, the state's steering functions are now transferred to the centralized administrative activity of the apparatus of domination – to government agencies, police, the army and the media. The result is a new synthesis of monopoly capitalism and state power that brings together the calculated interests of the major corporations and the planning capacity of the state organs in a technical rationality that dominates all aspects of society and quashes all opposition either by terror or by consumerist incorporation.

Developments in Europe, the Soviet Union and the United States all seemed to reveal the same tendencies. On Adorno's view, modernity comes to represent a new system of total domination characterized by manifestations of alienation, administrative manipulation, and by uniform subordination and depersonalization. With its new power (increasing bureaucratic reach) and technological means (radio and television), the state is able to expand its influence. It now enters and administers every facet of life (*DE*, C: 133; J: 105–6; C: 137; J: 109). Everything that cannot be subordinated to the demands and logic of the system will be processed, re-educated, dispensed with. Uniformity inevitably replaces individuality. The notion of the "totally administered society" has its complement in "the end of the individual".

With his Frankfurt School colleagues, Adorno drew upon a psychoanalytic interpretation of the family to explain how the administered society came to be lived, not as an imposition upon, but as formative of, the modern personality. Fromm had proposed that Freudian developmental psychology offered a diagnosis of socialization mechanisms in the nineteenth-century family which had produced the bourgeois individual as the bearer of a private will.[10] Overcoming the fear of the Oedipus complex, the male child was supposed to emerge from his traumatic identification with the father to become the inner-directed ego of the classical liberal age. However, the family had eroded as a strong institution, and the position of the patriarch or entrepreneur in developed capitalism had faltered. As a result, individuals were compelled to seek beyond the family for the fulfilment of their unconscious identificatory needs; they looked to leaders and broader peer and social groups.

Adorno thinks that David Riesman captures well the displacement of the family as the primary site of socialization with his distinction between "inner"- and "other"-directed personalities. Internalizing the authority of their parents, earlier generations of Americans were inner-directed. By contrast, today's "other-directed" American is "in a characterological sense more the product of his peers – that is, in sociological terms, his 'peer groups', the other kids at school or the kids in the block".[11] For his part, Adorno suggests that a "culture industry" has largely replaced the family as the primary site of social-ization. The tempestuous drama of self-formation enacted in the old bourgeois family has changed into the easeful assimilation of cultural norms offered by a total system of consumption. Entertainment, distraction, conspicuous consumption all play a part in promoting a popular perception of contentment. Individuals enjoy leisure; felt needs are satisfied (DE, C: 139; J: 110–11).

The term "culture industry" was deliberately chosen to eliminate any positive overtones arising from alternative expressions such as "mass culture" or "popular culture". Adorno and Horkheimer refute the idea that contemporary mass culture (film, radio, records, popular literature) was in any way a spontaneous, popular creation of the masses. It is not the organic product of a vibrant low culture that reflects the forms and activity of the masses, of their own cultural creativity. Contemporary mass culture is in no way spon-taneous and has little to do with the genuine demands of the masses.[12]

The hegemony of mass culture today means that art and culture are no longer authorized to inhabit their own autonomous sphere from whence they might open up new possibilities and reveal critical insights into prevailing social arrangements. Culture now becomes an industry, subordinated like all others to the overriding imperative of economic profit and administrative need. As it becomes increasingly dependent on industrial and finance capital, culture must be primarily saleable and reassuring. For Adorno and Horkheimer, then, the term "culture industry" does not simply signify that cultural production has become industrial: a creature of big business. It also suggests that contemporary culture is increasingly standardized with only a "pseudo-individualization", or marginal differentiation, of cultural products. "Not only are the hit songs, stars, and soap operas cyclically recurrent and rigidly invariable types, but the specific content of the entertainment itself is derived from them and only appears to change. The details are interchangeable" (*DE*, C: 125; J: 98). Despite the ideology of individualism that motivates much consumption in advertising and popular culture, the basic tendency of the culture industry is to eliminate all vestiges of individuality in favour of a predictable and calculable standardization and uniformity.

For all that, contemporary mass culture is not usually experienced as an authoritarian imposition of attitudes and worldviews. The great uncertainties of the twentieth century have engendered a widespread fear and anxiety about security and employment that generates ego weakness and neurosis. These conditions rob individuals of their independence and expose them to manipulation. Finding it difficult to cope, people take flight in entertainment: it offers fun, relaxation and relief from the boredom of work and from the fruitless, enervating efforts of the everyday. In this relaxed state, their irrational susceptibilities are open to manipulation by the mass media.

Adorno makes the point that these ideological effects do not rely on the self-conscious intentions of their producers. "The script does not try to 'sell' any idea."[13] The pursuit of popularity alone is sufficient to structure an ideologically potent fusion of messages in the products of the culture industry. On the one hand, the standardized character of popular culture reassures the dependent and insecure masses that everything is "somehow predestined" and that nothing will be asked of them except their "unreflecting obedience".[14] This authoritarian message is fused with, and cloaked by, an overt affirmation of the ideals of plurality and individual autonomy. "Pseudo-individuality is rife": individuality is reduced to a mere option to choose between mass-produced "styles". Individuals are "like Yale locks, whose only difference can be measured in fractions of millimeters" (*DE*, C: 154; J: 125).

Entertainment and the distractions of the culture industry serve to reconcile the masses to the drudgery and meaninglessness of everyday life in the totally administered society. As such, the reign of the culture industry is an index of the truth that people feel oppressed by the lack of control they have over their own lives. This is the basis of Adorno's critique of the symptomatic character of the pursuit of pleasure. To be pleased means to be in agreement, not having to think about suffering. "Basically it is helplessness." It is flight, not only as it asserts "flight from a wretched reality, but from the last remaining thought of resistance" (*DE*, C: 144; J: 115–16).

Reviving a critical pulse: the rationality potentials of intimacy

This brings us to the central dilemma thrown up by Adorno's critical exploration of the administered character of contemporary society. Earlier we saw that Adorno thinks we can measure the irrationality and illegitimacy of this kind of society by the hurt and damage that it does to us. His comprehensive critique holds an authoritarian culture industry to account for a zero-sum game that trades the longing for liberty against the quest for contentment. Objective conditions of the twentieth century have conspired to sap the confidence and the spirit of individuals, thus denying to them all sense of the damage that is daily being done to them.

However, as Axel Honneth points out, Adorno was determined to "guard against the impression that the capitalistic organization of life could ever close itself off into a smoothly self-reproducing functional whole".[15] What, then, does he offer by way of hope?

In his search for a critical normativity, Adorno rules out two major candidates. In the Enlightenment affirmation of reason he espies only the repressive bid to impose instrumental purposes and interests as a normative grid upon all human variety. The identity thinking upheld by the ideal of a civilizatory reason is the last place Adorno is going to look to articulate his critique of the distortions of social life. At the same time, his sociological account of the triumph of a reconciled, "happy" consciousness appears to block any chance that a critique of administered life might be grounded in a dynamics that is immanent in everyday life. J. M. Bernstein describes the apparent impasse as follows: "Adorno's philosophy is routinely interpreted as directly embodying the pessimism implied by the intersection of the sociological picture of a rationalized society and the philosophical dilemma of being left without a useable conception of reason."[16]

Adorno's last work, unfinished at his death, addressed the question of the cultural remainders that might allow us to cling to critical awareness. *Aesthetic Theory* set out to defend the resistive power of modernist art as the last refuge for an unreconciled subjectivity. Art that refuses the beautiful image of an integrated, reconciled world and opts for the atonal can mimetically capture the experience of unreconciled, discordant, subjectivity. The atonal, the ugly, which form the "organizing and unity constitutive moment"[17] of the modernist work, is the porthole through which the suffering angst of displaced subjectivity can make itself known.

Adorno is not claiming that autonomous art offers some pure Archimedean point from which the irrational distortions of an administered social life can be gleaned. Alienation from the "logic of domination" is expressed as suffering anxiety through the compositional forms of the modernist work, and this signifies its deep social mediations. However, the point has frequently been made that the critical negativity that Adorno finds stored up in modernist art remains trapped there, devoid of social consequence. He offers no hope that the work of art might set up a receptive relationship with an empirical consciousness that could turn its anxieties into a defiant vision of alternative ways of living. If aesthetic autonomy gives sanctuary to images of unreconciled subjectivity, it also seals them into a "speechless accusation" that provides nothing by way of a utopian vision with practical significance.

Perhaps, though, we can look to other dimensions of Adorno's social philosophy to find an escape route from its "praxial paralysis".[18] In what follows I shall look at what Adorno has to say of the critical needs that cling to the lived tensions of contemporary intimacy.

We have already seen that, for Adorno, the contemporary family has been rationalized to conform to the logics and comply with the purposes of the completely administered society. What partly attracts him to psychoanalytic theory is its insight into the traumas of the bourgeois family that formerly produced inner-directed personalities who were able to sustain an ethically distinct private life. Today the family has become nothing more than a conduit for the demands of the totally administered society. Subjectivity loses its normative ground and is determined only by the need to cope.

Sometimes Adorno appears quite nostalgic:

> With the family there passes away, while the system lasts, not only the most effective agency of the bourgeoisie, but also the resistance which, though repressing the individual, also strengthened, perhaps even produced him. The end of the family paralyses the forces of opposition. The rising collectivist order is a mockery of a classless one: together with the bourgeois it liquidates the Utopia that once drew sustenance from motherly love. (*MM*: 23)

The strong self-directed personality forged through the Oedipal drama had looked to the loving family as an ethical haven from the heartless world of commercial life. It might appear, then, that Adorno's critical diagnosis of life in the administered society draws its normative charge from the image of the ethical personality constructed in the bourgeois household.

Martin Jay thinks that the evidence points this way.[19] However, it seems to me that Rahel Jaeggi is on stronger grounds when she draws attention to Adorno's problematization of the ideal of an ethical, "right", life in a "wrong" society.[20] If we are to chart our way out of crippling alienation we need first to understand what a good way of being with others looks like. Adorno offers some grounds for hope that critical, ethical motivations might be located in the dialectics of intimacy.

Along with other commentators on the "disorganisation of transition" that was affecting postwar private life,[21] Adorno seemed to be alert, not just to the crushing new burdens placed on the weakened family, but to the prospect that the normative contents locked in its institutional conventions might be opened up to a new self-reflexiveness and renegotiation. He is by no means investing romantically in the idea of the natural power of love to break through an alienating sociality. Actually, he is highly sceptical of the ideological functions of romantic images of the individual as a merely feeling self.

Everywhere bourgeois society insists on the exertion of will; only love is supposed to be involuntary, pure immediacy of feeling. In its longing for this, which means a dispensation from work, the bourgeois idea of love transcends bourgeois society. But in erecting truth directly amid the general untruth, it perverts the former into the latter (*MM*: 172).

Posing as a sanctuary for particular natural subjectivity, the idealization of passionate, involuntary love offers society "an alibi for the domination of interests and bears witness to a humanity that does not exist". Since it falls for conventional attractions, romantic love "runs away" when the going gets tough and the needy particularity of the other starts to be felt. So love, it seems, can survive only if it becomes a chosen fidelity to the object of involuntary passion. While love's own chances depend on forging a unity of involuntary passion and elected loyalty, its dialectical unities can also help us to begin to think in a non-ideological way about the meaning of autonomy (*MM*: 172).

Adorno wants to learn from the insights of a complex ethical, not just natural, love. If love is to represent a better society,

> it cannot do so as a peaceful enclave, but only by conscious opposition. This, however, demands precisely the element of voluntariness that the bourgeois, for whom love can never be natural enough, forbid it. Loving means not letting immediacy wither under the omnipresent weight of mediation and economics, and in such fidelity, it becomes itself mediated, as a stubborn counterpressure. (*MM*: 172)

But love alone cannot provide sanctuary to the hope for a decent life. There is: "No emancipation without that of society". The "peaceful enclave" is not immune to the divisions, inequalities and insecurities of an alienated sociality and, indeed, it can be the site of a special, perceptive cruelty: "false nearness incites malice" (*MM*: 173). However, Adorno makes the point that the dialectics of intimate life can at least offer an image of non-instrumentalizing interactions between particular individuals. A natural romantic passion turns out to carry various cultural conventions and expectations that are not reflected upon. Yet the longing it expresses that particular unrepeatable subjectivity might achieve non-alienated recognition can provide the hook on to which an ethical, chosen, love can attach itself. The negotiation between reason and passion forged in an ethical intimacy is an index to the hope that a Romantic love for the particular might not always be at the mercy of a subduing enlightenment reason.

Bernstein insists that "Adorno is not providing a sociology of marriage or love but taking the pulse of the moral possibilities and hence the *rationality potential* latent in them".[22] However, Adorno's insight into the normative ambiguities of intimate life is not meant as a positive orientation to how we might live reasonably and decently with each other. "Wrong life", he tells us, "cannot be lived rightly" (*MM*: 39). He grimly supposes that the totally administered society finally invades and overwhelms the potentials for a rational mode of interaction that peeps through the dialectics of love. "Privacy has given way entirely to the privation it always secretly was, and with the stubborn adherence to particular interests is now mingled fury at being no longer able to perceive that things might be different and better" (*ibid.*: 34). The ethical power of intimacy rests on the capacity to negotiate and live with its normative ambiguities. But ambiguity is anathema to the management imperatives of the totally administered society. And, corrupted by the distorted motivations of a wrong life, love can turn into exquisite cruelty.

Conclusion

What can we do? Adorno always invests in understanding. He believes that "only by making this situation a matter of consciousness – rather than covering it over with sticking plaster – will it be possible to create the conditions in which we can properly formulate questions about how we should lead our lives today". The most we may be able to say "is that the good life today would consist in resistance to the forms of wrong life that have been seen through and critically dissected by the most progressive minds" (*PMP*: 167–8).[23]

However, it seems that all that critical theory has to offer is an impotent clairvoyance. It can help us thematize how we might use our diverse cultural resources to imagine a non-repressive mode of interacting with others. It can analytically demonstrate why there can be "no emancipation without society". Finally, it can critically dissect the mechanisms employed by the totally administered society to distort and confuse emancipatory motivations. Yet Adorno seems to be prepared to sacrifice an engaged role for critical theory to preserve the philosophical radicalism of his critique of a totally alienated present.

Adorno never had much interest or confidence in the feminist politics he saw taking shape in his last years.[24] However, there seem to be missed opportunities here for a mutually enlightening dialogue. In the first instance, it would seem that the feminist movement stands awkwardly in front of the totally administered society thesis as testament to a complex set of pathways, running in both directions, between critical motivations that germinate in contemporary intimate life and the expectations of civic and legal freedoms.

With the later Habermas, we can suggest that the social and political reform agendas of contemporary feminism have disclosed and exploited aspects of a latent critical normativity in liberal democratic institutions that were obscured in Adorno's despairing diagnosis of the totally administered society.[25] It might also be said that a modern feminist movement demonstrates that emancipatory needs nursed in an ethically complex private life can achieve public significance and help shape civic and political reform agendas. The strong thesis of the "unholy alliance" between administrative state power and monopoly capital that dominates Adorno's description of contemporary alienation tells an important story about contemporary social life, but it is not the only one worth telling.

This is a two-way street. Adorno also has something useful to say to the fraught, internally divided, character of feminism's reflections on the sources of its critical and utopian energies. This social movement has sometimes interpreted its hopes for an autonomous life within a romantic framework, as the aspiration of a, supposedly irreducible, natural feminine difference. Here Adorno's commentary on the conventional cultural descriptions that can overtake Romantic thinking might be allowed as a useful note of reservation. More than this, perhaps his outline of an ethics that draws upon diverse cultural legacies can offer a useful corrective to the stalled debate within contemporary feminism over the ideational sources of the emancipatory hopes that have fuelled it.

As we have seen, Adorno is persuaded that we have to utilize a range of emancipatory interests, both Romantic and reflective Enlightenment, if we are to have any hope of breaking the hold of contemporary alienation. While the unilateralism of the totally administered society thesis leaves us in the dark on the *how*, Adorno never has any doubt about the *why*. A humanistic conviction that people, "who are even now better than their culture" (*MM*: 46), deserve something much better than a totally administered society never leaves him.

Notes

1. J. E. Grumley, *History and Totality: Radical Historicism from Hegel to Foucault* (1989), 169.
2. *Ibid.*, 170.
3. Max Horkheimer, "The Authoritarian State", *The Essential Frankfurt School Reader* (1978), 95–118.

4. Axel Honneth, "A Physiognomy of the Capitalist Form of Life: A Sketch of Adorno's Social Theory", *Constellations: An International Journal of Critical and Democratic Theory* **12**(1) (March 2005), 51.
5. Adorno, "Television and the Patterns of Mass Culture", *Mass Culture: The Popular Arts in America* (1957), 477.
6. Max Horkheimer, *Eclipse of Reason* (1974), 139.
7. *Ibid.*, 141.
8. Friedrich Pollock, "State Capitalism: Its Possibilities and Limitations", *The Essential Frankfurt School Reader* (1978), 71–95.
9. *Ibid.*, 80–81.
10. Erich Fromm, "The Method and Function of an Analytic Social Psychology", *The Essential Frankfurt School Reader* (1978), 477–97.
11. David Riesman, in collaboration with Reuel Denney & Nathan Glazer, *The Lonely Crowd: A Study of the Changing American Character* (1950). Cited by Adorno in "Television and the Patterns of Mass Culture", 477.
12. See Robert W. Witkin's chapter on the philosophy of culture in this volume (Chapter 10) for further discussion of Adorno's views about the culture industry.
13. Adorno, "Television and the Patterns of Mass Culture", 480.
14. *Ibid.*, 477.
15. Honneth, "A Physiognomy of the Capitalist Form of Life", 60.
16. J. M. Bernstein, *Adorno: Disenchantment and Ethics* (2001), 20.
17. Jürgen Habermas, "The Entwinement of Myth and Enlightenment: Rereading 'Dialectic of Enlightenment'", *New German Critique* **26** (1982), 21.
18. Bernstein, *Adorno*, 58.
19. Martin Jay, *Adorno* (1984), 92.
20. Rahel Jaeggi, "'No Individual Can Resist': *Minima Moralia* as Critique of Forms of Life", *Constellations* **12**(1) (2005), 69. For further discussion of Adorno's views about living right life in a wrong society, see Fabian Freyenhagen's chapter in this volume (Chapter 6).
21. See, for example, Talcott Parsons & Robert F. Bales, with the collaboration of James Olds, Phillip Slater & Morris Zelditch, *Family, Socialization and Interaction Process* (1955).
22. Bernstein, *Adorno*, 58.
23. Cited by Jaeggi, "'No Individual Can Resist'", 70.
24. Stefan Müller-Doohm, *Adorno: A Biography* (2005), 475–6. Müller-Doohm describes the brutality of some of Adorno's women students in April 1969; they were seemingly motivated by a crass "sexual liberation" agenda.
25. Jürgen Habermas, *Between Facts and Norms: Contributions to a Discourse Theory of Law and Democracy* (1996), 244–5.

EIGHT

Political philosophy

Marianne Tettlebaum

Introduction

In the mid-1960s, Adorno delivered a series of lectures on history and freedom. In a lecture on the concept of progress, he urges his students not to capitulate to sceptics who argue that concepts that are not easily defined are meaningless. Adorno counters that no matter how difficult or vague concepts such as progress or freedom might be, one must attempt to understand rather than dismiss them. To this end, he offers his own "remedy" for combating sceptics: "when someone asks what freedom is . . . tell him that he needs only to think of any flagrant attack on freedom" – which he illustrates with the following example, based on his own experience: "I am content to be able to say of freedom – by this I mean political freedom, not the free will – that being free means that, if someone rings the bell at 6.30 a.m., I have no reason to think that the Gestapo . . . or the agents of comparable institutions are at the door and can take me off with them without my being able to invoke the right of habeas corpus" (*HF*: 140).

A house search by the Gestapo could be a matter of life and death. Adorno emerged from his own search, which occurred during the early years of fascism, physically unscathed, but the consequences could easily have been dire. The incident serves, therefore, not only as an example of what freedom is not – the possibility of being carried off from one's own home by the Gestapo – but also an intimation of what it might be – the possibility of living without fear.

As distant as we may believe ourselves to be today from the first possibility involving the Gestapo, Adorno would argue that we are equally distant from the second: a life without fear.

Adorno's focus on the difficulty, rather than on the likelihood, of achieving true freedom – on what freedom is not, rather than what it is – has led to the charge that his philosophy is apolitical. Politics is, admittedly, not a concept that explicitly guides his thought. Moreover, because he offers neither a circumscribed field of study that could be called politics nor a definition of the political, locating the political dimension of his work is no straightforward endeavour. That dimension, however, as the above example demonstrates, is crucial to his theoretical project.

At the moment of "that ominous knock at the door" before the house search (*HF*: 20), the occupant faces, at one extreme, the possibility of losing her life, and, at the other, the possibility that she has nothing to fear. The political dimension of Adorno's work, I suggest, lies in the spaces between these possibilities, the spaces, that is, between what was, what is and what ought to be. His political thought aims at analysing and understanding the "societal play of forces", to use his term, that comprise this space, determining both the occupant's expectations and the actual outcome (*CM*: 203). This "play of forces" involves everything from a society's history and economic structure to the concrete experiences of the individuals who comprise it. Only a thorough understanding and critique of all these aspects, rather than some kind of immediate action, can achieve anything resembling the second possibility of freedom while excluding anything resembling the first.

The lingering possibility of "that ominous knock", even in so-called free societies, pervades Adorno's writings. The powerlessness of intellectuals in the face of fascism's rise in the 1930s, and the general lack of resistance to it in the German population, left a profound impression on him. He was horrified, above all, by the atrocities of the concentration camps and the fact that such atrocities could occur in a civilization that called itself advanced. He argues, therefore, in "Education after Auschwitz", that the central idea of political instruction ought to be "that Auschwitz should never happen again" (*CM*: 203).

In the history and freedom lectures, Adorno contends that "if Auschwitz could happen in the first place, this was probably because no real freedom existed . . . [T]he misdeeds of Auschwitz were only possible . . . in a political system in which freedom was completely suppressed" (*HF*: 202). We must prevent another Auschwitz, not only because of the terror and injustice associated with the concentration camps, but also because the very existence of such camps testifies to the oppression and domination – the "unfreedom" – inherent in the societies in which they exist. To say that Auschwitz should never happen again is to say that the oppressive political and social conditions that permitted Auschwitz should never be allowed to proliferate. As long as the possibility of another Auschwitz exists, we remain fundamentally unfree.

Adorno believed that in order to ensure that Auschwitz does not happen again, we must understand the circumstances that led to it. He came to realize that no single factor could account for Hitler's rise to power, the horrors inflicted by the Nazis and, most puzzling of all, fascism's seemingly spellbinding effect on the German population. More problematic still, from a philosophical perspective, fascism arose despite the strong German enlightenment tradition of rational and independent thought as well as of moral and cultural education or *Bildung*. The tradition that ought to have been a source of powerful resistance to a development such as fascism was all too easily co-opted in favour of an uncritical German nationalism. Adorno argued that if that intellectual tradition was to continue to have the validity necessary for the success of political instruction, if not of education in general, then it had to be completely rethought. Even its most vaunted concepts, such as reason, had to be subjected to "critical treatment" (*CM*: 203).

Adorno's commitment to education rather than direct political action as a means of combating the legacy of fascism and other social ills in postwar Germany made him a controversial figure during the student uprisings of the late 1960s. In principle, students shared many of his concerns: they were disillusioned by what they perceived as the failure of their parents' generation to come to terms with its Nazi past; by the dulling effects of capitalism on society; and by a conservatism latent in public institutions, especially the university. But Adorno was sceptical of the students' leap into direct political action. The rise of the oppressive Stalinist regime in the Soviet Union made him, and other members of the Frankfurt School, wary of revolutionary Marxism. For Adorno, the potential for any kind of socialist revolution, even in postwar Germany, was long past, if, indeed, it had ever really existed. He believed, moreover, that political action that is not grounded in extensive thought and self-reflection risks, by its refusal of critical distance, perpetuating the very repressive conditions it seeks to change. Thinking, therefore, is ultimately a more effective means of resistance than action.

The students, however, saw Adorno's focus on thinking rather than action as a form of resignation and as an inadequate if not unjust response to their concerns. Their perception of his stance was only confirmed by his decision to call the police when they occupied the Institute of Social Research. In August 1969 Adorno was publicly humiliated by students who interrupted him during a lecture at the university and called on him to renounce his decision to call the police during the occupation of the Institute. Adorno refused and left the lecture hall. The incident left an indelible blemish on the perception of his political thought. From the students' perspective, Adorno was unable to actualize the potential for resistance that is inherent in his thought. The conservatism of his old age, they claimed, was inconsistent with the spirit of his earlier philosophy.

But the incident admits of another reading. Adorno's refusal to acquiesce in the face of the students' demands was itself a form of political resistance, an individual denial of the logic of force, and an invocation of precisely that right of *habeas corpus* he had been unable to invoke in the face of the Gestapo. Indeed, given the current political climate in the West, where the use of force has become synonymous with realizing freedom, Adorno's example is especially relevant. The continued prevalence of violence on a global scale has rendered action more suspect than ever before, for action serves largely to perpetuate the very fear it is meant to eradicate, fear that has, in turn, become an instrument of unfreedom, grounds for revoking the right of *habeas corpus* even in a democratic society. Now more than ever, thought is needed to unmask the repression and oppression at the root of violence. The use of freedom as a battle cry can only be the harbinger of unfreedom. Thinking, in fact, may be the only way to avoid total destruction.

In our current political climate, the student of politics who turns to Adorno will find his writings remarkably prescient. The most accessible and potentially relevant of these, from a political standpoint, are found in the collection *Critical Models*. For those who want to understand the development of Adorno's political thought in the context of the German philosophical tradition, the lectures on *History and Freedom* are an ideal place to start. The ideas Adorno introduces in these lectures receive their final formulation in the sections on Kant and Hegel in *Negative Dialectics*. In what follows, I draw on these and other writings[1] to elaborate the concepts I deem most salient, not only to Adorno's political thought, but also to its continued relevance.

Individual and state

Adorno considers the relationship between individual and state to be one of the fundamental concerns of political philosophy since Plato. Crucial to his understanding of this relationship is the notion that both individual and state are historical categories: they arose and developed in response to particular historical circumstances. As the categories of individual and state evolve, so does the relationship between them.

In Adorno's view, that relationship has become largely antagonistic. In "Individual and State", written shortly after his return to Germany, but unpublished during his lifetime, he examines the historical and theoretical roots of the increasing alienation that modern individuals experience with respect to the state. The state, he suggests, may have begun as an "organized society" to enable the survival of the human race in the face of "the forces of nature".[2] Eventually, however, with the advent of market economies that pitted the very individuals the state was supposed to protect against each other in competition, the state became an entity in its own right, seemingly independent of the individuals who constitute it.

As Adorno explains, however, the organization of society into states that came to have an existence larger than their individual members is only partially to blame for the alienation of individuals. Ever since the Greeks made the individual central and "determined its happiness to be the highest good", the individual, in its efforts to secure its own happiness, lost sight of its relationship to the state and society as a whole: "through its unrestrained liberation, the individual simultaneously prepared the ground for its oppression".[3] The very category of the individual, in other words, as it arose during the phase of the Greek city-states, contained the seeds of its own oppression. The more the individual made its own interests a priority, the less it seemed to need the state, the purpose of which was initially to protect those interests. Just as the state came to seem larger than and separate from the individuals it was supposed to serve, so the individual and its own interests came to seem larger than and separate from the state it was supposed to support.

In modernity, where all the functions of the state are more tightly incorporated and where, therefore, state power seems overwhelming and all-encompassing, the individual comes to feel not only that its interests are contrary to those of the state but also, more critically, that it is powerless in the face of the state. From this feeling of powerlessness, Adorno argues, arises a feeling of apathy toward the state and, hence, the alienation of the individual from the state – the sense that nothing one does would make a difference anyway. For this very reason, "the call for participation in things related to the state is, in truth, not so empty as it sounds to people. Their own fate, in fact, will depend, ultimately, on the consciousness of the necessity to form their state themselves."[4] The key to fostering such a consciousness, at least in the social sciences, is to bring to light the ways in which the problematic relationship between state and individual has its roots in the life of society.

Class

According to Adorno, an individual's relationship to the state is always mediated by the role of class in society. His acknowledgement of the centrality of class is evidence of his indebtedness to Marx. Yet, as he argues in "Reflections on Class Theory" (1942), in a society dominated by advanced or monopoly capitalism, class no longer functions as Marx argued it did. Although class still exists, it has become an instrument of conformity rather than a source of resistance. Class has become largely synonymous with the supposedly egalitarian bourgeoisie, which has become so prominent that the notion of it as a "class" no longer seems to apply. Purged of its critical potential by its association with what seems to be the norm – the bourgeoisie – class comes to seem useless and outdated.

By becoming less visible, class differences have become less potent: "The distinction between exploiters and exploited is not so visible as to make it obvious to the exploited that solidarity should be their ultima ratio; conformity appears more rational to them. Membership in the same class by no means translates into equality of interests and action" (*CLA*: 97). The working class loses sight of its own oppression and thus of the desire for a change in the system. In fact, changing the system seems as though it would threaten rather than increase freedom. But the bourgeoisie, too, suffers: its less prosperous members are "denied individuality" by their lack of wealth (*ibid.*: 108). The general elevation of the standard of living in Western society serves only to propagate the false impression that society has progressed.

In "Late Capitalism or Industrial Society?", Adorno reformulates the problem of the apparent disappearance of class in terms of the relationship between the forces and the relations of production. He argues that while the forces of production – the raw materials and labour required to produce goods – have been modernized with the most advanced technology, the relations of production – the system of the ownership and administration of capital – have remained stagnant. As he explains, "The forces of production are mediated more than ever by the relations of production . . . They are responsible for the fact that, in crazy contradiction to what is possible, human beings in large parts of the planet live in penury" (CLA: 121). Adorno's logic is hard to deny; the technological level of advancement reached by modern forces of production ought to allow for the worldwide elimination of poverty. Instead, wealth, influence and power remain concentrated in the hands of the few. If society were as advanced and civilized as it claims to be, then relations of production would facilitate rather than hinder a more equitable distribution of capital.

Under monopoly capitalism, Adorno argues, not only the state and the economy, but also the forces and relations of production, appear to be one. This appearance or "illusion" of unity is "socially necessary" (CLA: 124): it ensures the stability of society by making it seem as if the interests of the relations of production really do coincide with those of the forces of production, as if what is best for the upper levels of the bourgeoisie is also what is best for the working class. The result, ultimately, is that the system itself takes on a life of its own; it becomes a self-perpetuating machine indifferent to the lives of the individuals, indeed even to the societies, supporting it.

Capitalism thus ends up suppressing the very individualism and difference it claims to be promoting. As Adorno and Horkheimer argue in *Dialectic of Enlightenment*, based largely on their experiences in the United States during their exile from Germany, the seemingly endless variety of goods offered the consumer is really an endless version of the ever-same. What has become true of things, moreover, has also become true of society as a whole, including its political institutions. The Fordist assembly-line model, in which goods are produced with standardized parts, has become the model of a supposedly well-functioning society in which individual labour and thus individuals themselves must conform to the same standards. Those who do not conform are ostracized because they threaten the total control of the self-perpetuating system.[5] Capitalism, like fascism in Germany, seems to have cast a potentially dangerous spell over the American population, making it indifferent to any real possibility for change.

Democracy

Breaking this spell of indifference is, for Adorno, especially crucial to the functioning of democracy. Although he believed in the potential of a democratic form of government, he also held that democracies, like any other form of state organization, are easily co-opted, leading to the unfreedom rather than the freedom of individuals. As he and Horkheimer write in "Democratic Leadership and Mass Manipulation": "To apply the idea of democracy in a merely formalistic way, to accept the will of the majority *per se*, without consideration for the *content* of democratic decisions, may lead to complete perversion of democracy itself and, ultimately, to its abolition" (DLM: 268). Democracy is more than a mere form of social organization in which the majority rules. Adorno and Horkheimer recognize, however, that encouraging individuals to think critically about, and take a stake in, the "*content*" of the democratic political process is a difficult task. The biggest obstacle, perhaps, is the indifference, if not hostility, that derives from the suspicion that politics is solely "the realm of initiated politicians, if not of grafters and machine bosses. The less the people believe in political integrity, the more easily can they be taken in by politicians who rant against politics" (*ibid.*: 271).

Such indifference is compounded by the "antidemocratic stimuli to which the modern masses are exposed" (*ibid.*: 272). Adorno and Horkheimer's experience with the rise of fascism in Germany taught them that democracy is not immune from authoritarian political attitudes. In the United States, they worked with the Berkeley Public Opinion Study Group on an empirical and theoretical study of "the problem of subjective susceptibility for antidemocratism and anti-Semitism" (*ibid.*: 274) – or an account of the relationship between individual psychology and social and political attitudes towards repression.[6] Adorno and Horkheimer believed that an analysis of the authoritarian traits that hinder democracy and foster movements such as fascism might, if widely available to the general public, "induce people to reflect on their own attitudes and opinions, which they usually take for granted, without falling into a moralizing or sermonizing attitude" (*ibid.*: 278). Self-reflection, they suggest, could weaken the violence that is inherent in prejudice.

For its part, democratic leadership must work towards "the emancipation of consciousness rather than its further enslavement":

Today perhaps more than ever, it is the function of democratic leadership to make the subjects of democracy, the people, *conscious of their own wants and needs as against the ideologies which are hammered into their heads by the innumerable communications of vested interests.*

(DLM: 268, emphasis in original)

Democratic leaders must treat people as subjects, capable of rational self-reflection, rather than as objects to be manipulated; they must abandon propaganda in favour of truth. According to Adorno and Horkheimer, those who "prate about the immaturity of the masses" overlook the "mass potential of autonomy and spontaneity which is very much alive" (*ibid.*: 272). Democratic leaders must recognize and foster this potential for self-reflection in the masses, for heightened political introspection goes hand in hand with the awareness of the prejudices that limit such introspection.

This insistence on the individual's political awareness and responsibility reflects the importance Adorno attributes to critique in the functioning of democracy. In "Critique" (1969), he argues that "[c]ritique and the prerequisite of democracy, political maturity, belong together". Echoing Kant's famous essay, "What is Enlightenment?", Adorno suggests that the person who is "politically mature" speaks "for himself, because he has thought for himself and is not merely repeating someone else; he stands free of any guardian" (*CM*: 281). Political maturity is a prerequisite for the critic, who must refuse to temper her criticism in the face of calls for something *"constructive"* or *"positive"*. She adheres, as Adorno argues, to the idea that "the false, once determinately known and precisely expressed, is already an index of what is right and better" (*ibid.*: 288). In a democratic society, the critic is, ultimately, the individual who guarantees the survival of individualism and, thus, the survival of democracy itself.

Theory and praxis

The high value Adorno places on the role of the critic reflects his view that theory – the critical examination of a given circumstance – is a more responsible and effective means of bringing about political change than praxis – the active intervention in that circumstance. Adorno's ideas about theory and praxis – outlined most extensively in "Marginalia to Theory and Praxis" (unpublished during his lifetime) – stem, on the one hand, from his disagreement with the goals of pragmatist philosophy, and, on the other, from his suspicion, rooted largely in his experience of fascism, that violence inheres in most collective movements. For Adorno, a philosophy directed towards practical application is automatically constrained by the very limitations of the situation it seeks to address. To get results, in other words, such a philosophy must start with what is possible within the framework of the system it wants to change, rather than with what ought to be. It must address itself to precisely those "constructive" and "positive" concerns that dilute the rigour of true critique.

Owing to the limitations inherent in a praxis-oriented philosophy, collective movements that seek to put that philosophy's ideas into practice or to change existing conditions based on that philosophy risk becoming dogmatic. In the process of actively seeking change, moreover, the means often overshadow the ends, with the result that the relation of praxis to its object is "a priori undermined" (CM: 259). As Adorno explains,

> the error of the primacy of praxis as it is exercised today appears clearly in the privilege accorded to tactics over everything else. The means have become autonomous to the extreme. Serving the ends without reflection, they have alienated themselves from them. (CM: 268)

Praxis becomes an end in itself, rather than a means towards achieving an end; overwhelmingly concerned with action, it abandons reflection. An unreflective practice, is, for Adorno, inevitably unfree, and risks turning to rage or violence. With its emphasis on the collective, praxis also too easily absolves the individual of any responsibility. Adorno thus rejects any notion of "collective reason" as purely irrational.

Although theory is not immune to the conditions of unfreedom that plague praxis, it is nevertheless capable of maintaining a greater degree of freedom. This is due, on the one hand, to theory's freedom from achieving explicitly practical aims and, on the other, to the roots of both theory and praxis in the division of physical from intellectual labour. "Praxis", according to Adorno, "arose from labor, from the need to work in order to survive." From the moment, however, that the working class wanted to determine the conditions of its life, rather than passively reproduce, through its labour, the conditions that enabled other classes to live, the concept of praxis became divided: praxis, as labour, was necessary for survival, but praxis was also the reaction against that necessity, the desire to be free from it. As Adorno explains, "Praxis was the reaction to deprivation; this still disfigures praxis even when it wants to do away with deprivation" (*CM*: 262). Even in its current form praxis cannot escape its ties to self-preservation, cannot do away with the moment of unfreedom that is a fundamental part of its concept. Contemporary political movements have forgotten the roots of praxis in labour and thus its contradictory double character, as both a means of survival and a deterrent to freedom.

The price that theory paid for the division of individual from physical labour was its alienation from practice. This alienation is especially problematic because theory is, in fact, itself a form of praxis; it is "an inalienably real mode of behavior in the midst of reality" (*CM*: 261). Those who denigrate theory as ineffective disregard the transformative potential of thought, which lies in its resistance to a given situation, in its refusal to accept that what is must be: "Whoever thinks, offers resistance" (*ibid.*: 263). Whoever thinks, moreover, and through such thinking refuses to accept "the already given", initiates a "practical impulse": "There is no thought, insofar as it is more than the organization of facts and a bit of technique, that does not have its practical telos" (*ibid.*: 265).

Truly transformative praxis, however, is not determined and planned out in advance by theory; rather, it must emerge of itself, spontaneously, from the very attempt to think something other than what is. The importance of spontaneity cannot be overemphasized, for, in a society dominated by monopoly capitalism, in which the total rationalization and monopolization of the means and ends of production – the "rationality of the eternally same" (*CM*: 260) – have blocked genuine experience, the ability to act spontaneously is one of the few measures of freedom.

The totalizing effect of monopoly capitalism on society pertains even at the level of individual experience; distinguishing one's own desires from those prescribed by the system becomes almost impossible. In the face of such an all-pervasive system of control, spontaneous action, action that has not been determined in advance by the very system it seeks to disrupt, becomes rare. Praxis, therefore, "is a source of power for theory but cannot be prescribed by it. It appears in theory merely, and indeed necessarily, as a blind spot, as an obsession with what is being criticized" (*CM*: 278). Praxis emerges from theory only at the moment when theory, completely enmeshed in its analysis of a given situation, is most oblivious (or "blind") to praxis: praxis emerges from theory when it is least expected.

Ultimately, the relationship between theory and practice is one of "qualitative reversal"; they "stand in a polar relationship. The theory that is not conceived as an instruction for its realization should have the most hope for realization" (CM: 277). Theory is realized only via the negation or refusal of every practical impulse. In Adornian terms, we might say that theory offers the negative image of a possible practice. As the potential for realizing what is not or not yet, theory is the most effective way of conceiving freedom. For freedom "can be defined in negation only, corresponding to the concrete form of a specific unfreedom" (ND: 231). Theory that enables us to think this negative image of freedom might one day be the means of its realization.

Freedom

For Adorno, no modern attempt to conceive of freedom can ignore the rise of fascism and the tragedy of the concentration camps. As discussed above, freedom is possible only if and when the reoccurrence of such a tragedy has become impossible. Even individual freedom remains "imperfect and incomplete . . . as long as and to the extent that it presupposes the unfreedom of other human beings" (HF: 178). Freedom, therefore, can be conceived only negatively, as freedom *from* rather than freedom *to*: only under utopian conditions could a positive freedom be said to exist. And yet we cannot give up on the concept of freedom, even if "this very freedom is something that cannot be found in the realm of factual reality" (*ibid.*: 177).

According to Adorno, "If we are to update the concept [of freedom], the biggest mistake we could possibly make would be to issue appeals to freedom, to popularize the idea of freedom as a slogan or to appeal to people's autonomy." General appeals to do something in the name of freedom, or unreflective celebrations of freedom, denigrate the very freedom they wish to extol by reducing it "to the level of a cliché". The better approach to understanding freedom "would be to take the question of what has become of freedom and what threatens to become of it in the future and to treat such questions as the precondition of any serious reflection on freedom" (HF: 201). The concept of freedom is, like those of theory and practice, a historical concept whose meaning is inseparable from a given context. Understanding this concept, therefore, requires a critique of the shifting and often contradictory moments or aspects that comprise it.

Adorno's own critique of this concept, both in his lectures on history and freedom and in *Negative Dialectics*, begins with Kant's *Critique of Practical Reason*. In Kant, Adorno sees the origins of our modern philosophical idea of freedom and the moments of unfreedom inherent in it. In determining a universal norm or categorical imperative to which all human actions must be held accountable, rather than holding them accountable to a particular set of empirical values, Kant lays the foundation for an "egalitarian idea" of ethics and freedom (*ND*: 236). But Kant's conception of the will, the human capacity to act freely according to laws, ultimately leads, Adorno argues, to a concept of freedom in which true freedom is repressed.

For Adorno, the problems with the Kantian notion of the will arise largely from the rift between his analysis of the transcendental subject and the empirical examples he uses to illustrate it. Kant assumes that the subject's decisions "roll off in a causal chain", whereas, for Adorno, "what occurs is a jolt" (*ND*: 226–7). Kant attempts to ground human decisions and action in laws of causality. In so doing, however, he leaves out the very aspect of those decisions that is most indicative of freedom, their "spontaneity" (*ibid.*: 229). His account of the will suppresses those spontaneous impulses that are not identical with the laws of causality by which it supposedly operates, impulses of which the subject itself might not be conscious. Thus, voluntary actions become equivalent to human consciousness of those actions. As Adorno explains, "the subject knows itself to be free only insofar as its action strikes it as identical with it, and that is the case in conscious actions only" (*ibid.*: 227). A subject that acts only according to laws of which it is aware, laws that accord with its consciousness of itself, may in Kantian terms be exercising its freedom in accordance with the moral law. In Adornian terms, however, it is acting under coercion. Grounding the will in causality corrupts freedom into obedience (*ibid.*: 232).

Adorno's aim in critiquing Kant is, ultimately, to bring to light the way that freedom, by being conceived of as obedience, has come to be equated with the acceptance of the world as it is. His aim, in other words, is to expose the structures of thought that led us to value a concept of freedom not worthy of the name. He argues that the limits Kant places on freedom reflect the ambivalent attitude to freedom of the general bourgeois consciousness. On the one hand, that consciousness "fears the limiting of freedom and the constraints placed upon it"; on the other hand, it "takes fright at its own courage and fears that a freedom made real might lead to chaos" (*HF*: 196). Bourgeois enlightenment thinkers such as Kant opted for a restricted concept of freedom as much out of fear as out of theoretical necessity.

In Adorno's view, we are still largely beholden to this Kantian idea of freedom, which leads us to accept less than we otherwise might: "Where it is maintained that the substance of freedom is that you are free when you freely accept what you have to accept anyway, you can be certain that the concept of freedom is being abused and is being twisted into its opposite" (*HF*: 197). Passive acceptance, even of the law of the land, without consideration for the content of such law, does not, for Adorno, constitute freedom. Moreover, if all behaviour were constituted by passive reactions, "there could be no thinking" (*ND*: 217). If the individual is only autonomous to the extent required of her by the current economic system in order to function, then she is not really autonomous at all.

At stake in this social illusion of freedom is nothing less than the concept of life itself. Adorno argues that life ought to presuppose "the possibility of things not yet included, of things yet to be experienced", but this possibility has "been so far reduced that the word 'life' sounds by now like an empty consolation" (*ND*: 262). Freedom that consists in nothing but obedience to the laws that govern the world as it is forecloses the possibility of anything different or unexpected – the possibility, in other words, of a truly full concept of life. In other words, "[w]ithin a reality modeled after the principle of identity there exists no positive freedom" (*ibid.*: 241). A concept of life that is identical with existence reduces life to mere self-preservation. An individual who cannot conceive of herself as other than she is will never "truly be a subject" (*ibid.*: 277). Adorno's term for this otherness, this moment of difference inherent in concepts and subjects, is "non-identity". Non-identity, like spontaneity, is ultimately the guarantor of freedom in a society dominated by unfreedom. It is the basis for resistance to the current situation, the promise of the possibility that what is might be otherwise.

Education

For Adorno, education is the most effective means of fostering the thought, critique and resistance necessary for freedom. As he explains in "Philosophy and Teachers" (1962), one of his duties as a member of the Philosophy Department at the University of Frankfurt was to hold examinations for future high-school teachers who were required to pass a general philosophy exam. These future teachers, he writes, are "burdened with a heavy responsibility for the spiritual and material development of Germany" (CM: 21). In order adequately to fulfil this responsibility, teachers must demonstrate in their exams that they can think for themselves. Rather than merely summarizing a predefined area of philosophic study, the teachers ought to be able to "experience and to engage with a topic in a free and autonomous manner" (ibid.: 25).

At stake in the ability to think for oneself is nothing less than the future of society. For the inability to think for oneself is a precursor of totalitarian attitudes such as fascism: "National Socialism lives on today less in the doctrines that are still given credence . . . than in certain features of thought." These features, which include submission to the values of the moment, lack of spontaneous relations to "people, things, ideas" and "compulsive conventionalism", have grave political implications (CM: 27). Teachers who cannot transcend the narrow limitations of established thought do an injustice to their future pupils: they prepare them for obedience rather than freedom.

In "Taboos on the Teaching Vocation" (1965), Adorno contends that in preparing students to think for themselves, education prepares the way for the "debarbarization of humanity", the elimination of "delusional prejudice, oppression, genocide, and torture". The "key to radical change", therefore, "lies in society and in its relationship to the school". For this reason, "it is so eminently important for society that the school fulfills its task and helps society to become conscious of the fateful ideological heritage weighing heavily upon it" (CM: 190).

If freedom, as Adorno suggests, "means to criticize and change situations, not to confirm them by deciding within their coercive structure" (ND: 226n), then an education that prepares its students to critique rather than confirm prepares them for the possibility of freedom. Conceived in its relation to society, therefore, education is the realm in which change becomes a possibility. As such, although Adorno himself never explicitly frames it this way, education serves as the truest form of praxis available to society. Education prepares us to recognize and understand the threat of "that ominous knock", so that we ourselves neither perpetuate nor experience it.

Notes

1. My account of Adorno's political thought is indebted to the more thorough accounts of Russell Berman, "Adorno's Politics", *Adorno: A Critical Reader* (2002), especially 126–31; Espen Hammer, *Adorno and the Political* (2006), especially 18–25; and Peter Uwe Hohendahl, *Prismatic Thought: Theodor W. Adorno* (1995). For an extensive account of, and documentation related to, the Frankfurt School and the student movements, see Wolfgang Kraushaar (ed.), *Frankfurter Schule und Studentenbewegung. Von der Flaschenpost zum Molotowcocktail 1964–95*, 3 vols. (1998).
2. Adorno, "Individuum und Staat", *Gesammelte Schriften* 20.1 (1986), 287. All translations are my own.
3. *Ibid.*, 288.
4. *Ibid.*, 292.
5. See especially, "The Culture Industry: Enlightenment as Mass Deception", *DE*, C: 120–67; J: 94–136.
6. That study, written with Else Frenkel-Brunswik, Daniel J. Levison & R. Nevitt Sanford, was published as *The Authoritarian Personality* (1950).

NINE

Aesthetics

Ross Wilson

Introduction

That part of Adorno's work which we might wish to label his "aesthetics" is not hard to identify. At the time of his death, Adorno was close to completing his *Aesthetic Theory*, which represents the culmination of his lifelong engagement with the various arts – especially music and literature – and their philosophy. The development of Adorno's aesthetics can easily be traced from his early account in *Philosophy of New Music* of the rival tendencies in twentieth-century music represented by the composers Arnold Schönberg and Igor Stravinsky, through his engagement with a wide variety of literary texts in *Notes to Literature*, to the posthumously edited and published *Aesthetic Theory* itself.

However, closer inspection of these works – and perhaps of *Aesthetic Theory* in particular – quickly complicates such a neat survey of what might be called Adorno's aesthetics. There are a number of significant reasons for this complication. First, the category of aesthetics is itself at issue in Adorno's thought. In his important commentary, Lambert Zuidervaart has described *Aesthetic Theory* as a "meta-aesthetics", which is to say that Adorno is concerned, among other things, to question the very possibility of philosophical aesthetics.[1] Adorno's considerations of the meaning of aesthetics do not simply aim at a clearer, sharper definition of this term. Instead, one of the main appeals of *Aesthetic Theory* is that it seeks to question whether aesthetics can – or ought to – stand alone as a subdiscipline of philosophy. Philosophical reflection on the nature and status of art, for Adorno, is metaphysical, logical and moral, as well as "aesthetic" in the usual sense of that term.

Secondly, Adorno claims that aesthetics cannot stand apart from consideration of both the social and historical situation and the development of art, usually viewed as the preserve of art history. This claim that aesthetics should be attentive to historical and social considerations in its discussion of art is not just the demand that aesthetics back up its general theses with particular examples. Rather, artworks in their historical and social specificity already demand philosophical reflection. Aesthetics must be concerned, not so much with articulating general principles and definitions which are then to be applied from above, as it were, to any given artwork, but much more with the philosophical significance already implicit in actual, particular artworks.

Thirdly, Adorno claims that the subject matter of aesthetics is no longer obvious. This difficulty is not cleared up with the common-sensical reminder – as if philosophers interested in aesthetics were simply forgetful – that aesthetics should be concerned with art: the concept of art itself has become unstable. The music of Arnold Schön-berg, the stories of Franz Kafka, the poetry of Charles Baudelaire, the paintings of Pablo Picasso – to cite only the most prominent examples – have disturbed established conventions of composition, form, decorum and meaning to such an extent that it is no longer possible to settle decisively on the defining features of art as such. The crisis in the concept of art, wrought by developments in artistic practice, is strikingly expressed in the first line of *Aesthetic Theory*: "It is self-evident that nothing concerning art is self-evident any more."[2]

These fairly brisk opening considerations already suggest that Adorno's work is as much concerned with questioning the status of the discipline of aesthetics as with simply contributing to it. Adorno wants radically to work through – not simply to abandon or destroy – the fundamental questions of the philosophical interpretation of art: what is aesthetics? And, what is art? In mapping his ways of formulating these questions and, indeed, of beginning to answer them, this chapter falls into three sections. The first gives a brief account of Adorno's relation to the two most influential figures in modern European aesthetics before him: Immanuel Kant and G. W. F. Hegel. The second shows how Adorno's distinctive negotiation of the opposition between Kant's subjective and Hegel's objective aesthetics shapes his account of aesthetic response; it then considers Adorno's insistence on the need for art to be interpreted philosophi-cally. The third section deals with Adorno's criticism of flawed types of philosophical interpretation of art and his criticism of politically committed art, before setting out his view of the relation between art and society.

Aesthetics before Adorno: Kant and Hegel

Adorno's work draws on a very broad range of writing in philosophical aesthetics, art history, and cultural and literary criticism. His aesthetics is especially concerned with a number of significant questions inherited from Kant's aesthetics and from Hegel's response to Kant. Central to any discussion of Adorno's aesthetics, therefore, is some account of Kant's *Critique of the Power of Judgment* (1790), and of Hegel's *Aesthetics: Lectures on Fine Arts*, first delivered in 1823, and published posthumously in 1835.

The central focus of Kant's aesthetics is aesthetic judgement, or, more particularly, the judgement of taste. According to Kant, aesthetic judgement is autonomous. This means that aesthetic judgement is distinct from other types of judgement such as cognitive judgement, which aims at knowledge, or moral judgement, which aims to tell us what we ought (and ought not) to do. The autonomy of aesthetic judgement has the consequence that I cannot decide upon criteria for whether I will find, say, a poem pleasing before I actually read it.

Imagine that I have been taught that a poem must tick certain boxes in order to be a good poem, that, for instance, it must use particular kinds of words and not others, that it must have rhythmically regular lines, and that it must have some sort of rhyme-scheme. Kant insists that if I approve of a poem that does not conform to these principles, then the pre-established principles that I have been taught – and not my judgement – are to be sacrificed. Likewise, if I dislike a play but am informed that, in fact, it conforms perfectly with rules for what and how a play ought to be, I should, Kant claims, be unmoved.[3] My taste is the only court of appeal for whether I approve of an object aesthetically. This is what Kant means by the autonomy of aesthetic judgement; it is neither possible to establish the features of an aesthetically pleasing object prior to submitting it to judgement nor, concomitantly, is it possible to make aesthetic judgements conform to predetermined standards.

Kant's insistence on the autonomy of aesthetic judgement means that aesthetic judgement must not be confused with cognitive or moral judgements. On the contrary, it must be radically distinguished from them. To return to my example, were I to reply to a question about whether I have found a poem beautiful by saying that I deplored it because of what I took to be its immoral message, I would have allowed a moral judgement to infringe on the autonomy of purely aesthetic judgement. When I am asked to judge the poem aesthetically, I have misunderstood the question if I respond that I dislike it because I take it to be wicked or, indeed, uninformative.

Such an account might seem to reduce aesthetic judgement to mere opinion: I know what I like, and you know what you like, and that's that. However, much of the first part of the *Critique of the Power of Judgment* is dedicated to the attempt to show that, although aesthetic judgements must in a certain sense be subjective, they can nevertheless legitimately claim the assent of everyone. This is what Kant means when he describes aesthetic judgement as making a claim to subjective universality.[4] While the word "beautiful" does not refer to a definable property of the poem, the judgement "this poem is beautiful" is meant to be accepted by all subjects. Thus I know what I like – and I demand that you agree with me.

Kant's *Critique of the Power of Judgment* is a densely argued book to which this kind of summary can only begin to do justice. For our purposes, it is chiefly necessary to bear in mind Kant's insistence on the autonomy of aesthetic judgement and on the separation of aesthetic judgement from cognitive and moral judgements. In his important thesis on "The Concept of Criticism in German Romanticism", Adorno's friend Walter Benjamin argued that the generation of German thinkers after Kant, and especially the philosopher and critic Friedrich Schlegel, "secured, from the side of the object or structure, that very autonomy in the domain of art that Kant, in the third *Critique* [*Critique of the Power of Judgment*] had lent to the power of judgment".[5] In other words, Schlegel extended Kant's insistence on aesthetic autonomy from aesthetic judgement to art itself. Indeed, central to Adorno's own aesthetics is the autonomy of art – and not just of judgement.

We might be able to grasp how judgement is to be autonomous – it refuses to be dictated by predefined rules – but how is an artwork autonomous? On the wall of my living room, I have a print of Cimabue's *Maestà*, the original of which is kept in the Galleria degli Uffizi in Florence. While Cimabue might now be considered an "artist" and his altarpieces "art", this was not always the case. Or, at the very least, "art" sometimes served purposes such as, in this instance, religious devotion. As an altarpiece ceases to perform this function, or ceases to be valued primarily for its facilitation of worship, it becomes "art" in the sense that we might now understand it. Thus, what we might now identify as an artwork may not always have been such. An artwork is autonomous when it obeys no criteria other than artistic ones; that is, when it serves no function other than to be art.

Benjamin claims that the German Romantics inaugurated a turn from Kant's focus on subjective aesthetic judgement to art objects. This refocusing is also central to Hegel's criticism of Kant's aesthetics. Although Kant argues that the subjectivity of aesthetic judgement does not mean that it relinquishes its claim to be binding, Hegel still sees Kant's aesthetics as culpably subjective. Kant's quite explicit admission that aesthetic judgement cannot offer knowledge of the objects that it judges is a major flaw, according to Hegel. Hegel argues that "the depths of the thing [the artwork] remained a sealed book to taste, since these depths require not only sensing and abstract reflections, but the entirety of reason and the solidity of spirit, while taste was directed only to the external surface".[6]

Although Hegel certainly does not wish to revert to a position back behind Kant – that is, to the reimposition of fixed rules for the creation and judgement of artworks – he does think that Kant pays too high a price for his insistence on the autonomy of art. Kant thinks that aesthetic judgements can legitimately claim to be binding on other human subjects, but not because these judgements pertain to the truth or untruth about objects. By contrast, aesthetics for Hegel must be precisely concerned "to determine what the beautiful is as such".[7]

Aesthetic response and philosophical interpretation

Whereas Kant's aesthetics is *subjective* in the sense that it focuses on aesthetic judgement, and Hegel's aesthetics is *objective* in the sense that it wishes to explore the truth of the aesthetic object, Adorno wishes to move beyond this stark opposition. It is important here briefly to recall Adorno's broader philosophical project. In *Negative Dialectics*, he seeks to remedy the consequences of Kant's focus on the subject by a renewed turn to the object. However, he does not simply respond to Kant's elevation of the subject with his own counter-elevation of the object. Rather, what is required is a reconfiguration of the relationship between subject and object in which it is precisely by way of the subject that the merely subjective is broken through and the object is reached (*ND*: xix–xxi).[8] This reconfiguration is all the more necessary in aesthetics, Adorno claims. It is central to his understanding of "dialectical aesthetics":

> As contrary poles, subjective and objective aesthetics are equally exposed to the critique of a dialectical aesthetics: the former because it is either abstractly transcendental or arbitrary in its dependence on individual taste; the latter because it overlooks the objective mediatedness of art by the subject.
>
> (*AT*: 166)

The kind of aesthetics conceived by Adorno seeks to avoid simply adopting the positions offered by either Kant or Hegel. Instead, Adorno's aesthetics rests on an account of the mutual implication of subject and object. This is the case even where he scorns the type of subjective relation to art that would log aesthetic experience in an account book with everything else:

> For him who has a genuine relation to art, in which he himself vanishes, art is not an object; deprivation of art would be unbearable for him, yet he does not consider individual works sources of pleasure. Incontestably, no one would devote himself to art without – as the bourgeois put it – getting something out of it; yet this is not true in the sense that a balance sheet could be drawn up: "heard the Ninth symphony tonight, enjoyed myself so and so much" even though such feeble-mindedness has by now established itself as common sense.   (*AT*: 13)

It is perhaps hard to keep track of exactly what is being said here because the categories of both subject and object are mutually qualified to such a profound degree. The attitude to works of art – such as Beethoven's Ninth Symphony – that Adorno attacks is one that he associates elsewhere in his authorship with the consumer's response to the products of the "culture industry". Products churned out on a large scale and distributed by industrialized methods are merely consumed by a mass audience, rather than adequately engaged with even when they in fact merit such engagement (*DE*, C: xvi; J: xviii–xix). The imaginary balance sheet that Adorno mocks in the above passage is drawn up by the mere consumer of an inert object.

Adorno contends that an adequate response to artworks involves a much more intricate involvement of subject and object. It is true that such a response relies on the devotion of the subject to works of art in the hope that something will be derived from them. But this kind of intense subjective devotion – the *pathos* of which contrasts sharply with the *bathos* of the bourgeois experience of Beethoven in the above description – leads, not to the aggrandizement of the subject over art, but rather to his or her disappearance in it. It might reasonably be thought that this disappearance of the subject means that the dominant aesthetic category has now become the object. But "art is not an object". It is important to emphasize that for Adorno the pair subject–object is operative only as a pair. If the subject is radically altered, so too is the object.

Adorno's aesthetics, then, inherits and attempts to overcome the opposition of Kantian and Hegelian aesthetics. For Adorno as for Hegel, Kant unduly restricts aesthetics to the investigation of subjective response. However, Adorno still insists that aesthetic response is fundamental to consideration of aesthetic objectivity. This must be a certain kind of response, involving more than mere pleasure.

Indeed, in terms explicitly derived from *Dialectic of Enlightenment*, Adorno denounces the separation of feeling from thinking:

> feeling and understanding are not absolutely different in the human disposition and remain dependent even in their dividedness. The forms of reaction that are subsumed under the concept of feeling become futile enclaves of sentimentality as soon as they seal themselves off from their relation to thought and turn a blind eye toward truth; thought, however, approaches tautology when it shrinks from the sublimation of the mimetic comportment. (*AT*: 331)

Feeling separated from thought is whimsical; thought separated from feeling turns in on itself and refuses to be stirred by what is external to it. Crucially, understanding artworks is an essential part of any response to them: "Critique is not externally added into aesthetic experience but, rather, is immanent to it" (*ibid.*: 347). For Adorno, this means both that understanding is not a higher, later stage of reaction and, significantly, that the initial, immediate response to artworks is already important for serious contemplation of them.

This insistence on the centrality of critique to aesthetic response is mirrored by Adorno's emphasis on the necessity of philosophical interpretation to artworks themselves. Just as critique is not additional to response, so interpretation is not exactly added to artworks that are otherwise indifferent to it. As Adorno puts it, "Art awaits its own explanation" (*AT*: 353). Adorno is again indebted to Benjamin's work on the concept of criticism in German Romantic philosophy.

Benjamin had shown that, for writers such as Novalis and Schlegel, criticism was the consummation – that is, the completion – of the work of art. This is not so much to say that art is missing something that criticism adds, but rather that criticism brings out the philosophical significance that is already latent – and mute – in art. Benjamin attempts to bring out the specific character of the knowledge of artworks that transpires in criticism by describing it as a kind of self-knowledge of the artwork.[9]

It is becoming clear that Adorno's idea of the philosophical interpretation of artworks does not simply imply that art should be knocked into philosophical shape. The philosophical interpretation of art is the complement to a requirement already evident in artworks themselves. Moreover, Adorno goes so far as to say that "Artworks that unfold to contemplation and thought without any remainder are not artworks" (*AT*: 121). Without relaxing his emphasis on the need for the closest scrutiny of the philosophical significance of art, Adorno wants to guard against the kind of criticism that would simply read philosophical or, as we shall see, political propositions and theses out of works of art. Connected to this is Adorno's refusal to see what he calls a work's "truth-content" merely in the stated ideas and theses it contains, or in the position that it might be thought to advance. For example, the interest of a work such as John Milton's *Paradise Lost* is not exhausted once it has been decided whether it advances a clearly republican position or whether it successfully manages to articulate a coherent theodicy.

None of this, however, is to relinquish the claim of poetry, for instance, to philosophical significance. Rather, it is to say that the philosophical significance of poetry lies as much in its diction, syntax and versification as in the statements that can be extracted from it, or the positions with which it can be identified. Adorno is suspicious of the kind of philosophical interpretation that finds in artworks only whatever it has already put into them:

> today philosophical interpretations of literary works . . . fail to penetrate the construction of the works to be interpreted and instead prefer to work them up as the arena for philosophical theses: Applied philosophy, a priori fatal, reads out of works that it has invested with an *air* of concretion nothing but its own theses.
> (*AT*: 352)

In contrast, Adorno denies the choice between a brand of mere aesthetic consumption and vague, tendentious philosophizing.

While acknowledging that art can never simply be converted into philosophy without loss, Adorno argues that the refusal to relinquish philosophical interpretation is especially necessary when confronted with some of the radical developments in the arts during the twentieth century. Anyone who has been frustrated in their initial attempts to read James Joyce's *Finnegan's Wake*, for instance, or to listen attentively to Schönberg's *Pierrot Lunaire* will probably admit that modernist works more frequently seem to rebuff interpretation than to encourage it. Adorno states that "in the contemporary situation, it is [artworks'] incomprehensibility that needs to be comprehended" (*AT*: 118).

Perhaps Adorno's most explicit statements on the way that modernist works disturb the assumption that art is straightforwardly interpretable are to be found in "Presuppositions" in which he reflects on a reading – if "reading" is really the right word – of *FA: M'AHNIESGWOW* by the experimental poet Hans G. Helms.[10] In his discussion of the ways in which interpretive understanding (*Verstehen*) is problematized in encounters with this kind of work, Adorno returns to some of the questions regarding the relation of subject to object in aesthetics that I discussed above. First of all, he questions whether interpretive understanding should begin with a consideration of the effect on the subject of a work such as *FA: M'AHNIESGWOW*. It is far from clear that the subject is able straightforwardly and accurately to grasp "the interior of the work" (*NLII*: 96). The model of a stable subject faced by an inert object is inadequate.

Criticism of this kind of model extends, not just to the view that artworks should simply be enjoyed, but also to the idea that they should be rationally unpacked by understanding. Philosophical interpretation, especially in this case, cannot mean the "rational grasping of something in some sense intended".

> If [interpretive understanding] is meant to indicate something adequate, something appropriate for the matter at hand, then today it needs to be imagined more as a kind of following along afterward [*Nachfahren*]; as the co-execution [*Mitvollzug*] of the tensions sedimented in the work of art, the processes that have congealed and become objectified in it. One does not understand a work of art when one translates it into concepts – if one simply does that, one misunderstands the work from the outset – but rather when one is immersed in its immanent movement; I should almost say, when it is recomposed by the

ear in accordance with its own logic, repainted by the eye, when
the linguistic sensorium speaks along with it.   (*NLII*: 96–7)

To return to an earlier point, Adorno's attempt to overcome the
solidified opposition between subject and object does not mean that
the subject must simply be sacrificed on the altar of the work. Rather,
rational understanding conducted by, and on the terms of, the subject
should give way to its performance along with and according to the
innermost characteristics of the artwork. Moreover, the requirement
for this distinctive philosophical response is not extraneous to
the immediate sensible intuition of works of art, but part of it (*ibid*.:
97).

Art, commitment and ideology

We have seen so far that Adorno is wary of directly reading theses
out of artworks or identifying them with certain positions. Specifically, he is suspicious of attempts to ally artworks with particular
political stances. It might be said, therefore, that his concern with art
is aesthetic, rather than directly political. (It is worth noting again
that Adorno's questioning of aesthetics does not entail that aesthetics should be abolished and replaced by something else; that is, the
questioning of aesthetics may equally involve a certain ambivalent
defence of it.) Adorno's refusal to apply philosophy directly to
artworks and his advocacy of radical modernist art need to be
considered in connection with his criticism of the kind of art that
explicitly espouses particular political commitments. Although
Adorno is interested in the relation of art to society, that relation
does not inhere, for him, in the explicit political commitments or
social criticism that artworks might be taken to advance.

Adorno was wary of the artistic and theoretical attempts by Jean-
Paul Sartre and, on a much higher level, by Bertolt Brecht to turn art
towards explicitly political ends. For Brecht, "[t]he aesthetic point of
view is ill-suited to the plays being written at present" because he
thinks that the purpose of contemporary theatre is to stage instances
of social conflict and provide political instruction.[11] However,
Adorno objects that such a view insufficiently recognizes the disruption to traditional aesthetic categories by the catastrophic events of
modern history; it also fails to see the socially critical tendency
already implicit in artworks. The rational, humanistic assumptions
behind aesthetic meaning have been damaged to such an extent that

it is no longer possible for artworks successfully to communicate meaning directly.

Furthermore, Adorno sees art's socially critical potential – that is, its opposition to the prevailing way of the world – as located, not in its message, but in the very fact of its being art. The response to a world in which freedom is in retreat is not to impose political purposes – however laudable they may be – on art: "No artist is able on his own to transcend the contradiction between unchained art and enchained society: All that he is able to do, and perhaps on the verge of despair, is contradict the enchained society through unchained art."[12]

Just as the artist's refusal to submit to pressures on the unhindered exercise of artistic freedom is potentially more politically powerful than the direct expression of social criticism or political propaganda in art, so the artwork's standing apart from the run of mere things suggests that a differently configured world might be possible. "Art is the social antithesis of society", Adorno comments near the beginning of *Aesthetic Theory*; it is "not immediately deducible from it" (*AT*: 8, tr. mod.). However, care should be taken with this statement. On the one hand, Adorno is clearly expressing the view that art as such is antithetical to society as it is currently constituted. On the other hand, art is "the *social* antithesis of society": art is opposed to what it is, at least to some extent. The paradox that art faces is twofold: first, it can arise only from and in the world as it currently is and, secondly, it must be real and exist along with everything else in society if it is to suggest that an alternative is really possible. "Indeed, artworks are only able to become other than thing by becoming a thing" (*ibid.*: 86).

The paradoxical nature of autonomous art in contemporary society – that is, of art that obeys no law other than its own – goes still further. Zuidervaart has insightfully commented that while autonomous art may suggest opposition to an unfree society, it may also falsely suggest that some consummate freedom from society is in fact possible.[13] It is for this reason – that in some respects art wants to keep society at arm's length and thus deny its implication in it – that "Brecht distrusts aesthetic individuation as an ideology" (*NL*II: 82). In fact, this is central to Adorno's difference from Brecht. For Adorno, Brecht's dismissal of aesthetics throws the autonomous baby out with the ideological bathwater. Art is both ideological and emancipatory.

In order fully to understand Adorno's argument here it is necessary to get some sense of what is meant by ideology. Ideology might be generally defined as false consciousness; it deceitfully portrays as universal law whatever serves the particular interests of a particular section of society. Beginning from this definition of ideology, Adorno also qualifies it in a number of extremely significant ways, not all of which can be explored here.[14] While ideology is certainly untrue for Adorno, it is so in a particular way: "it is not ideology in itself which is untrue but rather its pretension to correspond to reality" (P: 32). Adorno is arguing that, while it is untrue to say that this really existing society is free, harmonious and just, the wish implicit in these statements that society be such is true. He remarks in *Negative Dialectics* that "the truth moment of ideology" is "the pledge that there should be no contradiction, no antagonism". That is, in declaring that there is no antagonism in society, ideology is false; but such declarations also harbour the wish that society indeed be free from antagonism. It is in this way that "the pragmatist, nature-controlling element [in ideology] already joins with a utopian element" (*ND*: 149–50).

Ideology is, therefore, not *simply* untrue. By making this point, Adorno wants to sharpen the otherwise very blunt instrument of the concept of ideology. He is also critical of accounts of ideology that, from the definition of ideology as false consciousness, conclude that all consciousness is false. For Adorno, this conclusion does not follow (*AT*: 252). He articulates a clear and extremely significant rebuttal of this kind of view in "On Lyric Poetry and Society" (originally broadcast as a talk on German radio):

Special vigilance is required when it comes to the concept of ideology, which these days is belabored to the point of intolerability. For ideology is untruth, false consciousness, deceit. It manifests itself in the failure of works of art, in their inherent falseness, and it is countered by criticism. To repeat mechanically, however, that great works of art, whose essence consists in giving form to the crucial contradictions in real existence, and only in that sense in a tendency to reconcile them, are ideology, not only does an injustice to their truth content but also misrepresents the concept of ideology. That concept does not maintain that all spirit serves only for some human beings to falsely present some particular values as general ones; rather, it is intended to unmask spirit that is specifically false and at the same time to grasp it in its necessity. The greatness of works of art, however, consists solely in the fact that they give voice to what ideology hides. Their very success moves beyond false consciousness, whether intentionally or not.[15]   (NLI: 39)

Two points in particular need to be drawn from this important passage. Adorno insists that the concept of ideology is not meant to be a general category applied blindly, in this instance, to art. Rather, what is required is specific attention to actual artistic phenomena. We should note that this makes Adorno a rather odd kind of literary or aesthetic *theorist* in that, even when he invokes an apparently theoretical category such as ideology, he insists on close scrutiny of actual artworks, not the application of pre-established categories to them.[16]

Adorno's refusal to accept a monolithic view of art as ideological is connected to his refusal to accept a monolithic view of ideology. We have seen that Adorno does not view ideology as *simply* untrue. Likewise, he states here that spirit – including art and the aesthetic in particular – is not to be dismissed wholesale as ideological from a position outside or before any consideration of a particular artwork. Indeed, if ideology and truth cannot decisively be disentangled, this seems particularly to be the case in art (*AT*: 234). The ideological supposition that culture is separate from the brutal enthronement of mere means as ends in contemporary society is also true in so far as it "implies, at least as an unconscious element, the promise of a condition in which freedom were realized" (*P*: 23). Artworks may inherently fail – note that Adorno does not refer to the failure of *bad* works of art in the passage from "On Lyric Poetry and Society" – in so far as they are ideological, but their very claim to freedom is also part of their wish for freedom, that is, part of their truth.

This investigation of the ways in which art's ideology points to both its truth and untruth clearly shows that Adorno's aesthetic theory is more a sustained investigation into the possibility and nature of a philosophical approach to art than an easily assimilated contribution to the established discipline of aesthetics. However, Adorno does not think that aesthetics should just be abandoned. Moreover, his interest in it is not motivated merely by intellectual–historical curiosity. Rather, one of the most striking and, for many, uncomfortable features of Adorno's work is that central questions in aesthetics also represent the most significant ways of thinking about the relation of subject to object, and about the hope for a world free of the antagonisms by which this one is riven.

Notes

1. Lambert Zuidervaart, *Adorno's Aesthetic Theory: The Redemption of Illusion* (1991), 8.
2. See also Adorno's consideration of the relation between the different arts and art as such in "Art and the Arts", *Can One Live after Auschwitz?* (2003), 368–87.
3. Immanuel Kant, *Critique of the Power of Judgment* (2000), 162–6.
4. *Ibid.*, 99.
5. Walter Benjamin, "The Concept of Criticism in German Romanticism", *Selected Writings*, vol. 1 (1996), 155.
6. G. W. F. Hegel, *Aesthetics: Lectures on Fine Art* (1975), 34.
7. *Ibid.*, 18.
8. See also *ND*: 40: "The Privilege of Experience". I explore aspects of Adorno's reception of Kant's supposed subjectivism in "Dialectical Aesthetics and the Kantian *Rettung*: On Adorno's *Aesthetic Theory*", *New German Critique*, forthcoming.
9. Benjamin, "The Concept of Criticism in German Romanticism", 143, 151 and 153.
10. For a brief but serviceable account of Helms's career, see Stefan Fricke's entry, "Helms, Hans G(ünter)" in *Grove Music Online*.
11. Bertolt Brecht, "Shouldn't We Abolish Aesthetics?", *Brecht on Theatre: The Development of an Aesthetic* (1964), 21. (Readers should note, and perhaps question, the subtitle of Brecht's writings on theatre.) For Sartre, see *What is Literature?* (1993).
12. Adorno, *Philosophy of New Music* (2006), 82.
13. Zuidervaart, *Adorno's Aesthetic Theory* (1991), 32.
14. Simon Jarvis has offered a subtle reading of Adorno's view of ideology. See in particular *Adorno: A Critical Introduction* (1998), 65–7, and with regard to art, 116–19. Readers of German might also consult "Beitrag zur Ideologienlehre" ("Contribution to the Theory of Ideology") *Gesammelte Schriften* 8 (1972), 457–77. An English version of this essay appears in Frankfurt Institute for Social Research, *Aspects of Sociology* (1972).
15. For an instructive reading of this essay – and its (mis)appropriation in subsequent accounts of ideology and literature – see Robert Kaufman, "Adorno's Social Lyric, and Literary Criticism Today: Poetics, Aesthetics, Modernity", *The Cambridge Companion to Adorno* (2004), 354–75.
16. Jarvis, *Adorno*, 137–8.

TEN

Philosophy of culture

Robert W. Witkin

Introduction

Many of Adorno's best-known writings on culture were produced during his sojourn in England (1934–38) and the United States (1938–47). Dark times and exile – the shadow of the Holocaust – are constant companions in these texts: their presence, unmistakable, imparts to his writing the urgent tone of a "wake-up" call.

Culture is ubiquitous: it mediates all consciousness, all mental life. We are never out of culture; for the most part we take it for granted, much as a fish takes water. Intellectual culture – philosophy, art, science and literature – is only one aspect of culture. More immediate are the everyday cultures of the workplace, of organizations, of public service, education, democratic politics and formal administration; the culture of intimacy, of family life and interpersonal relations; newspapers, magazines, and all the varieties of *leisure* culture – mass entertainment, radio, television, film, records, music and theatre.

Most people do not think of everyday culture – the culture of business life or of pop music – as toxic, even less as belonging to the same mind-set that led to the worst horrors of the twentieth century. The apocalyptic tone of Adorno's philosophy of culture is directed to persuading his readers of the pathology of modern culture and of the fate he believes awaits those who do not resist the cultural hegemony of a late capitalist society, who allow themselves to be assimilated, to become "apologists" for a barbarous world. His critique of culture is oriented, not simply to understanding culture, nor restoring its remnants to past glories but, uniquely, to renewing Culture[1] as a living process, one that refuses closure, remaining ever conscious of its difference from the world. While philosophy, art, morality, ideas, can never be reconciled to the world as it is, the aspiration to achieve reconciliation grounds moral praxis.

Adorno's ideas evolve, in essay form, through a complex and allusive interplay among many discourses. A labyrinth of originating texts is seamlessly woven into the fabric of his writing. His knowledge of philosophy, music, art and literature, both modern and classical, was vast and detailed. He was not just an erudite scholar, but an accomplished musician – a pianist and a composer, a pupil of Alban Berg and a member of the Schönberg circle. His critique of modern popular culture and mass entertainment took in astrology, variety theatre, *film noir*, jazz, radio and television. He associated personally with many important contributors to twentieth-century culture, both serious and popular.

In Adorno's philosophy, all culture is formed in the crucible of material economic relations (*P*: 23ff). This was as true of the Culture of the enlightenment, which was integral to the formation of the capitalist society that emerged from feudalism, as it was of the mass culture produced by the culture industries in the twentieth century. Both can be understood only in relation to society. Culture, in Adorno's utopian sense of enlightenment Culture, is formed in the effort to serve the spiritual element in life, to bring the subject, through expression, to self-understanding. But the achievement of integrity, of harmony and reconciliation in ideas or works of art, also comprises the sense of Culture's utopian difference from, and incompatibility with, an antagonistic world. The modern world is antagonistic to the extent that it is constituted as *objective* life from which the spiritual element is expunged. A living Culture that expresses the subjective spirit must, necessarily, apprehend its difference from an object world that lacks it. Conversely, a culture that identifies completely with that world lacks subjective spirit and cannot sustain the spiritual element in life.

Culture, on Adorno's view, must resist or suspend its own *objecthood* if it is to serve the spiritual needs of the subject. It must avoid closing with its objects. A living Culture is historical. To remain so, it must critically interrogate its continually changing relationship to its objects. To benefit the living subject, Culture must constitute itself as a coded set of possibilities for forming experience anew under changed and changing social conditions. That is, it must avoid the temptation to provide tablets of truth received from on high. It must, instead, provide *forms* that give its recipients something to *work* with; forms that engage them in the process of striking meaning anew from them. Works of art and Culture undergo change; they experience an outer history as they are engaged by new recipients under new historical conditions. Adorno refused to allow thought to rest upon its objects; he made the non-identity of concept and thing – of individual and society, part and whole, Culture and world – an object of critical attention (*AT*: 176).

The tragedy of culture

Intellectual culture – art, science, morality, etc. – can be seen from two distinct perspectives. In one, cultural forms express the life-process of the subject; works of art and science are oriented to the self-understanding of the subject (individual and collective), its spiritual development; they are intrinsically meaningful, valued as ends in themselves. In the second perspective, culture is instrumental; it is practically oriented, as *means*, to the attainment of worldly ends (both subjective and objective). The relationship between these two perspectives, one inward and the other outward, figures in different ways in the founding discourses of sociology.

A figure of key importance in the development of the philosophy of culture was Georg Simmel;[2] he had an unmistakable influence on scholars of Adorno's generation such as Georg Lukács and Adorno's close friend and early tutor, Siegfried Kracauer.[3] Jürgen Habermas has argued that social theories which originated in Max Weber and are constituted as diagnoses of the time (including Adorno and Horkheimer's) all draw from Simmel's philosophy of culture.[4] For Simmel, Culture is formed in the subject's self-objectification through expression (the soul objectified in its forms). Bringing together elements of its life-process as whole and expressing that process outwardly (the objectification of spirit), the subject, reflected in the myriad aspects of the world, returns to itself, enriched in self-understanding.

The "tragedy of culture", for Simmel, lies in the fact that the modern subject no longer directs this process. Once formed, objective culture (objectified spirit) yields to the demands of material life and breaks away from the subjects who created it. It no longer serves an individual's spiritual needs once it is identified with a material world that has ceased to recognize the spiritual. Science, technology, morality and so on come to form more or less closed material contexts that are opaque to subjective spirit. The growth of the money economy and of the division of labour has accelerated the growth of objective cultures, despiritualizing them at the same time: "Because of modern differentiation . . . the objective mind lacks this spirituality. This may be the ultimate reason for the present-day animosity of highly individualistic and sensitive people to the 'progress of culture'."[5]

In *The Philosophy of Money*, Simmel developed this point concerning the rapid increase in objective (material) culture. The (subjective) culture of the individual lags far behind the development of objective culture: our understanding of the most familiar things in daily use such as radios, the internal combustion engine, electricity and so forth lags behind the scientific and technical culture that produced them. Simmel argued, as Adorno would do, that an individual's spiritual needs are best served by observing a certain ascetic restraint in respect of objective culture. "Every day and from all sides, the wealth of objective culture increases, but the individual mind can enrich the forms and content of its own development only by distancing itself still further from that culture and developing its own at a much slower pace."[6]

Simmel draws conclusions about this process in respect of the development of modern societies. In a few lines he encapsulates the very essence of the thesis of *Dialectic of Enlightenment* developed by Adorno and Horkheimer some four decades later.

The preponderance of means over ends finds its apotheosis in the fact that the peripheral in life, the things that lie outside its basic essence, have become masters of its centre and even of ourselves. Although it is true to say that we control nature to the extent that we serve it, this is correct in the traditional sense only for the outer forms of life. If we consider the totality of life then the control of nature by technology is possible only at the price of being enslaved in it and by dispensing with spirituality as the central point of life. The illusions in this sphere are reflected quite clearly in the terminology that is used in it and in which *a mode of thinking, proud of its objectivity and freedom from myth, discloses the direct opposite of these features.*[7]

Culture and pseudo-culture

Adorno develops an argument similar to Simmel's, counterposing Culture to what he terms "pseudo-culture" (TPC). He uses the former term to refer to the great systems of thought and ideas associated with the European enlightenment, together with the art and music that developed with them. Enlightenment Culture was imbued with a consciousness of itself as serving the subject's spiritual needs, as being – in the Kantian sense – "purposefully purposeless". The role of Culture in the reproduction and development of material life was obscured by the idea, immanent in Culture, of Culture's own "autarchy". Adorno sets that autarchy, dialectically, against its opposite: modernity's adaptive, means-oriented culture which is directed solely to the mastery of the material world. Such a culture identifies itself with its objects, expunging everything within itself (subjective spirit) that is not instrumental and outwardly effective until individuals become objects to themselves, their lives as subjects virtually extinguished.

Adorno directed his critique at both aspects of culture. All culture is formed in response to material social life. But the division of mental and physical labour conceals this origin and allows those privileged by the division to think of Culture as autarchic. Adorno rejected claims that made Culture a self-contained and self-sufficient entity, existing for its own sake. The ideology of the autarchy of Culture was in any case dangerous, he argued. During the Nazi period, individuals who possessed the most refined tastes in art and music participated, willingly, in the torture of their fellow citizens, thus demonstrating the lie in all the claims of so-called high Culture to enrich the humanity of the subject. Moreover, when Culture claims to be self-contained and existing for itself, it becomes "cultural goods" and untrue.

On the other hand, pseudo-culture, oriented to adaptation, to fitting in, to assimilation by the collective machinery of the administered world, heralds the extinction of the individual and the very possibility of freedom; it capitulates to barbarism. Its growth erodes both the spirit and the Culture that sustains it. Industries centred on the production of culture for the masses have grown to such a degree that millions are inundated with cultural goods – disseminated via the mass media – that were inaccessible in times past. Adorno does not see this as a benefit but as a toxin. Mass culture is not a means of self-expression, of the self-development of the subject, but its antithesis; it appeals to the passive, regressive and self-indulgent in people. To participate, without resistance, in pseudo-culture is to extinguish one's life as a subject.

More than a collection of cultural goods, pseudo-culture is a dynamic process that grinds all culture in its mill. Even works of so-called high Culture are first stripped of everything that equips them to serve the development of spirit, and then assimilated to the rigid form of pseudo-culture. They become indistinguishable from cultural goods produced by the culture industry. As the older entrepreneurial capitalism in which individualism flourished gave way to the totally administered world of monopoly capitalism, so genuine Culture retreated before the advance of pseudo-culture. The vast proliferation of adaptive culture, information, advertising, mass entertainment and so on does not just displace genuine Culture; it degrades Culture, fuelling its own development, as pseudo-culture, by feeding upon it. The culture industry makes old art into its material. Even a Beethoven symphony, in the mill of the mass media, gets ground down into pseudo-culture, into a stream of neat tunes linked together by nothing very important (*EM*: 251–70). The works of great philosophers such as Spinoza are reduced to *digests* of their ideas, a few handy formulas. The individual cannot use these, actively, to engage with Spinoza's ideas, because they are torn from the entire edifice of philosophical discourse which alone makes them intelligible for those who actively develop their understanding through thinking (TPC: 31).

A dynamic process of understanding demands something like a composed reading in which one "forms" one's idea of the whole structure of Spinoza's system from a detailed grasp of its elements and their relations. These elements constitute a force-field of energies that is open to development both in respect of its internal relations and, externally, in relations with other systems of ideas. The state of part–whole relations that Adorno viewed as healthy, as indicating moral integrity, is one in which the whole structure develops out of interactions among its elements. Open and responsive to each other, these elements change and are changed by each other; in turn, the totality or whole that emerges from them remains open and responsive to them. Thus, while Adorno's model of moral responsibility and freedom rests upon the free and spontaneous initiative of the elements or parts of a system – whether elements in a philosophical system, musical *motifs* in a sonata, or individuals in a social system – it rests equally upon the responsiveness of these parts or elements to each other, their mutual mediation, and their reflexive relationship with the emergent whole that they are in the process of forming.

This treatment of part–part and part–whole relations derived as much from Adorno's musical background – his familiarity with Heinrich Schenker's musicology[8] – as from his reading of Emile Durkheim's sociology. In his analysis of the formation of both aesthetic and social systems, Adorno is even more explicit than Durkheim about structuration as moral work and as an index of truth-value.[9] A basic formulation of part–part and part–whole relations, a set of fundamental conditions, recurs in all his discussions of form and structure, from social formation to the musical formation of the sonata or rondo. The totality, as living Culture, exists only in its emergent formation from the details – from the elements and relations that constitute it. In a dynamic process of understanding, the subject engages with the material, discovering new possibilities in the system of ideas. Thus Spinoza's philosophy is not closed, hermetically sealed against change and development; it participates, through reception, in an outer history and is changed. No such dynamic understanding is possible when the whole is torn from the details and assumes the rigid form of a summary list.

What ceases to develop in time has become pseudo-culture. Contributing nothing to it, its elements merely decorate it. Culture thus degrades with the growth of cultural goods. Only Culture that resists closure and remains critically open can escape the fate of becoming "cultural goods". For the individual whose knowledge of the world comes in the form of digests, of pseudo-culture, there is no real understanding, only an authoritarian submission to assertions that are not truly understood. Education cannot provide the solution to the degrading of Culture; education is itself degrading along with Culture, of which it is a part. Adorno insists, nevertheless, that those who resist assimilation by the administered world hold on to Culture (as dynamic understanding) after society has deprived it of its foundation: "For the only way spirit can possibly survive is through critical reflection on pseudo-culture, for which Culture is essential" (TPC: 33, tr. mod.).

The culture of administration

Modern societies have seen the development of social organizations that approximate to rational–technical machineries for the exploitation of material and natural resources. Weber's analysis of means–end rationality, disenchantment and depersonalization, informs Adorno's critique of culture generally, and *Dialectic of*

Enlightenment in particular. The image of a total system for the mastery of material nature, and the mutilation of the human spirit involved in this process, can be projected from Weber's model of formal administration, of *bureaucracy*.

Fundamental to bureaucracy as a system of offices is the individual's separation from the office; organizational relations in Weber's *ideal-type* of bureaucracy are formal, depersonalized and instrumental. Recruitment by public examinations, the hierarchical principle in assigning a compass of responsibility to each office, the proliferation of records and of systems for managing them, together tend to objectify the office-holder who becomes a functionary – not a subject but an object of the collective machinery of administration. The relentless pursuit of mastery of material resources, through rational technical means–end efficiency, progressively extinguishes all elements of sensuous and non-rational life, all spiritual life that does not attach itself like a limpet to the world to be mastered.

While Marx argued that the labourer is expropriated from the means of production, Weber argued that economic expropriation in modern society is only one type. The soldier is expropriated from the means of making war and the bureaucrat is expropriated from the means of administration. The expropriation of the subject is a feature of the ubiquitous march of rationality.[10] What was taken from the subject as agent was given to the organization as a collective machinery. Law, morality and religion – indeed all cultural spheres – were no less subject to the progressive march of rationality and, with it, to the "disenchantment" of the world.

From this point of view, an economic revolution that abolished private ownership would enslave the world further rather than liberating it because the technical demands of economic management under collective ownership would require an intensification of rational–technical authority, of bureaucracy. (Recent history would appear to vindicate Weber on this point.) In Weber's march of rationality, expropriation threatens to become total, to expropriate spirit from the world on every level. On a literary plane, Franz Kafka conveyed, with chilling effect, in *The Castle* and *The Trial*, the nightmare of a legal–rational existence bereft of spiritual life, of a subjectivity that filled out empty forms as its historical core.

In the first chapter of *Dialectic of Enlightenment*, Adorno and Horkheimer fixed upon the Culture of enlightenment associated with the development of bourgeois societies. Their critique is directed against the claim of enlightenment Culture to have dispelled the ignorance and darkness of myth by enthroning science and reason in its place. The authors deny the implicit theory of progress: that culture, and with it society, moves from barbarity and ignorance towards the individual's freedom and enlightenment. Science indeed succeeds in displacing myth but science and reason themselves bring about a society from which subjective spirit is driven to the margins. A rational–technical society proves its command over nature and the object world by extinguishing everything within itself that is not identified with the object world and its mastery. Society as the would-be master of nature does not liberate but enslave itself; men and women become objects to themselves in a spiritually degraded world.

Although Adorno and Horkheimer's treatment of the Culture of enlightenment clearly accords with Weber's thesis concerning the role of rationality in the disenchantment of the modern world, they treat the prehistory of the modern world differently. Weber contrasted the characteristics of "legal–rational" society with those of "traditional" societies. He did not subscribe to a theory of progress any more than did Adorno but, unlike Adorno, he did not subscribe to a theory of development either. Adorno and Horkheimer make the principle of the technical mastery of nature into a unilinear developmental principle that takes society from its beginnings to the twentieth century. In *Negative Dialectics*, Adorno put this most clearly:

> Universal history must be construed and denied. After the catastrophes that have happened, and in view of the catastrophes to come, it would be cynical to say that a plan for a better world is manifested in history and unites it. Not to be defined for that reason, however, is the unity that cements the discontinuous chaotically splintered moments and phases of history – the unity of the control of nature, progressing to rule over men, and finally to that over men's inner nature. *No universal history leads from savagery to humanitarianism, but there is one leading from the slingshot to the megaton bomb* . . . Under the all-subjugating identity principle, whatever does not enter into identity, whatever eludes rational planning in the realm of means, turns into frightening retribution for the calamity which identity brought on the nonidentical.
>
> (*ND*: 320, emphasis added)

From the beginning, Adorno and Horkheimer argue, culture is oriented to the mastery of nature through the social organism's disciplining of itself. An adaptively formed culture is rigidly bound to its material context. The myths of earlier times had this rigid and unchanging character. Science, which claimed to enlighten the world through overcoming myth (which it treated as false idea) is, in reality, the successor myth. It is a more complete or perfect instrument for the mastery of nature and with it the mastery of society. Myth and enlightenment are shown not to be radically opposed. Both have the same purpose and the same structure as objective spirit. Both subscribe to the tyranny of means which consists in control over the labour of others, whether in the culture of rational administration in the modern world, or in the culture of class domination on board Ulysses' vessel in his encounter with the Sirens.[11]

Commodity fetishism

Perhaps the best-known and most accessible chapter in *Dialectic of Enlightenment* is "The Culture Industry", where Adorno and Horkheimer mount a sustained critique of popular culture in all its varieties. Marx's contribution is clearest here. For Marx, capitalism is a system of commodity production. In simple or *traditional* societies, production is oriented to fulfilling the known local needs of people pursuing a traditional way of life. It is possible to imagine that the life-process of the individual and the community (political, religious and aesthetic, as well as economic) is reflected in the society's material culture, is integral to the life-process of the community (political, religious and aesthetic, as well as economic), filling it out as its spiritual core. Commodities, however, are goods made purely for sale in a mass market. They are (economic) goods devoid of a spiritual core.

Marx claimed that those who labour to produce commodities are alienated from the products of their labour; commodities are not *their* products and do not express their life-process as individuals or members of communities. Workers are alienated too from the process of production: they work under conditions determined by the capitalist system that employs them. Finally, they are alienated from each other in a production process that desociates them as it deskills them.[12] In Taylorism–Fordism, for example, as the extreme form of the microdivision of labour, this desociation is taken to the limit and workers engage in mindless repetitive activity; coordination of action no longer requires social interaction and cooperation; all is synchronized by the machinery of the production line.[13]

The commodity itself becomes a fetish-object. Because the commodity is not the outcome of *expression*, of subjective spirit, it appears to consciousness in a form that elides the process of its production, so that it seems not to be the outcome of real relations among human beings but to belong to an autochthonous world of things. Anything detached from living history, from becoming, presents itself to the mind as *sui generis*, as self-contained and complete; it is a fetish-object. The disparity in power between the alienated subject and the commodified world engenders dependence and ego-weakness; the latter manifests, in the commodity, as the power of its appeal, of its promise to gratify. The realm of the commodity is a "phantasmagoria".[14]

Adorno treats the commodity as the form of all objective spirit that has detached itself from subjective spirit. Emptied of history, the commodity does not participate in living relationships. With the expansion of a monolithic global economy, the commodity form becomes insatiable, colonizing every domain of social life, extinguishing the remnants of subjective spirit wherever it finds them. The individual's relationship to the commodity becomes one of authoritarian submission as it does for all relations that are no longer historical.

Heavens above

Adorno is a master of conceptual modulation. He opens up possibilities in concepts such as that of the commodity, developing them to the point where they shade into other concepts drawn from different theoretical contexts. Thus the alienated forms of life represented by the commodity and bureaucracy also characterize the world of compulsive neuroses and paranoid delusion, of authoritarianism, the irrational and totalitarian terror. In the modern world, with its vast depersonalized administrative structures and its endless production of commodities, the disparity in power between the individual and society is immense.

In "The Stars Down to Earth", Adorno performed an impressive deconstruction of the daily horoscope "Astrological Forecasts" by Carroll Righter in the *Los Angeles Times* (November 1952–February 1953). He aimed to expose the social pathology that sustains indulgence in this particular form of the irrational. The astrology column purports to represent authority, the authority of the stars. But this authority simply projects the dependence and powerlessness experienced by individuals in the face of the real collective forces in society that control their daily lives. The stars are assumed to influence and shape events in daily life, and to provide individuals with opportunities they can take advantage of provided only that they act appropriately and in a timely fashion. The column's endorsement of the relentless pressure to succeed in life equates success with activity that is narrowly focused on the personal and particularistic interests of the individual. Rather than associating individuality with a self-possessed potency or the possession of intrinsic powers, the column promotes a sense of individuality as consisting in personal qualities such as "magnetism" and "charm". It stresses the capacity to fit in, to hold one's own in a group setting, to conform.

The stars appear to be in complete agreement with established ways of life and the habits and the institutions of the age. The effect of the column is to reproduce in its readers precisely that state of mind which the status quo induces in them daily: it shares this with all pseudo-culture. The culture industry's products are not harmless: all serve to secure the individual's adaptation to life in a spiritually degraded world. In Adorno's analyses, the reader can experience the link between the most ordinary aspects of everyday consciousness and the darkest compulsions of the irrational in social life:

> In astrology, as in compulsive neurosis, one has to keep very strictly to some rule, command or advice, without ever being able to say why. It is just this blindness of obedience which appears to be fused with the overwhelming and frightening power of the command. Inasmuch as the stars are viewed in astrology as an intricate system of do's and don'ts, this system seems to be a projection of a compulsive system itself.[15]

Popular music

Popular music in general, and jazz in particular, are instances of what Adorno calls cultural commodities, not simply because they are made by the culture industries – major recording companies, film studios, broadcasting media – but because they are manufactured, like all commodities, solely to realize their exchange value on the market. Songs are written to make money, to capture the attention of a mass audience and to sell many records. Song writers are not creative individuals who do what they do out of a genuine desire to express themselves. Nor is the culture industry simply the technical means for connecting them with an appreciative public. Successful artists, including the most talented, belong to the culture industry long before it ever agrees to display their wares (*DE*, C: 122; J: 96). Economic relations of commodity production are not incidental but enter into every aspect of the creative process, stamping its products with the characteristics of all commodities. Manufacture for the mass market demands nothing less.

Music is part of an *effect culture*. Knowing in advance what will "appeal" to an audience, what will "turn it on", enables the cultural entrepreneur to achieve a degree of market prediction that is essential for the kind of investment that has to be made. Commodities must be reliable stimuli, sufficiently similar to those that have, in the past, triggered the appropriate response in the record-buying or film-going public. The task is made relatively easy because the repetitive demands of meaningless work in modern society have numbed the masses, causing them to seek an escape both from boredom and effort. They respond to whatever is most familiar; and in the endlessly repetitious forms of commodified music, they experience an after-image of the production process itself (*DE*, C: 137; J: 109).

The principal characteristic of all pseudo-culture, all products of the culture industry, is "standardization". Each new song must be like all the others (Adorno discusses such things as the 32-bar song form, the limitation of all musical intervals to one octave and one note, the positioning of elements in relation to the bridge, and so forth) to elicit the recognition necessary to connect with an audience. The standardized commodity is a closed form. Its power to elicit a response (an effect) depends upon this closure. It cannot be a vehicle for expression because, to serve in this way, culture must be open; it must reflect the subject's life-process, embodying its (historical) development in its internal relations and, through reception, in its external relations.

Expressive culture is *historical*; pseudo-culture is not. Commodities come under the law of repetition. They offer more of the same. The proliferation of cultural goods and their apparent variety only masks the fact that what you get is essentially the same song, the same TV soap. Variations and apparent novelty and variety are superficial; Adorno describes them as instances of *pseudo-individualization*. Standardization, in popular music, means that the culture industry does the listener's listening for her, in advance. If the songs were identical, however, she would soon tire of them. Pseudo-individualization makes each song look as if it was new by marrying its standardized form to a distinctive feature, a catchy rhythm, melodic phrase, etc. (*EM*: 437–69).

Serious music

Music was central to Adorno's life and work. In his many publications devoted to music, structural considerations are paramount. At the very centre of European art music, in Adorno's writings, was Beethoven. The sonata as a musical form was perfected in Beethoven's middle period, when his major symphonies were composed. These can be thought of as large-scale sonatas. A symphony, such as Beethoven's Fifth, consists in a few fundamental elements or *motifs* which are repeated and varied in different ways: for example rhythmically, harmonically, through juxtaposition, inversion, modulation, melodic decoration, timbral changes and so forth. The composition as a whole is thus *thematically developed* through the repetition and variation of these *motifs* (AT: 100–101). In Adorno's analysis, this developmental process appears to proceed spontaneously and freely as though determined immanently from below (rather than transcendentally from above); that is, the composition appears to be the outcome of the free movement of the elements themselves.

Because the "thematic particles" – the *motifs* – of a Beethoven symphony are identical with their development, they become *historical* figures. In both the sonata form and the novel, the "subject" is marked by its historicity. We might say that, at any moment of existence, the "subject" of the sonata or the narrative is what it is by virtue of its "historicity"; by virtue, that is, of possessing a development, an unfolding biography or history in and through which its identity is conserved. Moreover, this development appears to proceed organically out of the subject's relations and encounters in the "text" and yet to lead, with a certain inevitability, to the fulfilment of its development as its *project*. Beethoven's development of the sonata allegro in his middle-period compositions reaches the pinnacle of the bourgeois effort to reconcile individual freedom and collective constraint in the medium of art.

The most obvious embodiment of this principle of developing variation occurs in the development and recapitulation of the sonata allegro, the structure Adorno considers essentially synonymous with Beethoven's second-period style. Development is the process through which the musical subject demonstrates its self-generated powers as it "goes out", in dialectical terms, from itself into the generalizing world of Other or object, through which it demonstrates, in other words, its freedom in objective reality. The emphatic reassertion of self in Beethoven's recapitulation is equally important. Through the recapitulation, the subject seems not only to bring together within

itself, but ac
dynamic deve
(unchangeable
of reality.[16]

Adorno's wr
Berg, Webern,
papers he wrot
the depth of th
From his early
later essays,[17] A
the alienated coi
against compose
lack of fulfilmen
alienation, throi
gether and retrea
tifying this appro
chiefly Igor Stravi
varieties of pher
respond to the c

what belonged to history. In many of Sc
turned its back on history, something
sky's music and jazz.

There were other
fiercely critical o
better know
dystopias
Horkh
con

domain of pure si ...... in both music and phenomenology, what was hypostatized as pure subjectivity or as pure music was, Adorno argued, empty. Its structural correlates were to be found in authoritarian submission and fascism as well as in all forms of pseudo-culture. Such music became *effect* music, purged of history and expression; a variant of the type produced by the culture industry.

Adorno was committed to the continuing relationship between subject and world – albeit a relationship of negative identity – and to the longing for reconciliation between them (*ND*: 149). For that to happen music must be expressive and dynamic; it must overcome alienation, not by seeking to abolish it through detaching subject from object, but through perfecting the expression of music's alienation on its outside. Schönberg, Berg and the composers of the second Viennese school of composition served as his models here. Even in the case of these composers, however, Adorno's approval was not total. He remained committed to Schönberg's revolution in atonal music around 1910 because it exemplified a music of suffering that was fully engaged with history, but he was ambivalent about Schönberg's later development of twelve-tone music, even though he himself used it in compositions. The apparently closed nature of the invariant ordering of twelve tones (the row) that was the basic building block of each composition appeared to hand to mathematics

önberg's followers, music
it shared with both Stravin-

er cultural critics

riters, contemporaries of Adorno, who were
modern culture and whose ideas, at the time, were
than his. These included the authors of literary
uch as *Brave New World* and *1984*. When Adorno and
mer had completed *Dialectic of Enlightenment*, they
ulted their friend, Leo Löwenthal, as to whom they might
pproach to help them publish the book. His witty reply, "Huxley,
as far as I know, does not read German, and Joyce is dead",[19]
acknowledged the discernible echoes in their work, both of *Brave
New World* and of the problematic language of *Finnegan's Wake*.
Prisms includes an essay on Kafka, whose books *The Castle* and *The
Trial* can also be seen as dystopias, and an essay on Huxley with a
very full critical discussion of *Brave New World*.

Other critics deplored the brash commercialized mass culture of
the modern world. Peter Hohendahl has drawn attention to the
American liberals of the 1940s and 1950s who, following the New
Deal, switched focus from the political-economic front to the critique
of modern culture, for example, Daniel Boorstin, Mary McCarthy,
David Riesman and others.[20] The apocalyptic dread of mass culture
took root in the academy, too. In England, the literary critic, F. R.
Leavis, taking his lead from Matthew Arnold's *Culture and Anarchy*,
where culture is described as "the best that has been known and
thought in the world",[21] wrote of the "dark prospects" for culture
which had now become incompatible with any concept of civilization
in the modern world.[22]

A third source for the critique of mass culture was the writing of
Clement Greenberg, arguably the most important American art critic
of the twentieth century. Greenberg had published his famous paper,
"Avant-Garde and Kitsch" in the *Partisan Review* in 1938,[23] some
nine years before the publication of *Dialectic of Enlightenment*. In
it, he anticipated many arguments about popular culture that
appeared later in Adorno and Horkheimer's chapter on the culture
industry. Like Adorno, Greenberg perceived that mass culture, which
used as its material the remnants of traditional art, posed a threat to
the autonomy and independence of the serious artist and thus the

possibility of establishing a critical relation to modern society. Like Adorno, he believed that critical culture was in danger of being sublated in mass cultural kitsch. Of the three sources of criticism mentioned, Greenberg's analysis in his major papers on art resonates in important respects with Adorno's own critique.

It is misleading to identify Adorno's critique of culture with cultural criticism that adopts apparently similar conclusions. Adorno himself was especially critical of those who treat culture as a value, who deplore the decline of serious Culture and its displacement by the vulgarities of mass culture; this was a type of criticism that issued in nostalgia for things past. For Adorno, criticism that tacitly accepts the world as it is, that complains of it but embodies no real resistance to it, is actually complicit in reproducing the existing state of affairs (P: 22–3).

The "cultural critic" imagines himself to be superior to the world he criticizes whereas in reality he is mediated to the very core by the object of his criticism, by the culture he criticizes. Because he does not really resist the reproduction of the status quo, even at the level of ideas, he helps to reinforce it: "As long as even the least part of the mind remains engaged in the reproduction of life, it is its sworn bondsman" (P: 26). Many so-called cultural critics, Adorno argued, are simply *apologists* for what they purport to criticize; their criticism reflects only the privilege granted by the separation of mental from manual labour. The superiority displayed in their writings is that of a ruling class which imagines itself to be in possession of higher spiritual values, to own the Culture that culture lacks. What is important in Adorno's philosophy of culture are not his specific conclusions but the continuous intense theoretical dynamic in and through which those conclusions, in response to continuously changing conditions, take on (new) meaning, and are themselves changed.

Notes

1. The word "culture" is capitalized where it refers to enlightenment Culture in Adorno's utopian sense of a culture that serves the spiritual needs of the subject. In every other sense of the word, as in "culture industry", "pseudo-culture", etc., the word "culture" appears in lower case.
2. See Georg Simmel, *Simmel on Culture: Selected Writings* (1997).
3. See Siegfried Kracauer, "Georg Simmel", *The Mass Ornament: Weimar Essays* (1995).
4. Jürgen Habermas, "Georg Simmel on Philosophy and Culture: Postscript to a Collection of Essays", *Critical Inquiry* 22(3) (Spring 1996), 403–14.

5. Georg Simmel, *The Philosophy of Money* (1990), 466–7.
6. *Ibid.*, 449.
7. *Ibid.*, 482, emphasis added.
8. See Robert Snarrenberg, *Schenker's Interpretive Practice* (1997).
9. See Emile Durkheim, *The Elementary Forms of the Religious Life: A Study in Religious Sociology* (1976).
10. For Weber's views on bureaucracy and the expropriation of the subject, see *From Max Weber: Essays in Sociology* (1948), 196–240.
11. For further discussion of the relationship between myth and enlightenment, see Alison Stone's chapter in this volume (Chapter 3).
12. Karl Marx, *The Economic and Philosophic Manuscripts of 1844* (1964), 106–16.
13. See Frederick Taylor, *Scientific Management* (1947).
14. Marx, *Capital: A Critique of Political Economy*, vol. 1 (1976), 165–8.
15. Adorno, *The Stars Down to Earth and Other Essays on the Irrational in Culture* (1994), 64.
16. Rose Subotnik, "Adorno's Diagnosis of Beethoven's Late Style: Early Symptoms of a Fatal Condition", *Journal of the American Musicological Society* 29(2) (1976), 249.
17. See, for example, Adorno's *Quasi Una Fantasia: Essays on Modern Music* (1992).
18. Adorno, *Philosophy of New Music* (2006), 107f.
19. Max Horkheimer, *Gesammelte Schriften* 17 (1996), 571. Cited in James Schmidt, "Language, Mythology, and Enlightenment: Historical Notes on Horkheimer's and Adorno's *Dialectic of Enlightenment*", *Social Research* 65(4) (Winter 1998), 808.
20. Peter Uwe Hohendahl, *Prismatic Thought: Theodor W. Adorno* (1995), 28f.
21. Matthew Arnold, *Culture and Anarchy, and Other Writings* (1993), 79f.
22. See F. R. Leavis, *Mass Civilisation and Minority Culture* (1930).
23. Clement Greenberg, "Avant-Garde and Kitsch", *Art in Theory: 1900–1990* (1992).

ELEVEN

Philosophy of history

Brian O'Connor

Introduction

The concept of history developed in a great array of directions during the period of modern German philosophy. Ranging from macrostructural analyses of the evolution of civilizations to descriptions of the temporal social experience of the individual, history was essentially a critical concept, one that sought to expose the allegedly naive idea of the fixed properties of culture and of the individuals who might live within them. Adorno belongs to this tradition of critical historical philosophy. His philosophy of history is strongly marked by various Hegelian, Marxian, Nietzschean and hermeneutical ideas.

A preoccupation with the idea of history is evident from the very beginnings of Adorno's career. From his *Habilitationsschrift* (1931) right up to *Aesthetic Theory* (incomplete at the time of his death in 1969), the issue is never far from central. To deal comprehensively with the range of influences and the multiplicity of applications of the concept of history in Adorno's work would be coextensive with a critical analysis of his *oeuvre*. This chapter will restrict itself to Adorno's engagements with what might be specifically regarded as "theories of history". The topics to be examined are Adorno's critique of (1) the idea of universal history and (2) progress; (3) his dialectical reading of the idea of natural history; and (4) his assessment of role of the totality in the production of history.

Universal history

The German idealist philosophies of history were essentially philosophies of progress. These theories rested heavily on the hypothesis of the existence of some collective phenomenon – the human species, civilization, or the human spirit – that could be interpreted as undergoing improvement across time. This process of improvement could be explained through "universal history", a narrative that traverses and somehow unites all historical epochs. The language of maturity, of completion, of realization is central to this narrative.

The idealist theory of history might be quickly rejected on the basis of its naive optimism and its metaphysical assumptions. Adorno recognizes the fundamental difficulties of the theory of universal history. Yet it is through critical engagement with this theory that Adorno achieves a distinctive articulation of the concepts of history and progress. As he programmatically announces: "[I]f you wish to say anything at all about the theory of history in general, you must enter into a discussion of the construction of universal history" (*HF*: 81).

It is important to be aware that Adorno's conception of the challenge of universal history takes different forms in the course of his career. Aspects of the position set out in the 1930s were sometimes subsequently reshaped by a philosophically expressed sense of crisis caused by the historical experience of the Holocaust. Before the war, Adorno's approach to the concept of history might be construed as a radical hermeneutics, one that set out to demonstrate the failure of the philosophical pretension to have achieved a totalistic grasp of the world. In a 1931 lecture Adorno states: "Whoever chooses philosophy as a profession today must first reject the illusion that earlier philosophical enterprises began with: that the power of thought is sufficient to grasp the totality of the real."[1]

The position that begins to emerge from *Dialectic of Enlightenment* onwards encompasses this view, but is not quite the same. It might be characterized as the effort to explore the destructive evolution of modernity with particular attention to the dynamics that reduce the possibilities of experience, a reduction that facilitated the perpetration of the Holocaust. Adorno and Horkheimer write: "we had set ourselves nothing less than the discovery of why mankind, instead of entering into a truly human condition, is sinking into a new kind of barbarism" (*DE*, C: xi; J: xiv). Positions developed before and after the war overlap at important points, however, leading to some tensions within Adorno's theory of history that become particularly evident in his critique of the idea of universal history. The impact of this tension will become clear once Adorno's fundamental commitments have been clarified.

At first sight Adorno's position will seem straightforwardly declinist. Declinism supposes a prior, satisfactory state of affairs which has been eroded by a clearly identifiable, irrevocable and inevitable historical process. Adorno is ostensibly committed to such a view when, in *Negative Dialectics*, he writes: "No universal history leads from savagery to humanitarianism, but there is one leading from the slingshot to the megaton bomb" (*ND*: 320). This is one of Adorno's most quoted passages, but it requires cautious interpretation as by itself it appears to propose a one-dimensional trajectory of destruction in bald opposition to the narratives of progress embodied by the idealist notion of universal history.

Although Adorno engages considerably with Kant's theory of history, he gives greatest attention to Hegel's version of the notion of universal history.[2] The problems of Hegel's philosophy of history are well known: individual freedom is subordinated to the unfolding of *Geist* (spirit); the horrifying episodes of history are justified as contributions to the maturation of *Geist*; *Geist* is one of modern philosophy's outstandingly gratuitous metaphysical theses. Hegel's theory, troubling though it may be, is nevertheless a powerful effort to ground the belief that there is something distinctive and superior about the period of modernity, a period for which all previous history has been somehow preparatory. Adorno sees Hegel's position as "seemingly absurd – masterfully absurd" (*HF*: 84). It is masterfully absurd in that it – like no other theory before or since – deals comprehensively with modernity's deepest assumption – the continuity of progress: universal history.

The very idea of universal history presupposes that time has a particular structure. Adorno, with Horkheimer, observes that the idea of universal history requires the foundation of a certain beginning – a point in the past – from which all subsequent events progressively follow. This is not simply a rational requirement of the theory, however. It is a thesis that enables authoritative claims about the shape of the present to be made: "Through the establishment of a unique past, the cycle takes on the character of inevitability . . . makes the new appear as the predetermined" (*DE*, C: 27; J: 21). The present is justified because it is inevitable; its inevitability is explained through its emergence from a certain point in the past.

Adorno's reaction to this thesis is not simply to turn it on its head. He asserts neither the discontinuity of historical facts nor the disconnectedness of historical events. As Simon Jarvis notes, Adorno "is not satisfied with presentation of history as sheer discontinuity, as though there were no connection whatsoever between different 'epochs' ".[3] The idea of history as essentially discontinuous, as an unstructured collection of disconnected events, is, in fact, a positivist view that Adorno dismisses on the grounds that it would encourage us to endorse "pure facticity as the only thing to be known and therefore to be accepted" (*ND*: 319–20). Again, Hegel's "masterfully absurd" system had brought the modernist notion of continuity to its fullest and most significant articulation. To reject it, as the positivist must, would be to reject without reflection a belief that has been part of modernity's self-understanding.

Nevertheless, the idea of the continuity of history, as expressed by universal history, cannot be endorsed since it cannot be articulated without doing violence to historical facts and thereby becoming a metaphysics detached from material reality. Adorno proposes to modify the thesis of continuity by placing it in dialectical tension with the notion of the discontinuity of history. Discontinuity is posited as a *feature* of history, not as an alternative theory of history. Discontinuity, as the basic condition of history, would preclude positivistically consciousness of the presence of patterns or forces of which historical actors are not always aware.

The notion of discontinuity tries to capture the idea that events and their actions are not intelligible simply as moments of time would be, that is, as transition points in the space between past and future. Events possess a significance – a structure – that is not made intelligible by reading them as either as the explication or development of earlier events, or as embryonic versions of later ones: "History is not an equation, an analytic judgment. To think of it this way is to exclude from the very outset the possibility of anything qualitatively different" (*P*: 66). Adorno insists that there are – contrary to all the universal narratives – qualitative differences across history. It is in the 1932 essay on "natural history" that Adorno sets out the framework within which his analysis is to take place: "history, as it lies before us, presents itself as thoroughly discontinuous, not only in that it contains disparate circumstances and facts, but also because it contains structural disparities" (INH: 266). These events are disruptive in that, we might say, they develop forms of life unique to themselves, not forms that are intelligible as incremental advances on their predecessors. This is the reality that prompts the hermeneutical task, or philosophy as interpretation.[4]

The example of democracy illuminates this difficulty. The Greeks are generally acknowledged as the progenitors of the institution of democracy. Yet their version is also recognized as being, not only different from that of today, but as containing elements that are anathema to our idea of democracy. In spite of that, the two versions are lined up at various points in a continuum and the incommensurabilities that are evident are glossed over as something quite incidental. It is precisely this kind of thinking that the idea of universal history embodies. Adorno rejects it in the name of the disparities that cannot be dismissed as incidental. He writes with his early essay in mind:

> The truth is that, while the traditional view inserts facts into the flow of time, they really possess a nucleus of time in themselves, they crystallize time in themselves. What we can legitimately call ideas is the nucleus of time within the individual crystallized phenomena, something that can only be decoded by interpretation. In accordance with this we might say that history is *discontinuous* in the sense that it represents life perennially disrupted. (*HF*: 91)

Adorno's substantiation of this idea of disruptive history is evident in his discussion of aesthetic phenomena. Art, he argues, is a constitutively historical phenomenon, not the material manifestation of atemporal aesthetic norms. Endorsing the Hegelian precept, he writes that the "vision of the possible death of art accords with the fact that art is a product of history" (*AT*: 3). This historical substance of art is embraced in authentic art: "authentic works are those that surrender themselves to the historical substance of their age without reservation" (*ibid*.: 182). In this way, however, they are disruptive phenomena in that they are "crystallized phenomena", nuclei of time. This is the point at issue in Adorno's claim that "history is not external to the work".[5] The intrinsic historicality of the work, however, renders aesthetic experience problematic if the experience is not contemporaneous with the production of the artwork: "Artworks may be all the more truly experienced the more their historical substance is that of the one who experiences it" (*ibid*.: 183).[6]

As mentioned, Adorno does not intend to replace the notion of universal history with that of discontinuity. He writes "discontinuity and universal history must be conceived together" (*ND*: 319). What emerges from this synthetic thought is the idea of history "perennially disrupted". The continuity of the historical process is explicable only as a series of disruptions. Adorno seems to mean this when he proposes that "[h]istory is the unity of continuity and discontinuity" (*ibid.*: 320).[7]

We must ask, though, what the unifying dimension could be. It cannot, after all, be adequate to say that what unifies history is that it has no unity. What Adorno in fact suggests is that "the unity that cements the discontinuous, chaotically splintered moments and phases of history" is "the unity of the control of nature, progressing to rule over men, and finally to that over men's inner nature" (*ND*: 320). In so far as this is Adorno's position, it is not unproblematic for the obvious reason that a narrative of the continuing control of nature is not discontinuous at all: periods of "crystallized time" (which we saw in Adorno's hermeneutic mood) turn out to be commensurable in so far as they share the dimension of domination. Ultimately Adorno's articulation of a dialectical structure of history, in which continuity and discontinuity are straining at each other, seems to favour a narrative that – in terms of the specifics of history at which it points – has a clear trajectory. Adorno's radical hermeneutics collides with a critical theory driven by the question of barbarism. The latter is pre-eminent, but this pre-eminence deprives Adorno of the space in which to position a unity of continuity and discontinuity. Although he is theoretically committed to the discontinuous dimensions – the "crystallized phenomena" – he assumes in practice the intelligibility of historical events through the perspective of the destruction of nature, and that reopens the possibility that he is engaged in a declinist universal history.

A possible defence might be garnered from one of Adorno's thoughts in *Minima Moralia*. There he writes:

> If Benjamin said that history had hitherto been written from the standpoint of the victor, and needed to be written from that of the vanquished, we might add that knowledge must indeed present the fatally rectilinear succession of victory and defeat, but should also address itself to those things which were not embraced by this dynamic, which fell by the wayside – what might be called the waste products and blind spots that have escaped the dialectic. (*MM*: 151)

This allusive passage refers to the continuity of domination ("the fatally rectilinear succession of victory and defeat") while also encompassing the sense of discontinuity ("the waste products and blind spots", the non-identical elements that cannot be encompassed within the grand narrative[8]). Also significant, perhaps, is Adorno's view of Otto Spengler's declinism. He dismisses its inevitabilist mechanisms of "plant-like growth and cultural decay" (*P*: 54) and criticizes Spengler's commitment to an ineluctable history of domination:

> His entire image of history is measured by the ideal of domination. His affinity for this ideal gives him profound insight whenever it is a question of the possibilities of domination and blinds him with hatred as soon as he is confronted by impulses which go beyond all previous history as the history of domination. (*Ibid.*: 61)

Within the history of domination – the continuous – there are moments that do not conform to the narrative, moments that in the end require the sort of historical interpretation informed by Adorno's hermeneutical background. Nevertheless the very status of the discontinuous – as that which is non-identical with the narrative of universal history – subordinates its fundamental meaning to that of continuity.

Progress

The claims of progress are criticized in Adorno's philosophy by means of the thesis of discontinuity. The disruptive phases of history deny modernity's narrative the possibility of its own continuing improvement. Importantly, though, critical theory must retain, in some form, the very idea of progress. Through its critique of society, critical theory understands itself to be contributing to a process of amelioration in which, for instance, reification might end. As a process the possibility of this critically induced progress cannot be explained by modifying the modernist teleology, that is, by disputing (against, say, some neo-Hegelian) the rightness of the present and pushing the *telos*, or goal of history, on to some further point in an indefinite future. Such a modification would be, in essence, an elongation of the universal history narrative. A new framework in which the concept of progress can be articulated needs to be developed.

Adorno's idea of what should be considered in the development of this framework is strongly coloured by the influence of Walter Benjamin. It is Benjamin who pushes Adorno into a deeper appreciation of what is entailed in conventional presuppositions about the nature of history, presuppositions that lend themselves to the progress thesis. Benjamin's thirteenth thesis on the philosophy of history states:

> Social Democratic theory, and even more its practice, has been formed by a conception of progress which did not adhere to reality but made dogmatic claims. Progress as pictured in the minds of Social Democrats was, first of all, the progress of mankind itself (and not just advances in men's ability and knowledge). Secondly, it was something boundless, in keeping with the infinite perfectibility of mankind. Thirdly, progress was regarded as irresistible, something that automatically pursued a straight or spiral course. Each of these predicates is controversial and open to criticism.[9]

Benjamin here furnishes Adorno with a basis for reflections on the location of progress or on the relationship of progress to time. For Adorno, the concept of progress confronts a dilemma: (a) progress cannot stand outside time, as something achieved only when history is somehow overcome;[10] yet (b) to articulate progress within history is to assume the progressive trajectory of universal history, a trajectory that sees progress as constantly transcending itself. As Adorno writes:

> If progress is equated with redemption as transcendental intervention per se, then it forfeits, along with the temporal dimension, its intelligible meaning and evaporates into historical theology. But if progress is mediated into history, then the idolization of history threatens and along with it . . . the absurdity that it is progress itself that inhibits progress.
>
> (CM: 147)

The very possibility of progress must be set within temporality, yet not within the narrative of universal history.[11] It requires a transformation of experience, not a messianic transformation of time.

Adorno's proposal for a way beyond this dilemma is what we might term a negativistic theory of progress. He states it in specific concrete terms: "whether humanity is capable of preventing catastrophe" (CM: 144). He comments: "I believe that you should start by taking progress to mean this very simple thing: that it would be better if people had no cause to fear: if there were no impending catastrophe on the horizon . . . For progress today really does mean simply the prevention and avoidance of total catastrophe" (*HF*: 143). This is the catastrophe brought about by allegedly progressive social integration achieved through the technologization of the lifeworld. The results of this integration are exemplified in the administered murder of the millions during the Holocaust: "Genocide is the absolute integration" (*ND*: 362). The question of the possibility of progress is set within history, yet it is not committed to a narrative of increasing improvement or progressions. It is negativistic in the sense that progress is intelligible only in so far as it is the prevention of catastrophe.

Adorno argues that a fundamental assumption needs to be abandoned if this alternative conception of progress is to be achieved. This is the assumption – as we saw above – identified by Benjamin: "Progress . . . was, first of all, the progress of mankind itself." This conventional assumption is, as Benjamin says, open to criticism, but it is Adorno who develops the criticism. He writes:

> no progress is to be assumed that would imply that humanity in general already existed and therefore could progress. Rather, progress would be the very establishment of humanity in the first place . . . [T]he concept of universal history cannot be saved; it is plausible only so long as one can believe in the illusion of an already existing humanity, coherent in itself and moving upward as a unity. (*CM*: 145)

Adorno contends here that the notion of progress has supposed a point from which progress can proceed. But we are not yet in some historical continuum in which we can say that such progress is plausible. It is this thought that gives rise to the negativistic idea that the process in which progress might take place has yet to begin (through avoidance of the threat generated by history). Progress is therefore not continuity, but a negation of the conditions of prior history: progress is "resistance to the perpetual danger of relapse" (*CM*: 160). On this basis, Adorno understands progress to contain the "aspect of redemption" (*ibid.*: 148), albeit in a non-theological sense for the reason described above.

It is in this way that the dilemma of progress is addressed. Progress is neither a detemporalizing act, since it is intelligible precisely as a response to historical experience; nor is it simply part of the historical continuum because it represents a disruption of that process. The way out of this dilemma requires that we break what Adorno terms the "magic spell" of progress, the belief of modernity that every new institution, for instance, is an incremental improvement on its predecessor (*CM*: 150). Catastrophe threatens for so long as we fail to realize that "the spell" assures us that progress will prevail. As Benjamin stated, we must criticize the idea that progress is "irresistible, something that automatically pursued a straight or spiral course". Such a view is the spell, which Adorno dialectically rejects in the very name of progress: "it could be said that progress occurs where it ends" (*ibid.*).

Natural history

Adorno's idea of natural history is a critical concept. It specifically questions the dualistic division of realms of human experience into the natural and historical. Adorno sets out to dissolve this dualism by showing that what is identified as natural bears historical dimensions, whilst what seems to be historical has natural foundations.

Adorno describes his critical approach as follows: "the attempt should be made to behold all nature, and whatever regards itself as nature, as history" (*HF*: 124). What this involves is an analysis of the concept of the natural, one that Adorno likens to "the concept of myth" (INH: 253). Mythic experience involves forces that both transcend human beings and cannot be altered by them. However, myths are, of course, products of human culture. The notion of the dissolution of the mythic – of the natural into the historical – is one of the fundamental tasks of the "consciousness-raising" programme of Adorno's critical theory. Typical of this programme is the following remark: "The mythic scientific respect of the peoples of the earth for the status quo, that they themselves unceasingly produce, itself finally becomes positive fact" (*DE*, C: 41; J: 33).

This is not a value-free account of how the social world evolves, of how the concept of nature can be shown to be produced by our social practices.[12] The historical processes in which our concepts of nature have been produced are those in which we have appropriated nature, and for Adorno these appropriations are destructive. The history of this process of appropriation begins with humanity's attempts to free itself from nature, "that mere state of nature from which it had estranged itself with so huge an effort" (*DE*, C: 31; J: 24). This is, in fact, the primal history of subjectivity, the history of the emergence of subjectivity. (This primal history has been heavily criticized for, among other things, its tendency to eternalize a particular version of subjectivity and its apparent over-reach.[13])

However, this emergence is a "two-sided process" that also takes the path of the domination of nature.[14] Gunter Rohrmoser puts it as follows: "Man cannot free himself from the natural state without overcoming nature and thereby mastering it."[15] Adorno describes this as a "reductio ad hominem",[16] a process of manipulation that unconsciously defines nature by the needs of human beings: "What men want to learn from nature is how to use it in order wholly to dominate it and other men" (*DE*, C: 4; J: 2),[17] What fails to be understood here is the degree to which we have appropriated nature. There is no consciousness of the fact that our concept of nature as something other than us is a product of our historical efforts to emerge from it. Instead we persist with the "mythic" image of nature as something that is simply there without history.

Adorno tries to show that just as nature has a history, history too has its relation to nature. This side of the dialectical conception of natural history criticizes the hypostatization of human history and human accomplishment. The Enlightenment philosophical claim – made most powerfully by Kant – of reason's achievements misconstrues reason as something above nature. Adorno counters that reason is, in fact, a piece of natural history. In this regard he discusses the idea of transcendental thought – that there are certain atemporal conditions of experience – and rereads them as a means by which the natural business of self-preservation is conducted:

> The definition of the transcendental as that which is necessary, a definition added to functionality and generality, expresses the principle of the self-preservation of the species. It provides a legal basis for abstraction, which we cannot do without, for abstraction is the medium of self-preserving reason.
>
> (*ND*: 179)

As the philosophical expression of a mode of self-preservation, reason must be traced back to a natural drive. As Deborah Cook writes, "the historical course of reason must be charted with reference to its relationship to the embodied subject and its drives".[18]

Adorno's dissolution of the dualism of nature and history applies with particular political intent to what, following Lukács, he calls second nature, "this world of things created by man, yet lost to him, the world of convention" (INH: 259–60). Adorno's work often tries to reveal the historical aspects in "the semblance of the natural" (*HF*: 121), most centrally the idea that capitalism represents a natural form of social organization is exposed as ideology. Indeed one might think of Adorno's *Ideologiekritik* as the critical investigation and exposure of "second nature". The narratives of universal history are also to be criticized as narratives of "second nature". Following the same thought, Adorno alleges that Hegel's concept of "world-spirit" "is the ideology of natural history" (*ND*: 365) in that it represents the process of domination as a dimension of the inevitable unfolding of world history. The philosophical dynamic which would ontologize realms of experience – render them beyond the reach of change and human history – is also an instance of the creation of this second nature. In this regard, Adorno instances the mathematical method of modern philosophy which "transforms logic by magic into a second nature and lends it the aura of ideal being" (*AE*: 65).[19]

In a number of discussions of the idea of natural history, Adorno gives his position greater sharpness through opposition to Heidegger, whose fundamental ontology provides an alternative account of the relationship between history and nature. Heidegger's idea of historical experience – which Adorno describes as an "unhistorical concept of history" (*ND*: 358) – fails to appreciate the entwinement of nature and history. This entwinement is a "painful antithesis" (*ibid.*: 359) in so far as it is a story marked by processes of domination. In his account of historicity – of the historical experience of human beings – Heidegger reduces history to a mode of human existence (INH: 256). This amounts to an ontologization of history in that it is a "historicity abstracted from historic existence" (*ND*: 358–9). In other words, it posits a capacity – a historical capacity – without realizing that historical experience is tied to the effort to emerge from the natural condition. Heidegger's notion of historicity emphasizes the "project" of *Dasein*, thereby missing the antagonistic relationship between history and nature.

Totality

History takes a particular direction in the dynamics of what Adorno describes as the "social totality". He holds that the social totality determines the individuals within it and increasingly brings all features of social life under these determinations. Because this relentless process of integration is incompatible with a critical consciousness, it threatens to lead us to catastrophe. At the same time, in a thinly hopeful possibility, only a collective subject would have the capacity to bring about resistance to the possibility of catastrophe.

Adorno's idea of totality is a complex critical reconstruction of Hegel's notion of *Geist*. In Hegel's account of progress, as discussed above, the agency of history – and therefore the repository and agent of its progress and continuity – is *Geist*. In his materialist reconstruction of Hegel, Adorno rereads the dynamic of *Geist* as the dynamic of the social totality: "The world spirit is; but it is not a spirit" (*ND*: 304).[20] He offers criticisms that try to show that the world spirit is, rather, a hypostasized historical–social process in which individual agency becomes subsumed in a self-reproducing totality. An understanding of this integrationist dynamic forms a key part of Adorno's philosophy of history.

Adorno's thesis is that society is a totality – that is, a phenomenon over and above a collection of discrete facts about individuals and institutions – because its cohesiveness is generated by a particular system of economic activity. This system, according to Adorno, comes ever more to determine all phenomena that appear within society. He writes: "What really makes society a social entity, what constitutes it both conceptually and in reality, is the relationship of exchange which binds together virtually all the people participating in this kind of society" (*IS*: 31). This binding is not, as the naive view might see it, the necessity of commerce, one that in its present form innocently involves fiscal exchange. Rather, the very activity of fiscal exchange determines our fundamental sense of our social reality. It gives expression to and consolidates a principle of modern rationality, the principle of equivalence. In this context equivalence means that any given phenomenon – an object, a product, a process – may be made relative to any other phenomenon by means of their supposed common translatability into fiscal value. As Adorno puts it: "Bourgeois society is ruled by equivalence. It makes the dissimilar comparable by reducing it to abstract quantities" (*ND*: 7).

The rationality required for the effective operation of exchange is the prevailing social rationality. For Adorno, the logic of exchange – a fundamental instrument of capitalism – informs the very processes of socialization. Indeed, he claims that "the exchange process" is "the underlying social fact through which socialization first comes about" (*IS*: 31). Set against this background, the idea that society is simply the sum total of the individuals who live within it is oblivious to the fact that the consciousnesses of individuals are shaped by forces in some way external to them, by "the totality which they form" (*S*: 145). This totality is ultimately a coercive historical process in which individuality is integrated to the requirements of the totality. And the prevalence of the exchange system is the ideational factor that stimulates this integration: "In the form of the exchange principle, the bourgeois *ratio* really approximated to the systems whatever it would make commensurable with itself, would identify with itself – and it did so with increasing, if potentially homicidal, success. Less and less was left outside" (*ND*: 23, tr. mod.).

This process of integration is what gives the history of the modern period – of the bourgeois age – its particular trajectory. The qualitatively different is brought ever closer through the increasing reach of the exchange system into all facets of life:

The exchange relationship largely endows the system with a mechanical character. It is objectively forced onto its elements, as implied by the concept of an organism – the model which resembles a celestial teleology through which each organ would receive its function in the whole and would derive its meaning from the latter. The context which perpetuates life simultaneously destroys it, and consequently already possesses in itself the lethal impulse towards which its dynamic is propelled.[21]

In dealing with Kant's "Idea for a Universal History from a Cosmopolitan Point of View", Adorno argues that the notion of progress has been intelligible in modernity as the growing sense of totality: Kant's notion of progress is articulated as the increasing rational unity of humanity. However, the problem with this sense of totality as progress is that it converts humanity into a collective agent in pursuit of an ideal. This collectivization determines that history must pursue a particular path: "But the dependence of progress on the totality comes back to bite progress". For Adorno, the integrationist dynamic of history, which understands progress as the development of the totality, is no progress at all: "If humanity remains entrapped by the totality it itself fashions, then, as Kafka said, no progress has taken place at all, while mere totality nevertheless allows progress to be entertained in thought" (*CM*: 145).

Adorno's description of the dynamic driven by the social totality may make it appear to be a metaphysical thesis after all, one which in the Hegelian manner posits a driving evolutionary process over and above human beings. However, the very enterprise of critical theory cannot allow the possibility of a historical process in which human beings are merely the material cause. Adorno acknowledges that human agency – albeit a distorted one in the current age – is operative in this process: "Society is a total process in which human beings surrounded, guided, and formed by objectivity do, in turn, act back upon society."[22] Or,

> [s]ocial totality does not lead a life of its own over and above that which it unites and of which it, in its turn, is composed. It produces and reproduces itself through its individual moments . . . System and individual entity are reciprocal and can only be apprehended in their reciprocity.[23]

The task of critical theory, of course, is to think through the conditions in which individuals might realize their capacity for agency, thereby reversing the destructive conditions of the totality, a phenomenon of second nature.

Adorno's critique of the social totality – his view that the totality encroaches and determines the course of life – might seem to amount to an argument in favour of the pre-eminence of the individual moment. However, the social totality – as we have just seen – also contains a commitment to the contributions that collective agents make to the reality in which they live. On this basis, Adorno can deny that he is a radical pluralist who would reject the totality in favour of free, self-determining individuals. He notes:

> it would be simplistic if you were to assume that, in what I have called the historical process or the world spirit that gives shape to the totality and draws it into itself, it is the particular that is in the right . . . while the totality is in the wrong. (*HF*: 95)

Somewhat tentatively and without systematic elaboration, Adorno proposes the possibility that collective action alone might be the agent of "redemption". The individual as part of a self-conscious totality – as opposed to the individualist who does not realize the foundational dimensions of her social determination – would be part of this agency: "The forms of humanity's own global societal constitution threaten its life, if a self-conscious global subject does not develop and intervene" (*CM*: 144).

At issue in the theory of progress is that progress – the step away from catastrophe – can occur only when collective agency is achieved. In this way we see that the possibility of emancipation from the totality lies within the totality itself: the historical process of integration that creates a coercive totality might also create the conditions for an agency adequate to the action required to resist the integrational historical process.

What Adorno posits here is consistent with his response to the dilemma of progress, the dilemma of the end of history, or progress as the continuity of universal history. The achievement of "a self-conscious global subject" might indeed be "the very establishment of humanity". Central to Adorno's contribution to this achievement is a critique of the naturalistic pretensions of the totalizing process.

Notes

1. Theodor W. Adorno, "The Actuality of Philosophy", Benjamin Snow (trans.), *The Adorno Reader*, Brian O'Connor (ed.) (2000), 24.
2. See in particular *ND*: 300–60.
3. Simon Jarvis, *Adorno: A Critical Introduction* (1998), 37.
4. This is the central contention of "The Actuality of Philosophy", in which the business of science is sharply distinguished from the practice of science.
5. Quoted by Susan Buck-Morss in *The Origin of Negative Dialectics: Theodor W. Adorno, Walter Benjamin, and the Frankfurt Institute* (1977), 43.
6. Interpretation in this way needs to be more than the hermeneutic treatment of historical experience. Adorno writes against Wilhelm Dilthey that he "did not engage facticity with sufficient seriousness; he remained in the sphere of intellectual history and, in the fashion of vague categories of styles of thought, entirely failed to grasp material reality" (INH: 265).
7. Mauro Bozzetti suggests that the opposition of continuity and discontinuity entails that "history must be thought simultaneously as progress and regress, viewed as humanity and barbarism". See Bozzetti, *Hegel und Adorno: Die Kritische Funktion des philosophischen Systems* (1996), 208.
8. Apropos: "The materialistic turnabout in dialectics cast the weightiest accent on insight into the discontinuity of what is not comfortingly held together by any unity of [the Hegelian notion of] spirit and concept" (*ND*: 319).
9. Walter Benjamin, "Theses on the Philosophy of History", *Illuminations* (1973), 262–3.
10. This is a very fundamental commitment which might be set against those readings of Adorno that align him with theological or messianic readings of history. As an instance of this see Rolf Wiggershaus, *Theodor W. Adorno* (1987), 31–2.
11. Adorno's criticism of Kierkegaard's "leap of faith" takes this same form: the leap represents an abandonment of the historical moment: "Precisely as the 'leap,' however, the appearance of the first is abstractly set apart from historical continuity; it becomes a mere means for the inauguration of a new sphere." Adorno, *Kierkegaard: Construction of the Aesthetic* (1989), 34.
12. One of Adorno's cue notes to himself states: "Laws of Nature not to be taken literally, not to be ontologized. In other words, the laws of nature capable of being abrogated" (*HF*: 115).
13. See Jürgen Habermas, *The Theory of Communicative Action*, vol. I (1984), 380, and Hauke Brunkhorst, *Adorno and Critical Theory* (1999), 73.
14. "The substance of Adorno's and Horkheimer's thesis is that the process of civilisation is already marked from its origins, by a fatal dialectic, because

the emancipation of men from scarcity, from subjugation to natural powers and to their own natural appetites, is achieved through a two-sided process, which on one side is liberation and the triumph of autonomy, and on the other is inextricably tied to domination and repression." Stefano Petrucciani, *Introduzione a Adorno* (2007), 53.

15. Günter Rohrmoser, *Das Elend der kritischen Theorie* (1970), 14.
16. Adorno *et al.*, *The Positivist Dispute in German Sociology* (1976), 6.
17. As Alison Stone points out, "Adorno asserts that nature is historical, but in a distinctive way. The history that shapes natural things, for Adorno, is the history of human efforts to dominate them, to mould them to human purposes in a way that negates their spontaneous modes of being." See Stone, "Adorno and the Disenchantment of Nature", *Philosophy and Social Criticism* **32**(2) (2006), 242.
18. Deborah Cook, *Adorno, Habermas, and the Search for a Rational Society* (2004), 91.
19. In *Against Epistemology* Adorno criticizes Husserl's "logical absolutism"; he endeavours to show that far from being "absolute", logic gains its validity through its contribution to the task of self-preservation and socialization.
20. See Michael Rosen, *Hegel's Dialectic and its Criticism* (1982), ch. 5 for a more detailed discussion of Adorno's materialist transformation of Hegel.
21. Adorno *et al.*, *The Positivist Dispute in German Sociology* (1976), 37–8.
22. *Ibid.*, 119.
23. *Ibid.*, 107.

Chronology

11 September 1903	Born in Frankfurt-am-Main, Germany.
1917	Meets Siegfried Kracauer.
1921–24	Studies philosophy at the University of Frankfurt; Hans Cornelius supervises his doctoral dissertation, *The Transcendence of the Material and Noematic in Husserl's Phenomenology*.
1923	Meets Walter Benjamin.
1924	Meets Max Horkheimer and Friedrich Pollock.
1925	Studies with composer Alban Berg in Vienna.
1926–27	Prepares his first *Habilitationsschrift*, *The Concept of the Unconscious in the Transcendental Theory of Mind*, under Hans Cornelius at the University of Frankfurt (the thesis was subsequently withdrawn).
1929–31	Prepares a second *Habilitationsschrift*, *Kierkegaard: The Construction of the Aesthetic*, under theologian Paul Tillich at the University of Frankfurt.
1931–33	Teaches at the University of Frankfurt.
1933	The Gestapo closes the Institute for Social Research on 13 March; Adorno's right to teach is withdrawn by the Ministry of Science, Art and Education on 7 April.
1934–37	Prepares a PhD thesis on Husserl at the University of Oxford under Gilbert Ryle.
1935	Becomes an official associate of the Institute for Social Research.
1938	Emigrates to New York with his new wife Gretel (*née* Karplus).
1939–40	Works with Paul Lazarsfeld at Princeton University on a radio research project funded by the Rockefeller Foundation.
1941	Moves with Max Horkheimer and other Institute members to Pacific Palisades in California.

1949	Returns to postwar Germany to teach again at the University of Frankfurt.
1950	Reopening of the Institute for Social Research in Frankfurt (where it continues to this day).
1956	Granted full professorship at the University of Frankfurt
1958–69	Becomes Director of the Institute for Social Research.
6 August 1969	Dies of a heart attack while on vacation in Zermatt, Switzerland.

References

Works by Theodor W. Adorno

Cited works by Adorno are listed by date of publication in English. The reference to the English work is followed by a reference to the original publication of that work in German or English (where no reference follows, the work was originally published in the year cited).

Adorno, Theodor W. (with Else Frenkel-Brunswik, Daniel J. Levison & R. Nevitt Sanford) 1950. *The Authoritarian Personality*, Max Horkheimer & Samuel H. Flowerman (eds). New York: Harper & Brothers.

Adorno, Theodor W. 1957. "Television and the Patterns of Mass Culture". In *Mass Culture: The Popular Arts in America*, Bernard Rosenberg & David Manning White (eds). London: Collier Macmillan.

Adorno, Theodor W. 1967. *Prisms*, Samuel & Shierry Weber (trans.). Cambridge, MA: MIT Press. [Originally published as *Prismen: Kulturkritik und Gesellschaft* (Berlin: Suhrkamp, 1955).]

Adorno, Theodor W. 1968. "Sociology and Psychology", Irving N. Wohlfarth (trans.), *New Left Review* 47. [Originally published as "Zum Verhältnis von Soziologie und Psychologie". *Sociologica I. Aufsätze, Max Horkheimer zum sechzigsten Geburtstag gewidmet* (Frankfurt: Europäische Verlags-Anstalt, 1955).]

Adorno, Theodor W. 1969–70. "Society", Fredric Jameson (trans.), *Salmagundi* 3(10–11), (Fall–Winter). [Originally published as "Stichwort Gesellschaft", *Evangelisches Staatslexikon* (Stuttgart: publisher unknown, 1967).]

Adorno, Theodor W. (with Max Horkheimer) 1972. *Dialectic of Enlightenment*, John Cumming (trans.). New York: Continuum. [Originally published as *Dialektik der Aufklärung: Philosophische Fragmente* (Amsterdam: Querido Verlag, 1947).]

Adorno, Theodor W. 1972. "Individuum und Organisation". *Gesammelte Schriften* 8. Frankfurt: Suhrkamp.

Adorno, Theodor W. 1972. "Die Revidierte Psychoanalyse", Rainer Koehne (trans.). *Gesammelte Schriften* 8. Frankfurt: Suhrkamp. [Originally published as "Revised Psychoanalysis", *Psyche* **VI**(1), 1952.]

Adorno, Theodor W. 1973. *Negative Dialectics*, E. B. Ashton (trans.). London: Routledge. [Originally published as *Negative Dialektik* (Frankfurt: Suhrkamp, 1966).]

Adorno, Theodor W. 1973. *The Jargon of Authenticity*, K. Tarnowski & F. Will (trans.). London: Kegan & Paul. [Originally published as *Jargon der Eigentlichkeit: Zur Deutsche Ideologie* (Frankfurt: Suhrkamp, 1964).]

Adorno, Theodor W. 1974. *Minima Moralia: Reflections from Damaged Life*, E. F. N. Jephcott (trans.). London: New Left Books. [Originally published as *Minima Moralia: Reflexionen aus dem beschädigten Leben* (Berlin: Suhrkamp, 1951).]

Adorno, Theodor W. 1974. *Philosophische Terminologie zur Einleitung*, Vol. 2. Frankfurt: Suhrkamp.

Adorno, Theodor W. (with Hans Albert, Ralf Dahrendorf, Jürgen Habermas, Harald Pilot & Karl Popper) 1976. *The Positivist Dispute in German Sociology*, Glyn Adley & David Frisby (trans.). London: Heinemann. [Originally published as *Der Positivismusstreit in der deutschen Soziologie* (Neuwied and Berlin: Leuchterhand, 1969).]

Adorno, Theodor W. 1983. *Against Epistemology: A Metacritique. Studies in Husserl and the Phenomenological Antinomies*, Willis Domingo (trans.). Cambridge, MA: MIT Press. [Originally published as *Zur Metakritik der Erkenntnistheorie: Studien über Husserl und die phänomenologischen Antinomien* (Stuttgart: Kohlhammer, 1956).]

Adorno, Theodor W. 1986. "Individuum und Staat". *Gesammelte Schriften* 20.1, Rolf Tiedemann (ed.). Frankfurt: Suhrkamp.

Adorno, Theodor W. (with Max Horkheimer) 1986. "Democratic Leadership and Mass Manipulation". *Gesammelte Schriften* 20.1, Rolf Tiedemann (ed.). Frankfurt: Suhrkamp.

Adorno, Theodor W. 1989. *Kierkegaard: Construction of the Aesthetic*, Robert Hullot-Kentor (trans.). Minneapolis, MN: University of Minnesota Press. [Originally published as *Kierkegaard: Konstruktion des Ästhetischen. Gesammelte Schriften* 2 (Frankfurt: Suhrkamp, 1979).]

Adorno, Theodor W. 1991. *Notes to Literature*, vol. I, Shierry Weber Nicholsen (trans.), Rolf Tiedemann (ed.). New York: Columbia University Press. [Originally published as *Noten zur Literatur* I (Berlin: Suhrkamp, 1957).]

Adorno, Theodor W. 1992. *Notes to Literature*, vol. II, Shierry Weber Nicholsen (trans.), Rolf Tiedemann (ed.). New York: Columbia University Press. [Originally published as *Noten zur Literatur* II (Frankfurt: Suhrkamp, 1961).]

Adorno, Theodor W. 1992. *Quasi Una Fantasia: Essays on Modern Music*, Rodney Livingstone (trans.). London: Verso. [Originally published as *Quasi una Fantasia. Musikalische Schriften* II (Frankfurt: Suhrkamp, 1978).]

Adorno, Theodor W. 1993. *Hegel: Three Studies*, Shierry Weber Nicholsen (trans.). Cambridge, MA: MIT Press. [Originally published as *Drei Studien zu Hegel* (Frankfurt: Suhrkamp, 1963).]

Adorno, Theodor W. 1993. "Theory of Pseudo-Culture", Deborah Cook (trans.), *Telos* no. 95 (Spring). [Originally published as "Theorie der Halbbildung", *Der Monat*, no. 152, 1959.]

Adorno, Theodor W. 1994. *The Stars Down to Earth and Other Essays on the Irrational in Culture*, Stephen Crook (ed.). New York: Routledge. [Originally published as "The Stars Down to Earth: the Los Angeles Times Astrology Column – A Study in Secondary Superstition", *Jahrbuch für Amerikastudien* 2 (1957: title essay).]

Adorno, Theodor W. 1997 *Aesthetic Theory*, Robert Hullot-Kentor (trans.). Minneapolis, MN: University of Minnesota Press. [Originally published as *Äesthetische Theorie*, Gretel Adorno & Rolf Tiedemann (eds) (Frankfurt: Suhrkamp, 1970).]

Adorno, Theodor W. 1998. "Husserl and the Problem of Idealism". *Gesammelte Schriften* 20.1. Frankfurt: Suhrkamp. [Originally published as "Husserl and the Problem of Idealism", *Journal of Philosophy* 37, 1940.]

Adorno, Theodor W. 1998. "Zur Philosophie Husserls", *Gesammelte Schriften* 20.1. Frankfurt: Suhrkamp.

Adorno, Theodor W. 1998. *Critical Models: Interventions and Catchwords*, Henry W. Pickford (trans.). New York: Columbia University Press. [Most of the essays in this volume were published in two collections: *Eingriffe: Neun Kritische Modelle* (Frankfurt: Suhrkamp, 1963) and *Stichworte: Kritische Modelle* 2 (Frankfurt: Suhrkamp, 1969).]

Adorno, Theodor W. 2000. *Introduction to Sociology*, Edmund Jephcott (trans.). Stanford, CA: Stanford University Press. [Originally published as *Vorlesung zur Einleitung in die Soziologie* (Frankfurt: Junius-Drucke, 1973).]

Adorno, Theodor W. *Problems of Moral Philosophy*, Rodney Livingstone (trans.). Stanford, CA: Stanford University Press. [Originally published as *Probleme der Moralphilosophie* (Frankfurt: Suhrkamp, 1996).]

Adorno, Theodor W. 2000. "The Actuality of Philosophy", Benjamin Snow (trans.). In *The Adorno Reader*, Brian O'Connor (ed.). Oxford: Blackwell. [Originally published as "Die Aktualität der Philosophie". *Gesammelte Schriften* 1 (Frankfurt: Suhrkamp, 1973).]

Adorno, Theodor W. 2001. *Metaphysics: Concept and Problems*, Edmund Jephcott (trans.). Stanford, CA: Stanford University Press. [Originally published as *Metaphysik: Begriff und Probleme* (Frankfurt: Suhrkamp, 1998).]

Adorno, Theodor W. 2001. *Kant's "Critique of Pure Reason"*, Rodney Livingstone (trans.). Stanford, CA: Stanford University Press. [Originally published as *Kants "Kritik der Reinen Vernunft"* (Frankfurt: Suhrkamp, 1995).]

Adorno, Theodor W. 2002. *Essays on Music: Theodor W. Adorno*, Susan H. Gillespie (trans.), Richard Leppert (ed.). Berkeley, CA: University of California Press. [These essays span the course of Adorno's professional life as a philosopher and musicologist.]

Adorno, Theodor W. (with Max Horkheimer) 2002. *Dialectic of Enlightenment: Philosophical Fragments*, Edmund Jephcott (trans.). Stanford, CA: Stanford University Press. [Originally published as *Dialektik der Aufklärung: Philosophische Fragmente* (Amsterdam: Querido Verlag, 1947).]

Adorno, Theodor W. 2003. "Art and the Arts". In *Can One Live after Auschwitz? A Philosophical Reader*, Rodney Livingstone et al. (trans.). Stanford, CA: Stanford University Press. [Originally published as "Die Kunst und die Künste". *Gesammelte Schriften* 10.1 (Frankfurt: Suhrkamp, 1977).]

Adorno, Theodor W. 2003. "Reflections on Class Theory". In *Can One Live after Auschwitz? A Philosophical Reader*, Rodney Livingstone et al. (trans.). Stanford, CA: Stanford University Press. [Originally published as "Reflexionen zur Klassentheorie". *Gesammelte Schriften* 8 (Frankfurt: Suhrkamp, 1972).]

Adorno, Theodor W. 2006. *Philosophy of New Music*, Robert Hullot-Kentor (trans. and ed.). Minneapolis, MN: University of Minnesota Press. [Originally published as *Philosophie der neuen Musik* (Tübingen: Mohr, 1949).]

Adorno, Theodor W. 2006. "The Idea of Natural History". In *Things Beyond Resemblance: Collected Essays on Theodor W. Adorno*, Robert Hullot-Kentor (trans.). New York: Columbia University Press. [Originally published as "Die Idee der Naturgeschichte". *Gesammelte Schriften* 1 (Frankfurt: Suhrkamp, 1973).]

Adorno, Theodor W. 2006. *History and Freedom: Lectures 1964–65*, Rodney Livingstone (trans.), Rolf Tiedemann (ed.). Cambridge: Polity. [Originally published as *Zur Lehre von der Geschichte und von der Freiheit (1964/65)* (Frankfurt: Suhrkamp, 2001).]

Other works

This section contains full bibliographical details for works by other authors that are cited in this volume.

Arnold, Matthew 1993. *Culture and Anarchy, and Other Writings*, Stefan Collini (ed.). Cambridge: Cambridge University Press.

Benhabib, Seyla 1986. *Critique, Norm, and Utopia: A Study of the Foundations of Critical Theory*. New York: Columbia University Press.

Benhabib, Seyla 1994. *The Reluctant Modernism of Hannah Arendt*. London: Sage.

Benjamin, Walter 1973. "Theses on the Philosophy of History", Harry Zohn (trans.). In *Illuminations*, Hannah Arendt (ed.). London: Fontana.

Benjamin, Walter 1977. *The Origin of German Tragic Drama*, J. Osborne (trans.). London: New Left Books.

Benjamin, Walter 1978. "On the Mimetic Faculty". In *Reflections: Essays, Aphorisms, Autobiographical Writings*, Edmund Jephcott (trans.). New York: Harcourt Brace Jovanovich.

Benjamin, Walter 1996. "On Language as Such and the Language of Man", Edmund Jephcott (trans.). In *Selected Writings*, vol. 1, Michael Jennings (ed.). Cambridge, MA: Belknap Press.

Benjamin, Walter 1996. "The Concept of Criticism in German Romanticism", David Lacterman, Howard Eiland & Ian Balfour (trans.). In *Selected Writings*, vol. 1, Michael Jennings (ed.). Cambridge, MA: Belknap Press.

Berman, Russell 2002. "Adorno's Politics". In *Adorno: A Critical Reader*, Nigel Gibson & Andrew Rubin (eds). Oxford: Blackwell.

Bernstein, J. M. 2001. *Adorno: Disenchantment and Ethics*. Cambridge: Cambridge University Press.

Bernstein, J. M. (ed.) 2003. *Classic and Romantic German Aesthetics*. Cambridge: Cambridge University Press.

Bozzetti, Mauro 1996. *Hegel und Adorno: Die Kritische Funktion des philosophischen Systems*. Freiburg: Karl Alber.

Brandom, Robert B. 1994. *Making it Explicit: Reasoning, Representing, and Discursive Commitment*. Cambridge, MA: Harvard University Press.

Brecht, Bertold 1964. "Shouldn't We Abolish Aesthetics?". In *Brecht on Theatre:*

The Development of an Aesthetic, John Willett (trans. & ed.). London: Methuen.

Bristow, William F. 2007. *Hegel and the Transformation of Philosophical Critique*. Oxford: Oxford University Press.

Brumlik, Micha 1992. *Die Gnostiker: Der Traum von Selbsterlösung des Menschen*. Frankfurt: Eichborn.

Brunkhorst, Hauke 1999. *Adorno and Critical Theory*. Cardiff: University of Wales Press.

Buck-Morss, Susan 1977. *The Origin of Negative Dialectics: Theodor W. Adorno, Walter Benjamin, and the Frankfurt Institute*. Brighton: Harvester.

Cartwright, Nancy 1999. *The Dappled World*. Cambridge: Cambridge University Press.

Cassirer, Ernst 2004. *Gesammelte Werke*, Vol. 17. Darmstadt: Wissenschaftliche Buchgesellschaft.

Cook, Deborah 2004. *Adorno, Habermas, and the Search for a Rational Society*. London: Routledge.

Demmerling, Christoph 1994. *Sprache und Verdinglichung*. Frankfurt: Suhrkamp.

Dews, Peter 1987. *Logics of Disintegration: Poststructuralist Thought and the Claims of Critical Theory*. London: Verso.

Durkheim, Emile 1976. *The Elementary Forms of the Religious Life: A Study in Religious Sociology*, Joseph Ward Swain (trans.). London: Allen & Unwin.

Ette, Wolfram, Günter Figal, Richard Klein & Günter Peters (eds) 2004. *Adorno im Widerstreit*. Munich: Karl Alber.

Figal, Günter 2006. *Gegenständlichkeit*. Tübingen: Mohr Siebeck.

Finlayson, J. Gordon 2002. "Adorno on the Ethical and the Ineffable", *Journal of European Philosophy* 10(1).

Franco, Paul 1999. *Hegel's Philosophy of Freedom*. New Haven, CT: Yale University Press.

Frankfurt Institute for Social Research 1972. *Aspects of Sociology*, John Viertel (trans.). Boston, MA: Beacon.

Freud, Sigmund 1975. *Civilization and its Discontents*, Joan Riviere (trans.). London: Hogarth Press.

Freud, Sigmund 1985. "Group Psychology and the Analysis of the Ego". *The Penguin Freud Library*, vol. 12: *Civilization, Society and Religion*, James Strachey (trans.). Harmondsworth: Penguin.

Freyenhagen, Fabian 2006. "Adorno's Negative Dialectics of Freedom", *Philosophy and Social Criticism* 32(2).

Fricke, Stefan. "Helms, Hans G(ünter)", *Grove Music Online*, http://www.grovemusic.com.

Fromm, Erich 1978. "The Method and Function of an Analytic Social Psychology". In *The Essential Frankfurt School Reader*, Andrew Arato & Eike Gebhardt (eds). Oxford: Blackwell.

Gadamer, Hans-Georg 1975. *Truth and Method*, Garrett Barden & John Cumming (trans.). New York: Continuum.

Geuss, Raymond 2005. *Outside Ethics*. Princeton, NJ: Princeton University Press.

Greenberg, Clement 1992. "Avant-Garde and Kitsch". In *Art in Theory: 1900–1990*, C. Harrison & P. Wood (eds). Oxford: Blackwell.

Grumley, J. E. 1989. *History and Totality: Radical Historicism from Hegel to Foucault*. London: Routledge.

203

Habermas, Jürgen 1982. "The Entwinement of Myth and Enlightenment: Rereading 'Dialectic of Enlightenment'", Thomas Y. Levin (trans.). In *New German Critique* 26.

Habermas, Jürgen 1983. "Theodor Adorno: The Primal History of Subjectivity: Self-Affirmation Gone Wild". In *Philosophical-Political Profiles*, F. G. Lawrence (trans.). London: Heinemann.

Habermas, Jürgen 1984. *The Theory of Communicative Action*, vol. I: *Reason and the Rationalization of Society*, Thomas McCarthy (trans.). Boston, MA: Beacon.

Habermas, Jürgen 1987. *The Theory of Communicative Action*, vol. II: *Lifeworld and System: A Critique of Functionalist Reason*, Thomas McCarthy (trans.). Boston, MA: Beacon.

Habermas, Jürgen 1993. "Morality, Society, and Ethics: An Interview with Torben Hviid Nielsen". In *Justification and Application: Remarks on Discourse Ethics*, Ciaran P. Cronin (trans.). Cambridge, MA: MIT Press.

Habermas, Jürgen 1993. *Postmetaphysical Thinking: Philosophical Essays*, William Mark Hohengarten (trans.). Cambridge, MA: MIT Press.

Habermas, Jürgen 1996. *Between Facts and Norms: Contributions to a Discourse Theory of Law and Democracy*, William Rehg (trans.). Cambridge, MA: MIT Press.

Habermas, Jürgen 1996. "Georg Simmel on Philosophy and Culture: Postscript to a Collection of Essays", Mathieu Deflem (trans.), *Critical Inquiry* 22(3): Spring.

Hammer, Espen 2006. *Adorno and the Political*. London: Routledge.

Hegel, G. W. F. 1969. *Science of Logic*, A. V. Miller (trans.). Atlantic Highlands, NJ: Humanities Press.

Hegel, G. W. F. 1970. *Philosophy of Nature*, vol. 1, M. J. Petry (trans.). London: Allen & Unwin.

Hegel, G. W. F. 1975. *Aesthetics: Lectures on Fine Art*, T. M. Knox (trans.). Oxford: Clarendon Press.

Hegel, G. W. F. 1991. *Elements of a Philosophy of Right*, H. B. Nisbet (trans.), A. Wood (ed.). Cambridge: Cambridge University Press.

Hegel, G. W. F. 1991. *Encyclopedia Logic*, T. F. Geraets, W. A. Suchting & H. S. Harris (trans.). Indianapolis, IN: Hackett.

Heidegger, Martin 1971. "The Origin of the Work of Art". In *Poetry, Language, Thought*, Albert Hofstadter (trans.). New York: Harper & Row.

Herman, B. 1993. *The Practice of Moral Judgment*. Cambridge, MA: Harvard University Press.

Hohendahl, Peter Uwe 1995. *Prismatic Thought: Theodor W. Adorno*. Lincoln, NE: University of Nebraska Press.

Honneth, Axel 1991. *Critique of Power: Reflective Stages in a Critical Social Theory*, K. Baynes (trans.). Cambridge, MA: MIT Press.

Honneth, Axel 2005. "A Physiognomy of the Capitalist Form of Life: A Sketch of Adorno's Social Theory", James Ingram (trans.), *Constellations: An International Journal of Critical and Democratic Theory* 12(1): March.

Horkheimer, Max 1939. "Die Juden und Europa". *Zeitschrift für Sozialforschung* 8(1–2).

Horkheimer, Max 1972. "Traditional and Critical Theory". In *Critical Theory: Selected Essays*, Matthew J. O'Connell (trans.). New York: Herder & Herder.

Horkheimer, Max 1974. *Eclipse of Reason*. New York: Continuum.

Horkheimer, Max 1978. "The Authoritarian State". In *The Essential Frankfurt School Reader*, Andrew Arato & Eike Gebhardt (eds). Oxford: Blackwell.

Horkheimer, Max 1993. "The Present Situation of Social Philosophy and the Tasks of an Institute for Social Research". In *Between Philosophy and Social Science: Selected Early Writings*, G. Frederick Hunter, Matthew S. Kramer & John Torpey (trans.). Cambridge, MA: MIT Press.

Horkheimer, Max 1996. *Gesammelte Schriften*, vol. 17: *Briefwechsel 1941–1948*, Gunzelin Schmid Noerr (ed.). Frankfurt: Fischer.

Husserl, Edmund 1969. *Ideas: General Introduction to Pure Phenomenology*, W. R. Boyce Gibson (trans.). New York: Humanities Press (*Ideas* I).

Husserl, Edmund 1970. *The Crisis of European Science and Transcendental Phenomenology: An Introduction to Phenomenological Philosophy*, David Carr (trans.). Evanston, IL: Northwestern University Press.

Husserl, Edmund 1970. *Logical Investigations*, vol. 1, J. N. Findlay (trans.). London: Routledge & Kegan Paul.

Husserl, Edmund 1989. *Ideas Pertaining to a Pure Phenomenology and to a Phenomenological Philosophy. Second Book: Studies in the Phenomenology of Constitution*, R. Rojcewicz & A. Schuwer (trans.). Dordrecht: Kluwer (*Ideas* II).

Husserl, Edmund 2001. *Natur und Geist*. Dordrecht: Kluwer.

Ingarden, Roman 1992. *Einführung in die Phänomenologie Edmund Husserls – Osloer Vorlesungen 1967*, Gregor Haefiger (ed.). Tübingen: Niemeyer.

Jaeggi, Rahel 2005. " 'No Individual Can Resist': *Minima Moralia* as Critique of Forms of Life", James Ingram (trans.), *Constellations: An International Journal of Critical and Democratic Theory* 12(1): March.

Jarvis, Simon 1998. *Adorno: A Critical Introduction*. Cambridge: Polity.

Jarvis, Simon 2004. "Adorno, Marx, Materialism". In *The Cambridge Companion to Adorno*, Tom Huhn (ed.). Cambridge: Cambridge University Press.

Jay, Martin 1973. *Dialectical Imagination: A History of the Frankfurt School and the Institute for Social Research, 1923–1950*. Boston, MA: Little, Brown.

Jay, Martin 1984. *Adorno*. London: Fontana.

Kant, Immanuel 1929. *Critique of Pure Reason*, Norman Kemp Smith (trans.). Basingstoke: Macmillan.

Kant, Immanuel 1959. "What is Enlightenment?". In *Foundations of the Metaphysics of Morals*, Lewis White Beck (trans. & ed.). Indianapolis, IN: Bobbs-Merrill.

Kant, Immanuel 1971. "Idea for a Universal History with a Cosmopolitan Purpose". In *Kant's Political Writings*, H. B. Nisbet (trans.), Hans Reiss (ed.). Cambridge: Cambridge University Press.

Kant, Immanuel 1996. *Practical Philosophy*, M. J. Gregor (trans. & ed.). Cambridge: Cambridge University Press.

Kant, Immanuel 2000. *Critique of the Power of Judgment*, Paul Guyer & Eric Matthews (trans.), Paul Guyer (ed.). Cambridge: Cambridge University Press.

Kaufman, Robert 2004. "Adorno's Social Lyric, and Literary Criticism Today: Poetics, Aesthetics, Modernity". In *The Cambridge Companion to Adorno*, Tom Huhn (ed.). Cambridge: Cambridge University Press.

Kern, Iso 1964. *Kant and Husserl*. The Hague: Martinus Nijhoff.

Kracauer, Siegfried 1995. "Georg Simmel". In *The Mass Ornament: Weimar Essays*, Thomas Y. Levin (trans.). Cambridge MA: Harvard University Press.

Kraushaar, Wolfgang (ed.) 1998. *Frankfurter Schule und Studentenbewegung. Von der Flaschenpost zum Molotowcocktail 1964–95*, 3 vols. Hamburg: Rogner & Bernhard.

Leavis, F. R. 1930. *Mass Civilisation and Minority Culture*. Cambridge: Minority Press.

Lepenies, Wolf 1992. *Melancholy and Society*, Jeremy Gaines & Doris Jones (trans.). Cambridge, MA: Harvard University Press.

MacIntyre, A. 1985. *After Virtue*, 2nd edn. London: Duckworth.

Marx, Karl 1964. *The Economic and Philosophic Manuscripts of 1844*, Martin Milligan (trans.). New York: International Publishers.

Marx, Karl 1976. *Capital: A Critique of Political Economy*, vol. 1, Ben Fowkes (trans.). London: Vintage.

McDowell, John 1994. *Mind and World*. Cambridge, MA: Harvard University Press.

Menke, C. 2005. "Virtue and Reflection: The 'Antinomies of Moral Philosophy'", James Ingram (trans.), *Constellations: An International Journal of Critical and Democratic Theory* 12(1): March.

Müller-Doohm, Stefan 2005. *Adorno: A Biography*, Rodney Livingstone (trans.). Cambridge: Polity.

O'Connor, Brian 2004. *Adorno's Negative Dialectic: Philosophy and the Possibility of Critical Rationality*. Cambridge, MA: MIT Press.

Paddison, Max 2004. "Authenticity and Failure in Adorno's Aesthetics of Music". In *The Cambridge Companion to Adorno*, Tom Huhn (ed.). Cambridge: Cambridge University Press.

Parsons, Talcott & Robert F. Bales, with James Olds, Philip Slater & Morris Zelditch 1955. *Family, Socialization and Interaction Process*. Glencoe, IL: The Free Press.

Passmore, John 1995. "Attitudes to Nature". In *Environmental Ethics*, Robert Elliot (ed.). Oxford: Oxford University Press.

Pauen, Michael 1994. *Dithyrambiker des Untergangs: Gnostisches Denken in Philosophie und Ästhetik der Moderne*. Berlin: Akademie Verlag.

Petrucciani, Stefano 2007. *Introduzione a Adorno*. Rome: Editori Laterza.

Pippin, Robert 1989. *Hegel's Idealism: The Satisfactions of Self-Consciousness*. Cambridge: Cambridge University Press.

Pippin, Robert 1990. *Modernism as a Philosophical Problem*. Oxford: Blackwell.

Pippin, Robert 2005. *The Persistence of Subjectivity*. Cambridge: Cambridge University Press.

Pollock, Friedrich (ed.) 1955. *Gruppenexperiment. Ein Studienbericht*. Frankfurt: Europäische Verlags-Anstalt.

Pollock, Friedrich 1978. "State Capitalism: Its Possibilities and Limitations". In *The Essential Frankfurt School Reader*, Andrew Arato & Eike Gebhardt (eds). Oxford: Blackwell.

Riesman, David (in collaboration with Reuel Denney & Nathan Glazer) 1950. *The Lonely Crowd: A Study of the Changing American Character*. New Haven, CT: Yale University Press.

Rohrmoser, Günter 1970. *Das Elend der kritischen Theorie*. Freiburg im Breisgau: Verlag Rombach.

Rosen, Michael 1982. *Hegel's Dialectic and its Criticism*. Cambridge: Cambridge University Press.

Sartre, Jean-Paul 1993. *What is Literature?* Bernard Frechtman (trans.). London: Routledge.

Schenker, Heinrich 2001. *New Musical Theories and Fantasies*, 3 vols, Ernest Oster (trans.). Oxford: Pendragon Press.

Schmidt, Alfred 1971. *The Concept of Nature in Marx*, Ben Fowkes (trans.). London: New Left Books.

Schmidt, James 1998. "Language, Mythology, and Enlightenment: Historical Notes on Horkheimer's and Adorno's *Dialectic of Enlightenment*", *Social Research* 65(4): Winter.

Schnädelbach, H. 2000. "Phänomenologie und Sprachanalyse". *Philosophie in der modernen Kultur*. Frankfurt: Suhrkamp.

Seel, Martin 2006. *Adornos Philosophie der Kontemplation*. Frankfurt: Suhrkamp.

Sellars, Wilfrid 1980. *Pure Pragmatics and Possible Worlds: The Early Essays of Wilfrid Sellars*, Jeffrey F. Sicha (ed.). Atascadero, CA: Ridgeview.

Sellars, Wilfrid 1997. *Empiricism and the Philosophy of Mind*. Cambridge, MA: Harvard University Press.

Simmel, Georg 1990. *The Philosophy of Money*, T. Bottomore & D. Frisby (trans.), D. Frisby (ed.). London: Routledge.

Simmel, Georg 1997. *Simmel on Culture: Selected Writings*, D. Frisby *et al.* (trans.), D. Frisby & M. Featherstone (eds). London: Sage.

Snarrenberg, Robert 1997. *Schenker's Interpretive Practice*. Cambridge: Cambridge University Press.

Stern, Robert 2002. *Hegel and the Phenomenology of Spirit*. London: Routledge.

Stone, Alison 2004. *Petrified Intelligence: Nature in Hegel's Philosophy*. Albany, NY: SUNY Press.

Stone, Alison 2006. "Adorno and the Disenchantment of Nature", *Philosophy and Social Criticism* 32(2).

Subotnik, Rose 1976. "Adorno's Diagnosis of Beethoven's Late Style: Early Symptoms of a Fatal Condition", *Journal of the American Musicological Society* 29(2).

Tassone, G. 2005. "Amoral Adorno: Negative Dialectics Outside Ethics", *European Journal of Social Theory* 8(3).

Taylor, Charles 1995. "Overcoming Epistemology". In *Philosophical Arguments*. Cambridge, MA: Harvard University Press.

Taylor, Frederick 1947. *Scientific Management*. London: Harper & Row.

Weber, Max 1948. *From Max Weber: Essays in Sociology*, H. H. Gerth & C. Wright Mills (trans. and eds). London: Routledge & Kegan Paul.

Whitebook, Joel 1996. *Perversion and Utopia: A Study in Psychoanalysis and Critical Theory*. Cambridge, MA: MIT Press.

Wiggershaus, Rolf 1987. *Theodor W. Adorno*. Munich: C. H. Beck.

Wiggershaus, Rolf 1994. *The Frankfurt School: Its History, Theories, and Political Significance*, Michael Robertson (trans.). Cambridge, MA: MIT Press.

Wiggershaus, Rolf 2000. *Wittgenstein und Adorno*. Göttingen: Wallstein.

Wittgenstein, Ludwig 1953. *Philosophical Investigations*. Oxford: Blackwell.

Zuidervaart, Lambert 1991. *Adorno's Aesthetic Theory: The Redemption of Illusion*. Cambridge, MA: MIT Press.

Index